NATIONAL
GEOGRAPHIC
KiDS

ALMANAC
2020

A red panda eats bamboo in Wolong National Nature Reserve in Sichuan Province, China.

ALMANAC
2020

NATIONAL GEOGRAPHIC
WASHINGTON, D.C.

National Geographic Kids Books
gratefully acknowledges the following people for their help with the
National Geographic Kids Almanac.

Jennifer Leff of the National Geographic Explorer Programs

Amazing Animals

Suzanne Braden, Director, Pandas International

Dr. Rodolfo Coria, Paleontologist, Plaza Huincul, Argentina

Dr. Sylvia Earle, National Geographic Explorer-in-Residence

Dr. Thomas R. Holtz, Jr., Senior Lecturer, Vertebrate Paleontology, Department of Geology, University of Maryland

Dr. Luke Hunter, Executive Director, Panthera

Dereck and Beverly Joubert, National Geographic Explorers-in-Residence

Nizar Ibrahim, National Geographic Explorer

"Dino" Don Lessem, President, Exhibits Rex

Kathy B. Maher, Research Editor (former), *National Geographic* magazine

Kathleen Martin, Canadian Sea Turtle Network

Barbara Nielsen, Polar Bears International

Andy Prince, Austin Zoo

Julia Thorson, translator, Zurich, Switzerland

Dennis vanEngelsdorp, Senior Extension Associate, Pennsylvania Department of Agriculture

Science and Technology
Space and Earth

Tim Appenzeller, Chief Magazine Editor, *Nature*

Dr. Rick Fienberg, American Astronomical Society, Press Officer and Director of Communications

Dr. José de Ondarza, Associate Professor, Department of Biological Sciences, State University of New York, College at Plattsburgh

Lesley B. Rogers, Managing Editor (former), *National Geographic* magazine

Dr. Enric Sala, National Geographic Explorer-in-Residence

Abigail A. Tipton, Director of Research (former), *National Geographic* magazine

Erin Vintinner, Biodiversity Specialist, Center for Biodiversity and Conservation at the American Museum of Natural History

Barbara L. Wyckoff, Research Editor (former), *National Geographic* magazine

Going Green

Eric J. Bohn, Math Teacher, Santa Rosa High School

Stephen David Harris, Professional Engineer, Industry Consulting

Catherine C. Milbourn, Senior Press Officer, EPA

Brad Scriber, Senior Researcher, *National Geographic* magazine

Paola Segura and Cid Simões, National Geographic Emerging Explorers

Dr. Wes Tunnell, Harte Research Institute for Gulf of Mexico Studies, Texas A&M University–Corpus Christi

Natasha Vizcarra, Science Writer and Media Liaison, National Snow and Ice Data Center

Culture Connection

Dr. Wade Davis, National Geographic Explorer-in-Residence

Deirdre Mullervy, Managing Editor, Gallaudet University Press

Wonders of Nature

Anatta, NOAA Public Affairs Officer

Dr. Robert Ballard, National Geographic Explorer-in-Residence

Douglas H. Chadwick, wildlife biologist and contributor to *National Geographic* magazine

Susan K. Pell, Ph.D., Science and Public Programs Manager, United States Botanic Garden

History Happens

Dr. Sylvie Beaudreau, Associate Professor, Department of History, State University of New York

Elspeth Deir, Assistant Professor, Faculty of Education, Queens University, Kingston, Ontario, Canada

Dr. Gregory Geddes, Professor, Global Studies, State University of New York–Orange, Middletown-Newburgh, New York

Dr. Fredrik Hiebert, National Geographic Visiting Fellow

Micheline Joanisse, Media Relations Officer, Natural Resources Canada

Dr. Robert D. Johnston, Associate Professor and Director of the Teaching of History Program, University of Illinois at Chicago

Dickson Mansfield, Geography Instructor (retired), Faculty of Education, Queens University, Kingston, Ontario, Canada

Tina Norris, U.S. Census Bureau

Parliamentary Information and Research Service, Library of Parliament, Ottawa, Canada

Karyn Pugliese, Acting Director, Communications, Assembly of First Nations

Geography Rocks

Carl Haub, Senior Demographer, Conrad Taeuber Chair of Public Information, Population Reference Bureau

Dr. Toshiko Kaneda, Senior Research Associate, Population Reference Bureau

Dr. Kristin Bietsch, Research Associate, Population Reference Bureau

Dr. Walt Meier, National Snow and Ice Data Center

Dr. Richard W. Reynolds, NOAA's National Climatic Data Center

United States Census Bureau, Public Help Desk

Contents

CONTENTS

WONDERS OF NATURE 200

HISTORY HAPPENS 220

GEOGRAPHY ROCKS 252

NATIONAL GEOGRAPHIC KIDS
ALMANAC CHALLENGE 2020

THE RESULTS ARE IN!

Which lion poster was the favorite in our 2019 online pole? *See page 191.*

Want to become part of the 2020 Almanac Challenge? Go to page 190 to find out more.

YOUR WORLD 2020

A surfer rides a wave in Fiji. Surfing will make its debut at the 2020 Olympic Games in Tokyo, Japan.

10 WAYS THE WORLD HAS CHANGED SINCE THE 2010 ALMANAC

PANDA BOOM

In 2010, China's Wolong National Nature Reserve was just beginning to rebuild after a devastating earthquake in 2008 that left dozens of pandas homeless. Today, Wolong—home to 10 percent of all living pandas in the world—has been rebuilt, and its breeding program recently welcomed 42 cubs. This panda boom means the beloved animals are now off the endangered list—hopefully for good.

FINAL FLIGHT

In 2010, NASA announced that its 30-year space shuttle program would fly its final mission in 2011. Now, NASA's focus is on exploring Mars, and scientists are using the Mars rovers to search for signs of life—and to determine if humans could one day live on the red planet.

OCEAN AID

Since 2010, large areas of the South Atlantic and South Pacific Oceans have been designated as Marine Protected Areas (MPAs). While only some 4 percent of the world's oceans are now protected from human activities like overfishing, it's a positive step toward saving our seas.

A BIG WORLD

The planet's population is growing—by the billions! It now stands at some 7.6 billion people, nearly a billion more than the population in 2010. And there's no sign of a slowdown: Experts estimate the number to hit 8 billion by 2023.

POWER UP

There were fewer than 17,000 electric cars on the roads around the world in 2010. Today, there are more than 3 million. While this may not mean the end of gas-powered vehicles for good, the electric car count is estimated to hit 125 million by 2030.

TABLET TAKEOVER

Back in 2010 when Apple first introduced the iPad, just about 5 percent of U.S. households owned a tablet. Now? More than half of the nation is tuned into such devices. Worldwide, some 20 percent of the population is on team tablet. But far more—66 percent—stick to smartphones.

POTTER MANIA

Millions of Muggles across the globe flocked to movie theaters in 2010 and 2011 to see *Harry Potter and the Deathly Hallows Part 1* and *Part 2*, the final films in the über-popular series. Today, Harry is as beloved as ever, with the hit play *Harry Potter and the Cursed Child* and several theme parks featuring all things Potter.

LOST AND FOUND

In 2018, the last remaining male northern white rhino passed away, marking a sad blow to this rare subspecies. While some animals' numbers are dwindling, others are just being discovered: Since 2010, scientists have found a walking catfish, a two-legged lizard, and the adorable olinguito (above), a small mammal native to South America.

SEEING THE FUTURE

In 2010, virtual reality prototypes were being developed but the tech was not widely available. A decade later, VR is used daily in places like hospitals, classrooms, museums, and in people's homes worldwide.

VIDEO VIEWS

In the past 10 years, YouTube's popularity has exploded. In 2010, some two billion videos were viewed a day. Today? That number exceeds five billion. One of 2010's most popular clips—a man emotionally showing off a double rainbow in his front yard—has been viewed nearly 50 million times since it was originally posted.

GOLDEN GATHERING

BOW, WOW: THIS CELEBRATION HAS GONE TO THE DOGS!

In 2018, the Golden Retriever Club of Scotland welcomed 361 golden retrievers from around the world to an estate in the Scottish Highlands. The occasion? The 150th birthday of the very first litter of golden retrievers, born in July 1868. Golden retrievers were originally bred by a Scottish politician and businessman known as Lord Tweedmouth to be hunting companions that could also swim far distances. Today, golden retrievers rank among the world's most popular and beloved dog breeds, paws down.

ICY MAZE

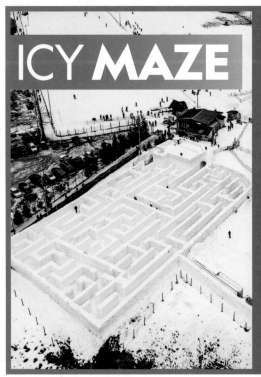

THIS LABYRINTH IN POLAND

is nothing short of a-*maze*-ing! Constructed out of some 60,000 individual blocks of ice and snow, the maze at Snowlandia Zakopane Park covers an area that's about the size of five basketball courts. Each winter, it takes some 50 workers about one month to build the maze, which features narrow passages with walls taller than most adults. And if you find your way out with time to spare, Snowlandia also offers its visitors a chance to explore a five-story snow castle, complete with an icy throne. Talk about some *royal* fun!

Olympic Fever

IN THE SUMMER OF 2020,

Tokyo will become the first Asian city to become a repeat host of the Summer Olympics, having welcomed the games to the Japanese capital in 1964. When the 32nd Olympic Games kick off on July 24, 2020, millions of ticket holders will watch athletes from around the world compete in 33 different sports. Which events are new this year? Women's softball and men's baseball are back on the program after being removed in 2008, and karate, sport climbing, surfing, and skateboarding will be competed on the Olympic stage for the first time ever. So even more athletes will have a chance to go for the gold.

Meet Miraitowa and Someity, the official mascots of the 2020 Olympics and Paralympic Games! Selected by elementary school children throughout Japan, the cheerful mascots are named for the Japanese words for future and eternity (Miraitowa) and mighty (Someity). Together, the mascots are meant to represent both tradition and innovation.

SPORTS FUNNIES
OLYMPIC EDITION

Hey, would you mind scratching my back while we're up here?

Team Canada competes in Team Synchronized Swimming at the London 2012 Olympic Games.

Team USA basketball players Kevin Durant and DeAndre Jordan joke on the podium after receiving gold medals at the Rio 2016 Olympic Games.

I can't believe I forgot to wish my mom a happy birthday ...

Real-Life TRANSFORMERS

When it comes to some robots, there's more than meets the eye!

Modeled after the popular Transformers toys, the J-deite RIDE robot is programmed to shift into a car and back to a bot again. The robot, which was designed by a team of Japanese engineers, is taller than an elephant and weighs about the same as a rhino. In about one minute, it can switch from a robot to a drivable car that seats two. As for its top speed on the roads? The J-deite RIDE top speeds of 37 miles an hour (60 km/h).

Hit a switch on a remote control and the J-deite RIDE returns to its robot form. While upright, it can walk about 328 feet (100 m) an hour. That pace is not nearly as speedy as the fictional Transformers, but it's not too bad for a real-life robot!

HOT MOVIES in 2020*

- Trolls World Tour
- Barbie
- Peter Rabbit 2
- Minions 2
- The Croods 2
- Sing 2
- The SpongeBob Movie: It's a Wonderful Sponge

*Release dates and titles are subject to change.

Walking Gorilla

WHEN LOUIS THE GORILLA wants to get around his habitat at the Philadelphia Zoo, he doesn't always move about on all fours like most apes. Instead, he walks on his own two feet, completely upright!

The strange sight is super uncommon for gorillas, who typically walk on two legs once in a while, and just for a few seconds. But six-foot (1.8-m)-tall Louis is seen standing quite often, taking quick strides across the yards, just like a human.

So why does Louis love to walk? Researchers who work with him at the Philadelphia Zoo say it has to do with his preference for keeping his hands clean. He walks when he's gathering food like tomatoes, leading experts to think that he doesn't want to crush the juicy snacks by walking on his hands. Louis also stands up and walks when his yard is muddy, and he has been seen using leaves to wipe dirt off his hands and feet. Sounds like Louis is one particular primate!

THERE ARE TORNADOES ... AND THEN THERE ARE *LAVANADOES*.
KILAUEA'S STRANGE PHENOMENON

A lavanado happens when a funnel forms over an active volcano, forming a twister of fire, smoke, ash, and, yes, even lava if it can stay suspended in the air. Recently, a lavanado was spotted over Kilauea on Hawaii's Big Island, the result of intense heat and high winds rising rapidly from the raging volcano. This terrifying twister, measuring some 200 feet (61 m) long, could be spotted whirling over the island from half a mile (800 m) away. Similar columns have been seen over large wildfires, also forming from a combination of high heat and wind.

While lavanadoes are rare, they are fascinating examples of the extreme weather produced around active volcanoes—and proof of just how powerful these forces of nature truly are.

Cool Events 2020

GILROY GARLIC FESTIVAL

Garlic ice cream? Why not! That's just one of the fun foods found at this festival showcasing the smelly veggie in northern California, U.S.A.

July 24–July 26

POLAR BEAR SWIM

100 years have passed since the first people plunged into the icy waters near Vancouver, Canada. Today, thousands of brave swimmers jump right into this New Year tradition.

January 1

SUMMER PARALYMPIC GAMES

LET THE GAMES BEGIN!
Thousands of athletes with various disabilities head to Tokyo.

August 25–September 6

WORLD FROG DAY

Ribbit, ribbit! Show your love for these hopping amphibians today.

March 20

WORLD SMILE DAY

SAY CHEESE!
Today, you've got plenty to grin about!

October 2

EARTH DAY

The **50TH ANNIVERSARY OF THIS EVENT** reminds us to protect the planet today—and every day.

April 22

MAYFLOWER VOYAGE

400TH ANNIVERSARY
It has been four centuries since the *Mayflower* brought the Pilgrims from England to America.

November

WORLD OCEAN DAY

Celebrate the seas and all of the living things that call our oceans home.

June 8

ROLL ON

As part of a Christmas Eve custom, the locals of Caracas, Venezuela, lace up their roller skates and glide to church.

December 24

ESCAPE ROOM

The lights turn off, and there you are: In a dark, windowless room, with your friends and family ... and no way out. Sound like the start of a scary movie? Not quite. You are in an escape room—and it's all for fun!

Escape rooms, which first started in Tokyo in 2007, have been popping up all around the world as a family-friendly activity. The concept is simple: Your group is locked in a room and is given about an hour to search for clues and solve puzzles to figure out how to exit. Cracking the code is all about teamwork and plenty of problem-solving. Escape rooms have become so popular that there is even an adventure park in Budapest, Hungary, where you can spend an entire day attempting to get out by conquering a series of physical and mental obstacles.

And if you don't crack the code in an escape room? It's okay! You still get to leave the room—and you're always welcome to come back for escape room redemption.

A Not-So-Great Escape!

While most people try to break out of an escape room, one harebrained burglar in Vancouver, Washington, U.S.A., went the opposite route. After breaking into an escape room (where he allegedly ate a burrito he brought with him and pocketed a remote control and a cell phone), the bad guy began to worry he couldn't actually, uh, escape. Scared, he called 911. And even though he eventually found an exit, the cops still busted him for burglary.

HIGH-TECH TEACHER

ROBOTS CAN DO JUST ABOUT ANYTHING THESE DAYS.

Including teach a class full of kids! At least that's what Elias the robot is doing in Finland. As part of a test program, Elias and three other humanoid robots are

programmed to work with students to teach subjects like math and language. He can speak 23 languages, ask questions, and even give feedback on the kids to human teachers. But Elias isn't just about reading and writing. He can break out some serious dance moves! Sounds like one rockin' robot.

A panther chameleon flashes a threat display in Masoala National Park, Madagascar.

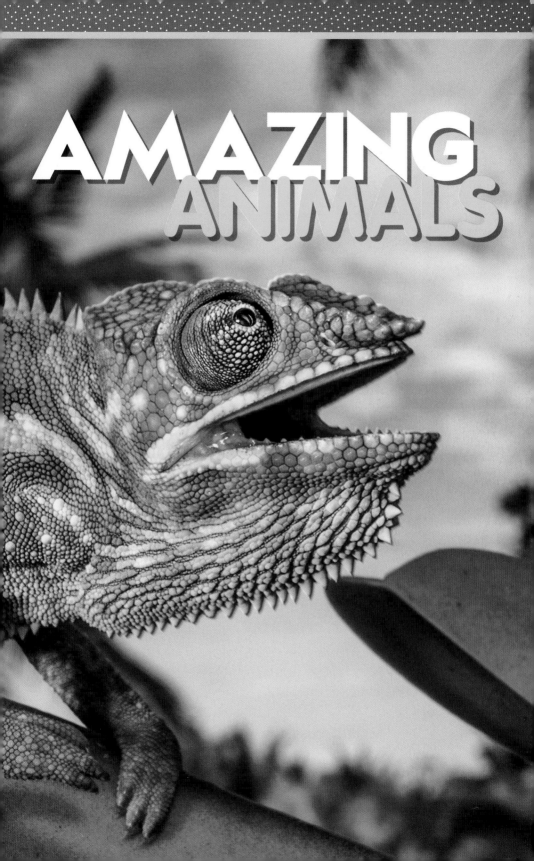

AMAZING
ANIMALS

EARTH EXPLORER

Meet **Krithi Karanth!**

This conservation biologist and National Geographic explorer is hoping to solve conflict between wildlife and humans in her home country, India.

From the time she was a kid, Krithi Karanth has been concerned about the need to protect wildlife. In fact, as the daughter of a conservationist, Krithi spotted her first tiger and leopard in the wild when she was just two years old. Today, as a conservation scientist, Krithi is focused on keeping the wildlife in her native India around for future generations.

One way she's doing just that? By trying to limit the conflict between farmers throughout the many villages in India and the wildlife that often wind up on their land. These animals—including feral pigs, tigers, leopards, and elephants—crush crops, mangle fences, and even harm farm animals.

"Spaces for wildlife are shrinking, and people are in closer contact with wildlife," explains Krithi. "As a result, the frustrated and sometimes furious farmers chase or harm animals."

Krithi is working to build tolerance by helping people report and get paid by the government for damage caused by wild animals. She created Wild Seve, a phone reporting system through which people in the field file reports of damage for farmers. Once a report is filed, the farmer receives payment for their losses from the Indian government.

"If farmers are covered for their loss, they will be less likely to retaliate," explains Krithi. She hopes this simple system will be a way to keep humans happy—and animals alive.

Krithi is also intent on raising awareness of India's unique wildlife to the rest of the world. She has even written her own children's book called *Will You Play With Me?* to introduce kids to animals found only in India—like the lion-tailed macaque and the wild dog—and to get kids excited about and to value the animals found in their own countries.

"It's easy to think that all of the discoveries have been done and the species have all been found, but that's not true," says Karanth. "There is still a lot of exploration left to do."

Female Asian elephants don't have tusks.

ASIAN ELEPHANTS

" The big question we have to ask in India is, 'Is there room for wildlife?' And the answer has to be yes. "

BENGAL TIGER

No two tigers have the same pattern of stripes.

CALL TO ACTION!

Pick a cause—whether it's saving big cats or boosting the bee population—and look into the ways you can support it. "You don't have to sit back and say 'I can't do anything,'" says Krithi. "Go out and learn everything you can about wildlife. Take pictures of animals and write about them." Who knows, maybe one day you'll play a major role in saving a species.

Extraordinary ANIMALS

KITTEN on WHEELS

Fort Langley, Canada

When the TinyKittens Society found a starving kitten suffering from a terrible injury to his back legs, they were shocked he was still alive. But his rescuers refused to give up on him. After amputating part of the cat's back legs, his medical team constructed slings, splints, and eventually a set of mini wheels to give his back end a lift and keep him mobile.

Throughout the process, the team documented the cat's progress on social media. He had tons of fans! Nobody would have guessed that after seven months of intensive physical therapy, the miracle cat—now called Cassidy—would be able to get around without the help of his wheels. These days he scoots around on his two front paws. Except when he's tired, of course—then he hitches a ride on his new family's robotic vacuum cleaner.

I rock ... and roll.

CASSIDY NO LONGER NEEDS WHEELS TO GET AROUND.

TOADZILLA!

"Hoppy" to see me?

TOADZILLA, A GIANT CANE TOAD, IS HANDLED BY THE TRACKER WHO LOCATED THE CREATURE.

Darwin, Australia

In the dark of night, a group of citizens set out to hunt down one of Australia's most menacing predators. Their prey? A giant toad nicknamed Toadzilla.

Looking like a cantaloupe with legs, Toadzilla is the largest cane toad on record in Australia, at about eight inches (20.3 cm) long and almost two pounds (0.9 kg). Why the toad hunt? Cane toads were brought to Australia all the way from Hawaii to eat crop-destroying beetles, but instead they gobble down just about anything they can get their mouths around. "Cane toads take away food from other predators and are killing many other native animals," says Graeme Sawyer of FrogWatch, which leads expeditions such as the one that netted Toadzilla.

Luckily cane toads are slow and easy to catch. Once Sawyer's team heard Toadzilla's distinctive mating call—"like a dial tone on a telephone," he says—a tracker grabbed the creature by hand.

Now instead of being a predator, Toadzilla is a teacher, visiting schools to educate kids about invasive species like the cane toad. Better listen to *this* teacher!

The birds ALL call me for fashion tips.

PARROT wears SWEATERS

Lecompton, Kansas

Chilly temperatures never get Javi the bird down. That's because the lesser sulphur-crested cockatoo (a type of parrot) owns plenty of sweaters to keep herself warm!

Normally birds rely on their feathers to stay toasty. But Javi—who was likely raised in harsh conditions before moving to the Tallgrass Parrot Sanctuary—probably plucked out most of her feathers because of stress. Caretakers weren't sure if her belly and chest feathers would grow back, but they knew Javi would be more comfortable with another layer covering her delicate skin. So they fitted her with a sweater.

Today the cockatoo owns more than 20 sweaters. They're made from colorful socks that Tallgrass co-owner Kail Marie makes herself. The fashions have caught the eye of Javi's bird friends, Sassy and Poppy. "Javi's the leader," Marie says. "They'll follow her anywhere." Looks like Javi got more than a new wardrobe—she got new friends as well.

Here we come to save the day!

PUPPIES save LOST BOY

Virgilina, Virginia

Jaylynn Thorpe's family was terrified when the three-year-old wandered off into the woods on a frigid 17°F (-8.3°C) night. Thankfully, Bootsy and Dipstick the puppies wandered off with him—and probably saved his life.

While rescue workers searched for Jaylynn with scent-sniffing dogs and a heat-seeking helicopter, the puppies nestled around the shivering boy. They pressed against him all night and kept him warm—and alive. "They treated him like another puppy in their litter," veterinarian Emily Kinnaird says. "They snuggled to keep warm."

Twenty hours later, rescuers were nearby. But a scared Jaylynn hid beneath a pile of leaves. Once again, the puppies played the heroes, barking to alert the rescue team. Jaylynn was reunited with his family, cold and hungry but unhurt. "The puppies were very important to his survival," fire chief Chad Loftis says.

RADIO FLYER

BOOTSY (LEFT) AND DIPSTICK

INCREDIBLE ANIMAL FRIENDS

I love ya, but I think your coat needs washing.

HIGHLAND BULL

ORIGIN Scotland; these bulls were brought to Australia (near New Zealand) by Scottish immigrants

WEIGHT 1,500 to 1,800 pounds (680.4 to 816.5 kg)

CLAIM TO FAME Highland cattle grow two coats of hair. The coarse outer layer protects the animals from wind and rain, and the soft bottom layer keeps them warm.

FUN TO KNOW Experts think Highland cattle have been around since the sixth century.

DOMESTIC GOOSE

ORIGIN Europe and Asia

WEIGHT 5 to 10 pounds (2.3 to 4.5 kg)

CLAIM TO FAME The goose is thought to be one of the first animals to be domesticated, probably in Egypt about 3,000 years ago.

FUN TO KNOW The wing-span of a domestic goose can be six feet (1.8 m) wide.

Step away from the bull!

GOOSE GUARDS BULL

GISBORNE, NEW ZEALAND

A big Highland bull like Hamish probably doesn't need a bodyguard, but this goose disagrees. Whenever the bull is grazing in the pasture, the goose watches for cattle that—in the bird's opinion—get way too close. "Then the goose will stretch out his neck, shriek, and chase the other cows and bulls away," says Kees Weytsmans, owner of the Knapdale Eco Lodge where the two live.

Hamish and the goose have been inseparable for 10 years—ever since the bird was found resting on Hamish's leg a week after the bull was born. Since then, the goose has rarely left Hamish's side. Weytsmans once moved Hamish to another rancher's pasture for a few nights. But one evening apart was all the goose could stand. "The next afternoon the goose traveled all by himself to the other pasture to find Hamish," he says. And though Hamish doesn't seem as eager for friendship as the goose, the bull doesn't mind his bodyguard. Otherwise, this bull would ruffle some feathers!

MONKEY DOTES ON IGUANA

KREFELD, GERMANY

This white-faced saki rarely scaled back her affection for her green iguana bestie. The saki, a type of monkey, loved petting and snuggling her reptile pal as they lounged together on tree branches at the Krefeld Zoo.

The saki and iguana met after they were placed in the zoo's Rain Forest House, a tree-filled enclosure that's home to 40 different types of animals from tropical areas. "Both green iguanas and white-faced sakis spend most of their time in treetops," zoo spokesperson Petra Schwinn says. "One day these two crossed paths." The curious saki examined the reptile, patting its skin with her long fingers.

The pals continued to have hangout sessions, eating together at the enclosure's feeding station. But most of their "playdates" were in the trees and involved the saki petting the iguana and tickling his chin. The reptile, meanwhile, seemed to soak up the attention.

Recently the animals moved to separate zoos. But keepers and visitors haven't forgotten about their friendship. "They made a good team," Schwinn says.

THE FEMALE SAKI PETS HER IGUANA PAL.

GREEN IGUANA

RANGE
Central and South America

WEIGHT
11 pounds (5 kg)

TALL TAIL
If it's caught by a predator, the green iguana can detach its tail and grow another.

FUNNY NAME
These animals are sometimes referred to as "bamboo chickens."

Hey, your beard feels a bit sharp. How about a shave?

WHITE-FACED SAKI

RANGE
South America

WEIGHT
around 4 pounds (1.8 kg)

FACE OFF
Only male white-faced sakis have white fur covering their faces. The fur on a female's face is mostly brown.

SWEET TREATS
Sakis eat fruit, honey, leaves, and flowers.

WHAT IS Taxonomy?

Since there are billions and billions of living things, called organisms, on the planet, people need a way of classifying them. Scientists created a system called **taxonomy,** which helps to classify all living things into ordered groups. By putting organisms into categories, we are better able to understand how they are the same and how they are different. There are eight levels of taxonomic classification, beginning with the broadest group, called a domain, followed by kingdom, down to the most specific group, called a species.

Biologists divide life based on evolutionary history, and they place organisms into three domains depending on their genetic structure: Archaea, Bacteria, and Eukarya. (See p. 85 for "The Three Domains of Life.")

Where do animals come in?

HEDGEHOG

Animals are a part of the Eukarya domain, which means they are organisms made of cells with nuclei. More than one million species of animals have been named, including humans. Like all living things, animals can be divided into smaller groups, called phyla. Most scientists believe there are more than 30 phyla into which animals can be grouped based on certain scientific criteria, such as body type or whether or not the animal has a backbone. It can be pretty complicated, so there is another, less complicated system that groups animals into two categories: vertebrates and invertebrates.

SAMPLE CLASSIFICATION
KEEL-BILLED TOUCAN

Domain:	Eukarya
Kingdom:	Animalia
Phylum:	Chordata
Class:	Aves
Order:	Piciformes
Family:	Ramphastidae
Genus:	*Ramphastos*
Species:	*sulfuratus*

TIP:
Here's a sentence to help you remember the classification order:
<u>D</u>id <u>K</u>ing <u>P</u>hillip <u>C</u>ome <u>O</u>ver <u>F</u>or <u>G</u>ood <u>S</u>oup?

BY THE NUMBERS

There are 13,267 vulnerable or endangered animal species in the world. The list includes:

• 1,204 mammals, such as the snow leopard, the polar bear, and the fishing cat.

• 1,469 birds, including the Steller's sea eagle and the black-banded plover.

• 2,386 fish, such as the Mekong giant catfish.

• 1,215 reptiles, including the American crocodile.

• 1,414 insects, including the Macedonian grayling.

• 2,100 amphibians, such as the Round Island day gecko.

• And more, including 170 arachnids, 732 crustaceans, 239 sea anemones and corals, 190 bivalves, and 1,992 snails and slugs.

ROUND ISLAND DAY GECKO

Vertebrates
Animals WITH Backbones

Fish are cold-blooded and live in water. They breathe with gills, lay eggs, and usually have scales.

Amphibians are cold-blooded. Their young live in water and breathe with gills. Adults live on land and breathe with lungs.

Reptiles are cold-blooded and breathe with lungs. They live both on land and in water.

Birds are warm-blooded and have feathers and wings. They lay eggs, breathe with lungs, and usually are able to fly. Some birds live on land, some in water, and some on both.

Mammals are warm-blooded and feed on their mothers' milk. They also have skin that is usually covered with hair. Mammals live both on land and in water.

BIRD: MANDARIN DUCK

AMPHIBIAN: POISON DART FROG

Invertebrates
Animals WITHOUT Backbones

Sponges are a very basic form of animal life. They live in water and do not move on their own.

Echinoderms have external skeletons and live in seawater.

Mollusks have soft bodies and can live either in or out of shells, on land or in water.

Arthropods are the largest group of animals. They have external skeletons, called exoskeletons, and segmented bodies with appendages. Arthropods live in water and on land.

Worms are soft-bodied animals with no true legs. Worms live in soil.

Cnidaria live in water and have mouths surrounded by tentacles.

MOLLUSK: MAGNIFICENT CHROMODORID NUDIBRANCH

SPONGE: SEA SPONGE

GARDEN SNAIL

Cold-blooded
versus
Warm-blooded

Cold-blooded animals, also called ectotherms, get their heat from outside their bodies.

Warm-blooded animals, also called endotherms, keep their body temperature level regardless of the temperature of their environment.

RISE OF THE TIGER

An adult male tiger can weigh the same as eight 10-year-old kids.

Tigers live in both cold and hot climates.

Scientists find good news with the help of secret snaps.

Recently, scientists have worked to get a current global estimate of how many wild tigers exist. As part of the effort, experts in countries throughout the tiger's range, including Russia, Bangladesh, Bhutan, India, and Nepal, trekked to forests and grasslands where the cats live to set up camera traps—motion-sensing or remote-controlled cameras that snap wildlife pics. They hoped the photos would give clues about the number of tigers in each nation.

Cats on Camera

To track down tigers, researchers focused on water holes and areas with boar and other tiger prey. There, they fixed multiple camera traps to trees to catch the cats from different angles. The camera's treelike disguise made them less likely to be destroyed by curious animals. After setting up the traps, the researchers journeyed home.

Take a Number

The cameras snapped pictures of any animal that walked in front of them, using night vision to get good photos in the dark, when tigers are most active. The researchers returned to collect the devices a few months later and uploaded their pictures to computers, which analyzed each tiger's coat pattern and recognized when a certain tiger appeared more than once. The computers then counted how many individuals appeared overall in the photos.

Using this data and other information, teams were able to estimate how many tigers lived in the countries studied. The final tally surprised them all.

Tiger Time

Researchers estimated that about 3,890 wild tigers exist on the planet. That's up from as few as 3,200, the estimated population in 2010. Experts say this bump may be partly due to conservation efforts made by several of the countries where tigers live, such as laws to protect the cats' habitats.

Still, experts emphasize that the rise in numbers doesn't mean that tigers are out of danger. In fact it's possible that better technology may have allowed researchers to photograph more tigers than before, making it seem as if the population is increasing. Still, analyzing these "selfies" is certainly a step in the right direction for the future of wild tigers.

A TIGER CUB INVESTIGATES A CAMERA THAT'S MOUNTED ON WHEELS AND CONTROLLED REMOTELY BY A RESEARCHER.

MARGAYS: OUT ON A LIMB

Meet the margays! These small wild cats, about the size of a house cat, are native to rain forests of Central and South America. Because of their secretive lifestyle—they spend a lot of their lives in trees, even hunting among the branches—catching a glimpse of these acrobatic cats in their natural habitat is no easy task.

BUILT TO CLIMB

With a body uniquely adapted to life in the treetops, a margay moves through the canopy like a feline gymnast. Unlike most wild cats, they can go down a tree headfirst. The margay's ankles can rotate all the way around to face backward, which allows the cat to quickly change direction while climbing.

A margay's feet are wide and soft, with flexible toes that allow it to grab branches. Its 17-inch (43-cm)-long tail provides balance as it moves around in the treetops.

TRACKING MARGAYS

Because they can stay hidden in the trees, experts use radio collars to track these cats and shed some light on their daily activities. As a result, the margay's characteristics and habits aren't a complete secret. Experts have observed that these solitary animals are active mostly at night (their huge eyes help them see in the dark), hunting for birds, snakes, rodents, and even small monkeys. It takes skillful climbing to accomplish that hunting feat.

SAVING MARGAY HABITAT

Though the overall margay population isn't in immediate danger, the cats are vulnerable. Margays need tropical forests to survive. Habitat destruction, especially clearing forests for farms and ranches, is their biggest threat. Today, scientists are working hard to save the habitat of these acrobats of the rain forest.

Climbing skills make margays the acrobats of the rain forest.

CLIMBING HEADFIRST DOWN A TREE IS A RARE ABILITY MARGAYS HAVE MASTERED.

TURBO-CHEETAH

A cheetah can cover 26 feet (8 m) in one stride.

SCIENTISTS USE CUTTING-EDGE TECHNOLOGY TO UNCOVER THE CHEETAH'S BIG SECRET.

The fastest land animal, cheetahs have been clocked going over 60 miles an hour (97 km/h). Naturally, scientists have attributed the cheetah's hunting success to its speediness—until recently. Using top-notch technology to research the feline's movements and hunting techniques, scientists found surprising answers to the question of what makes the cheetah a first-rate predator.

CUTTING-EDGE COLLARS

Until recently, people assumed that the animal's swiftness was what allowed it to snag prey so effectively in the wild. But some experts weren't so sure. So one team, led by Alan Wilson, trekked to Botswana, a country in Africa with one of the world's largest cheetah populations, where they encountered several of the cats on grassy terrain. After zapping them with tranquilizer darts, the scientists fitted them each with a special fashion accessory: a tricked-out radio collar to monitor their movements.

Over the next 18 months, the gadgets sensed when each cheetah was running (which meant that it was hunting), then recorded the cat's location and speed. After 367 runs, the scientists began analyzing the data they'd collected. They knew that the cheetahs were chasing prey. If a cat's run ended with quick, jerky movements and then mostly stillness, they could tell that it had wrestled with and taken down its target.

SMOOTH MOVES

Looking at the cats' speed and the paths in which they ran, the scientists realized that it's not just speed that makes the cheetah a talented hunter—it's the animal's ability to slow down quickly and make sharp turns. Take the antelope, which runs in a zigzag in an attempt to lose its pursuer. The study showed that, like the antelope, the cheetah slows down, makes a tight turn, and speeds off in the same direction—all within seconds. This is a skill cheetahs start to develop as cubs, and with claws that act like running cleats and a long tail to keep them balanced, a cheetah's body is built for making difficult hairpin turns.

All of this makes the cheetah a champion predator. And now that researchers are more aware of this feline's hunting habits, the data may help conservationists create nature reserves where cheetahs can thrive.

A cheetah can take four strides in one second.

Collar Connection

The high-tech collars used by Alan Wilson's team had accelerometers to measure increases and decreases in the feline's speed. They also included gyroscopes that could sense when a cheetah twisted or turned to change direction, and GPS to allow the scientists to pinpoint the felines' exact locations on the savanna.

LIONS OF THE KALAHARI DESERT

ROARRR!
On a still night, the sound of lions roaring can carry for five miles (8 km). Roaring often is used to tell other lions, "This is my piece of land."

E yes half-closed against the wind-blasted sand, a sleek, black-and-gold-maned lion (above) strides along a dry riverbed in the Kalahari Desert. He is one of the lions that roam the desolate sand dunes of southern Africa's Kalahari and Namib Deserts. These lions thrive in an intensely hot landscape. They have learned how to go without water for weeks.

Life for a desert lion is very different from life for a lion in the grassy plains of Africa, such as in the Serengeti of Kenya and Tanzania. There, large prides of up to 20 lions spend most of their time together. A pride is very much like a human family.

Fritz Eloff, a scientist who spent 40 years studying the desert lions of the Kalahari, found that desert lions live, on average, in small groups of fewer than six. Family ties are just as strong, but relationships are long-distance. Desert lions often break up into even smaller groups.

BUSY NIGHTS

Life for Kalahari lions is a constant battle against thirst and high temperatures. In summer during the day, the surface temperature of the sand can be 150°F (66°C). That's hot enough to cook an egg.

Not surprisingly, Kalahari lions hunt mostly after the sun has gone down. The big cats usually rest until the middle of the night, waiting for a cool desert wind. Then they spend the rest of the night walking—looking for food.

In the Serengeti, food is very plentiful. Lions rarely have to walk more than a couple of miles before they find a meal. But life in the desert is not so easy. With only a few scattered animals such as porcupines and gemsboks—horse-size antelopes—for prey, desert lions have to walk farther and work harder to catch dinner.

DANGEROUS DINNER

When Kalahari lions do find something to eat, it is usually spiky or dangerous. One out of every three animals they catch is a porcupine. The desert lion's main prey is the gemsbok, which can provide 10 times as much meat as a porcupine. But gemsboks are difficult to bring down; they've been known to kill lions by skewering them on their three-foot (0.9-m)-long, saberlike horns.

Water is scarce in the Kalahari, so the desert lions have to be as resourceful at finding a drink as they are at finding a meal. One hot day, just as a light rain began to fall, Eloff watched two lionesses. Side by side, they licked the raindrops off each other.

These lean, strong lions have amazingly learned to survive, and by cooperating, they manage to thrive in an inhospitable, almost waterless world.

Surprise Party!

Red-eyed tree frogs astonish others with their weird behavior.

Looking for a snack, a 30-inch (76-cm)-long viper slithers down a tree in a steamy rain forest in Central America. Suddenly it sees a tasty-looking, three-inch (7.6-cm)-long red-eyed tree frog resting on a nearby leaf. The reptile lunges forward and snatches up the tiny croaker in its fanged mouth. But the snake's in for a not-so-pleasant surprise—the frog tastes terrible! The snake immediately spits out the amphibian. Landing unharmed on the forest floor, the frog blinks its big red eyes, then hops off to safety.

Red-eyed tree frogs have some features and behaviors that surprise other animals in their rain forest home, as well as the experts who study them. Discover how these jaw-dropping jumpers turn their habitat into one big surprise party.

The red-eyed tree frog oozes stinky, slightly toxic slime through its skin when a predator is near. It also doesn't taste very good!

A FROG LEAPS TO CAPTURE A TASTY CRICKET.

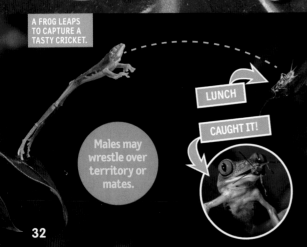

LUNCH

CAUGHT IT!

Males may wrestle over territory or mates.

Ambush and Eat

A red-eyed tree frog might jump through the air to get closer to an insect it wants to eat. This animal also uses the element of surprise. Known as an ambush predator, the amphibian sometimes hides among the leaves in its rain forest home. The frog waits patiently until a tasty-looking moth or cricket comes within striking distance. Then it fires out its long, sticky tongue to capture the insect and pull the meal into its mouth. Now *that's* some fast food.

Eye Spy

These nocturnal animals may spend the day lazing on plants, but they can still spy on their habitat. Thanks to a see-through third eyelid

that closes over their eyeballs when resting, the amphibian can stay on the lookout for trouble while it reenergizes. If a hunter does approach, the frog can leap away, startling its pursuer. The eyelid's stripes also may help hide the frog's bright red eyes from would-be predators.

A RED-EYED TREE FROG IN THE COUNTRY OF COSTA RICA SCALES A PLANT SHOOT.

One of the frog's calls sounds like a baby rattle.

Stick to It

Slick surfaces aren't a problem for this frog. It can easily clamber across wet leaves. Instead of hopping, the animal takes careful steps like a pro rock climber. It also has rounded toe pads that stick to surfaces like suction cups, and its feet produce gluey mucus to help it grip slippery surfaces. It can even cling to the undersides of leaves to hide from predators—Spider-Man-style. That's a sticky surprise.

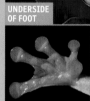

UNDERSIDE OF FOOT

Shake It Off

When researchers visited the country of Panama to study these frogs, they saw something that gave them a jolt: a male frog shaking the shoot of a plant with his hind legs, similar to a person strumming a guitar string! They realized that males do this when other males come too close to their turf. The shaking creates vibrations, which intruders interpret as a signal to back off.

Why not just croak loudly to ward off intruders? "They don't want to reveal their location to the entire pond, including enemies such as frog-eating bats," biologist Michael Caldwell says. That'd shake things up *way* too much.

NORTH AMERICA
ATLANTIC OCEAN
PACIFIC OCEAN
SOUTH AMERICA

Gulf of Mexico

Caribbean Sea

MEXICO
BELIZE
HONDURAS
GUATEMALA
NICARAGUA
EL SALVADOR
COSTA RICA
PANAMA
PACIFIC OCEAN
COLOMBIA

Where red-eyed tree frogs live

Meerkat CITY

Meerkats always have something to do. These mongoose relatives live in busy communities, with no time to sit around being bored. In their family groups of up to 40 members, everyone pitches in to get all the jobs done.

Guards

Meerkats are very territorial. Guards, called sentinels, are always on the lookout for rival meerkats that try to move in on their territory. If a sentinel (left) spots any intruding meerkats, it sends out an alarm call. The whole group gathers together and stands tall to try to scare away the rivals. If that doesn't work, meerkats quickly decide whether to fight or retreat.

Predators such as eagles or jackals rate a different warning call. When the sentinel spots a predator, it lets out an alarm call that sends all the meerkats scurrying into the nearest bolt hole—an underground safety den where the eagle can't follow.

A SENTINEL KEEPS WATCH.

Diggers

Picture yourself looking for a tasty bug to eat (below) when suddenly you hear the alarm call for "eagle." You dash left, you dash right, and you finally find a bolt hole.

Bolt holes provide fast getaways for meerkats in danger. Members of the group cooperate to make sure bolt holes are properly dug out, that nothing is blocking the entry, and that there are enough bolt holes in every area.

Meerkats are built to be super diggers. All four of their paws have long, sturdy claws that they use like rakes. They dig to find food, such as lizards and other small reptiles, insects and their larvae, and scorpions.

Babysitters

Within a meerkat group, the alpha, or leader, female and the alpha male are usually the only ones that have babies. When their babies are too young to follow along while they search for food, meerkat parents have to go without them. So they leave their pups with babysitters—other adult meerkats in the group. The pups stay inside their family's underground burrow for the first three weeks of life, protected and cared for by the babysitters.

HOME SWEET BURROW

DIGGING FOR FOOD

WILD DOGS OF AFRICA

The puppy-dog eyes and pleading squeals of a five-month-old African wild dog named Cici can mean only one thing: dinnertime. An older sister in Cici's pack responds, dragging over a meaty impala bone. In African wild dog society, puppies have all the power. "It's up to the older siblings to take care of the puppies," says Micaela Gunther, a scientist who studies wild dogs, including Cici's family. "The doting grown-ups even deliver toys, such as a strip of impala skin perfect for puppy tug-of-war." Imagine your big brother or sister working hard to hand you snacks and games while you eat, play, and rest all day.

DOG DAYS

Like wolves, wild dogs live in packs of about 15 dogs. Pups stay in the pack for about two years. Then some may break off to start packs of their own, while others stay with their mom and dad.

When the pups are newborn, every member of the pack works together to provide for them. At first the puppies stay near the den, often under the watch of a babysitter, while the pack hunts. Returning pack members throw up meat for the pups. Sound gross? Puppies love these leftovers.

PACK ATTACK

By the time the pups are six months old, they join the pack on hunting expeditions. First they learn how to stalk prey, and eventually they participate in the kill. Single 60-pound (27-kg) dogs rarely catch larger prey on their own, but a pack of 20 proves that there really is strength in numbers. Together they can take down a zebra or wildebeest weighing up to 1,000 pounds (454 kg).

Hunting wild dogs often pursue herds of gazelle for miles, fresh dogs trading places with tired ones. Eventually the weakest of the chased animals tires. The dogs surround it and attack from every direction. This teamwork is bred from the pack's intense social bonding, such as puppy play sessions. Team-building is the reason wild dogs spoil the pups, who grow up united and ready to contribute to the strength of the pack.

SCALY SUPERHEROES

Discover the hidden powers of the pangolin.

Clark Kent and Peter Parker—the alter egos of Superman and Spider-Man—don't really stand out. And neither do pangolins in the tropical forests or grasslands of Africa and Asia where they live. But like your favorite movie heroes, this animal has a few hidden superpowers. Check them out here.

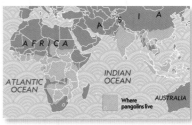

ASIA
AFRICA
INDIAN OCEAN
ATLANTIC OCEAN
AUSTRALIA
Where pangolins live

SPIDER-MAN STICKINESS!

SPIDER-MAN

Spider-Man shoots out sticky strands of webbing from his wrists to swing from one skyscraper to another. When a pangolin is hungry, it shoots out its sticky tongue, which extends up to 16 inches (40.6 cm) past its mouth. Coated in gluey saliva, the licker scoops up ants and termites, the pangolin's favorite snacks. In all, the mammal can eat some 70 million insects a year. Makes sense that this superhero-like creature would have a super appetite.

WOLVERINE CLAWS!

WOLVERINE

During fights with villains, Wolverine defends himself with long, sharp claws that pop out of his knuckles.
Pangolins have claws on each of their front feet used to rip up ant and termite nests as they search for dinner. Claws also help them clutch onto branches or dig burrows for sleeping. Whether you're a superhero or a pangolin, claws really come in handy.

Eight species of pangolins exist in all.

The animal emits a stinky odor when threatened.

IRON-MAN ARMOR!

CLOSE-UP OF SCALES

IRON MAN

Iron Man sports a high-tech suit of armor that shields the superhero from weapons hurled by enemies. Pangolins wear armor, too. Their "suits" consist of rows of overlapping scales that resemble a pinecone. Made out of keratin—the same substance in your fingernails—the pangolin's armor is so tough that predators such as lions can't bite through it. It's too bad that this armor doesn't come with built-in jets!

ANT-MAN MOVES

ANT MAN

When he senses trouble, Ant-Man shrinks to the size of, well, an ant. Pangolins, which can be almost six feet (1.8 m) long from head to tail tip, have their own way of shrinking. If the mammal notices a nearby predator, it'll curl into a small ball less than half its normal size and shield its stomach and face. Unable to find a vulnerable part of the pangolin to strike, many enemies give up. Tiny can be tough.

TONGUE TIME

Up to 28 inches (71 cm) in all, a pangolin's tongue can be almost as long as its body (minus the tail)! How does it fit inside the mammal? The tongue runs from its mouth down its sternum (or breastbone). The back end curves around organs in the lower abdomen, arching toward the backbone. At rest, the tongue's front end is coiled inside the pangolin's mouth. The animal flicks out its licker to snag grub.

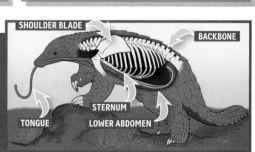

SHOULDER BLADE

BACKBONE

TONGUE

STERNUM

LOWER ABDOMEN

The Secret Language of Dolphins

I t's no secret that dolphins are able to chat with each other. Using squawks, clicks, and chirps, these smart animals communicate with distinctive dolphin chatter. But what are they saying? Scientists are trying to find out by studying wild and captive dolphins all over the world to decipher their secret language.

CHATTY Mammals

In many ways, you're just like the more than 30 species of dolphins that swim in the world's oceans and rivers. Dolphins are mammals, like you are, and must swim to the surface to breathe air. Just as you might, they team up in pods, or groups, to accomplish tasks. And they also talk to each other. "Sometimes one dolphin will vocalize and then another will seem to answer," says Sara Waller, who studies bottlenose dolphins off the California coast. "And sometimes members of a pod vocalize in different patterns at the same time, much like many people chattering at a party." And just as you gesture and change facial expressions as you talk, dolphins communicate nonverbally through body postures, jaw claps, bubble blowing, and fin caresses.

THINKING Dolphin

Scientists think dolphins "talk" about everything from basic facts like their age to their emotional state. "I speculate that they say things like 'Good fish are over here,' or 'Watch out for that shark because he's hunting,'" says Denise Herzing, who studies dolphins in the Bahamas. Sometimes, dolphins call for backup. After being bullied by a duo of bottlenose dolphins, one spotted dolphin returned to the scene the next day with a few pals to chase and harass one of the bully bottlenose dolphins. "It's as if the spotted dolphin communicated to his buddies that he needed their help, then led them in search of this guy," says Herzing, who watched the scuffle.

Want to have some fun?

Let's chase bubbles!

Back off, bud!

Toss me a treat!

If you were a bottlenose dolphin, you could swim at a speed of 20 miles an hour (32 km/h). That's about four times as fast as an Olympic swimmer.

Let's play!

5 to 20: individual dolphins in an average pod

Over 4: types of vocalizations dolphins use (These include squawks, whistles, clicks, and squeaks.)

12 miles (19 km): distance high-frequency whistles can travel

Over 30: nonverbal behaviors (for instance, tail slapping or rubbing fins) dolphins use to communicate

2 months: time before a baby dolphin is born that a mother might start "singing" to her unborn calf

LANGUAGE Lessons

Experts use high-tech gear to record and analyze every nuance of the dolphin language. But they're far from speaking "dolphin" yet. Part of the reason is because dolphins are hard to keep up with. Very fast swimmers, they stay underwater for up to 10 minutes between breaths. Also, their language is so dependent on what they're doing, whether they're playing, fighting, or going after tasty fish. It's no different for humans. Think about when you raise a hand to say hello. Under other circumstances, the same gesture can mean goodbye, stop, or that something costs five bucks. It's the same for dolphins. During fights, for example, dolphins clap their jaws to say "Back off!" But they jaw clap while playing too, as if to show who's king of the underwater playground. It's all a bit of a mystery.

So while scientists haven't completely cracked the code on dolphin chatter just yet, they're listening ... and learning.

I'm tougher than I look!

SEA OTTERS:
Super Cute, Super Tough

ULTIMATE FUR COAT

A sea otter wears a luxurious fur coat made up of about 800 million hairs. A shield from the sea, the coat is covered in natural oils that keep the skin and underfur dry. Because its fur is the only thing protecting a sea otter from the heat-stealing ocean water, the marine mammal spends nearly half of its day cleaning, combing, and fluffing its coat.

Only a female and her pups will hunt in groups or share food.

FEEDING FRENZY

To stay warm, an otter also relies on a super-revved metabolism. It must eat three times more calories than a kid needs in order to survive. A daily menu might be 7 abalone, 37 cancer crabs, 50 sea urchins, or 157 kelp crabs—that's about equal in calories to 42 scoops of chocolate ice cream! Otters also have to work for their food: To eat 150 kelp crabs, the otter needs to make at least 150 dives!

Sea otters may look like cute, gentle balls of fur, but they're actually rugged, resilient predators that battle prey, the environment, and other otters every day. Here's why they deserve a reputation as the tough guys of the ocean.

SEA SURVIVOR

A sea otter is about the same size as an 11-year-old kid—but a whole lot tougher. A human would be lucky to last 20 minutes in an otter's home just beyond the breaking waves before hypothermia—a drop in body temperature—set in and their body shut down. Unlike whales and walruses, otters don't even have blubber (a thick layer of fat) to keep them warm. So how do they survive?

Sea otters are related to skunks, weasels, badgers, and river otters.

SUPER STRENGTH

Sea otters are like superheroes when it comes to strength. A hard clam or mussel shell is no match for an otter's extremely powerful jaws and strong teeth. A person would have to use a special sharp tool to pry a firmly anchored abalone from its rock. An otter has only its paws and an occasional rock. The otter also uses its strong paws to snatch and overpower large crabs while avoiding their dangerous claws.

Super swimmers, super eaters, super divers—sea otters definitely deserve their rep as supertough marine mammals.

Incredible Powers of the **OCTOPUS!**

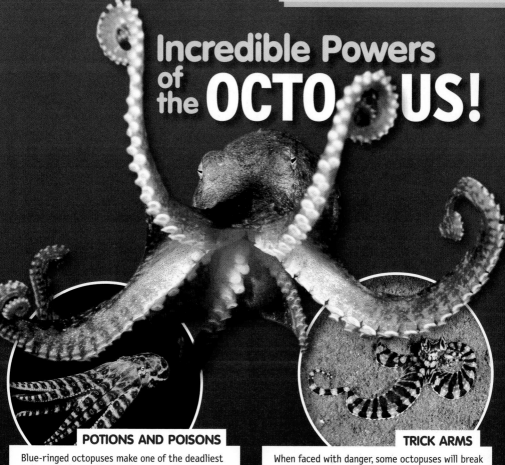

POTIONS AND POISONS

Blue-ringed octopuses make one of the deadliest poisons in the world. They have enough poison in their saliva to kill a human, though these mollusks mostly use their venom to paralyze prey or to defend themselves from enemies.

TRICK ARMS

When faced with danger, some octopuses will break off an arm and scoot away. The arm keeps wriggling for hours, sometimes crawling all over an attacker and distracting it. The octopus grows a new arm out of the stump.

THE OCTOPUS IS THE TALLER LUMP ON THE RIGHT. THAT'S BRAIN CORAL ON THE LEFT.

ESCAPE ARTIST

To confuse attackers, an octopus will squirt a concentrated ink out of its backside that forms a smokelike cloud. This allows enough time for an octopus to escape.

MAGICAL MOVES

Octopuses can squeeze through tiny holes as if they were moving from room to room through keyholes. Some can even swim through the sand, sticking an eye up like a periscope to see if the coast is clear.

OCEAN SUPERSTARS

The fascinating lives of 6 sea turtle species

Think all sea turtles are the same? Think again! Each of these species stands out in its own way.

1 GREEN SEA TURTLE: THE NEAT FREAK

In Hawaii, U.S.A., green sea turtles choose a "cleaning station"—a location where groups of cleaner fish groom the turtles by eating ocean gunk, like algae and parasites, off their skin and shells. In Australia, the turtles rub against a favorite sponge or rock to scrub themselves. Neat!

2 KEMP'S RIDLEY: THE LITTLE ONE

They may be the smallest sea turtles (babies shown here), but they're not so tiny: Adults weigh as much as many 10-year-old kids, and their shell is about the size of a car tire. They're speedy, too: It takes them less than an hour to dig a nest, then lay and bury their eggs.

3 OLIVE RIDLEY: THE ULTRA-MOM

Every year, hundreds of thousands of female olive ridley sea turtles take over beaches to lay their eggs and then bury them before disappearing back into the sea. Call it safety in numbers: With thousands of turtles swarming the shoreline, they're sure to overwhelm any predator.

4 LEATHERBACK: THE MEGA-TURTLE

These giants among reptiles have shells about as big as a door and weigh as much as six professional football players! Their size doesn't slow them down, though. A leatherback can swim as fast as a bottlenose dolphin.

5 HAWKSBILL: THE HEARTY EATER

What's the hawksbill's favorite snack? Sponges! These turtles gobble about 1,200 pounds (544 kg) of sponges a year. The turtles can safely eat this sea life, which is toxic to other animals. That means there are plenty of sponges to snack on!

6 LOGGERHEAD: THE TOUGH GUY

The loggerhead sea turtle's powerful jaws can easily crack open the shells of lobsters, conchs, and snails to get at the meat inside. Some loggerheads swim a third of the way around the world to find food.

Animal

Red Fox

A newborn red fox hangs on a small shrub, likely accidentally dropped by his mother as she carried her litter to a new den. Without his mom to keep him warm on this winter night, he won't survive.

The next morning, a couple notices the kit. The woman scoops up the newborn in her hands, and feels him twitch. He's alive, but just barely.

OUT OF THE WOODS

The fox—now named Albert—is rushed to a wild animal veterinary hospital. Staff place Albert in a toasty incubator, and bottle-feed him formula. They also set a teddy bear beside him for snuggling. Within a few days, Albert perks up and scarfs down his meals.

FOX FRIENDS

When spring arrives about eight weeks later, Albert joins other rescued kits in a large enclosure next to the sanctuary. The little foxes chase and wrestle one another, practicing their stalking and pouncing skills—two abilities that will help them survive in the wild. Caregivers also hide dead squirrels and mice in their pen so the youngsters can practice hunting.

HOME STRETCH

Seven months after Albert's rescue, Albert and his fox pals are placed in a pen at the wooded release site, adapting to the sights, smells, and sounds of the wild. One night, Albert and the other foxes quietly slip back into the forest. They are back where they belong.

DINNER IS SERVED.

Bats

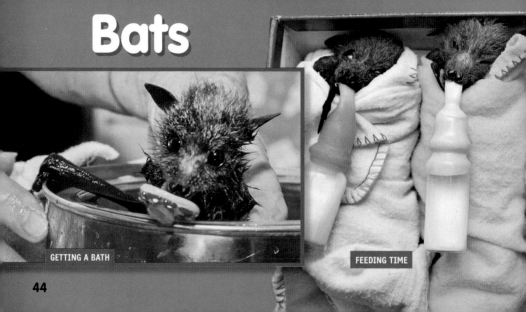

GETTING A BATH

FEEDING TIME

Rescues

Walking along the road at the foot of a hill in China's Sichuan Province, a group of people notice a giant panda on the hillside. Dazed, freezing, and starving, the panda has collapsed and is near death. The humans rush to alert officials—there is not much time left.

TO THE RESCUE

A rescuer shoots the panda with a tranquilizer dart, and the panda drifts off to sleep. They gently carry her down the hill and race her to a veterinary hospital. The underweight panda is infected with parasites and is suffering from hypothermia—when body temperature drops very low. With just some 1,800 giant pandas left in the wild, the caretakers know just how important it is to save this animal.

BAMBOO BONANZA

At first, the panda, Wolong II, just lies in her pen. But after a few days of rest and medicine, she sits up and begins munching on bamboo. The animal quickly gains more than 20 pounds (9 kg).

About six weeks after her rescue, Wolong II is healthy enough to return to the wild. She's secured in a metal crate and lifted into a truck. The rescue team carries the crate into the woods, and lays it down in a quiet spot surrounded by bamboo trees. They open its hatch, and Wolong II lumbers off into the forest without looking back.

Giant Panda

CARETAKERS AT THE HOSPITAL GIVE THE PANDA OXYGEN TO HELP HER BREATHE.

In eastern Australia, hundreds of baby bats were in trouble. The gray-headed flying foxes—who had not yet learned to fly—clung to their mothers, hanging high in a tree. But as a violent storm intensified, the wind knocked the babies from the shelter of their mothers' wings, and they fell to the ground. Wildlife volunteers rushed to the scene and discovered dozens of baby flying foxes lying helpless on the ground, 30 feet (9 m) below the tree.

The situation was scary, but after three long days, more than 350 little flying foxes were gently transported to a clinic. Bones were set, and antibiotics were given. Volunteers bottle-fed milk formula to the newborns every three hours. Soon, they graduated from bottles to solid foods, chowing down on chopped apples. They also learned to lap up nectar and finally figured out how to fly. After two and a half months at the clinic, the bats moved into an outside enclosure and eventually began to explore the wild, where they continued to thrive within the forest.

45

According to an ancient Native American legend, the Raven turned one out of every ten bears white to remind people of a time when Earth was covered by snow and ice.

Secrets
of the **Spirit Bear**

A rare animal creates a mysterious sight in the forest.

O n a cold, rainy October night in the rain forest, a hulking white form with a ghostly glow appears in the distance. No, it's not the ghost of a black bear. It's a spirit bear, also called a Kermode bear, which is a black bear with white hair. Spirit bears live almost exclusively in one place: the Great Bear Rainforest along the coast of British Columbia, Canada. Researchers want to figure out why the bears with white coats have survived here. Fewer than 200 spirit bears call this area home.

WHITE COAT CLUES
For many animals, unusual white coloration can make it hard to survive because they may have trouble hiding from predators. But the Kermode bear's coloring may actually help it survive and give it an edge while catching salmon.

"A white bear blends into the background during the day and is more successful catching fish," explains biologist Thomas Reimchen. "There is an advantage to one bear in some conditions and the other in different conditions."

TALE OF TWO ISLANDS
Canada's Gribbell Island has the highest concentration of Kermode bears, followed by neighboring Princess Royal Island. These isolated islands may be another key to the bears' survival, since there's no competition from grizzly bears, and wolves are the only natural threat. The islands' trees provide shelters, and rivers are filled with salmon.

Even though spirit bears have flourished on these islands, new threats such as logging worry scientists and the members of the Native American Gitga'at First Nation, who have lived with and protected spirit bears for centuries. That's why researchers are working hard to understand the biology of the spirit bear. As they do, they can find the best ways to ensure its survival.

MONKEY TROUBLE
A YOUNG BABOON TAKES A DANGEROUS SWIM.

It's a chilly winter morning in Botswana's Okavango Delta in Africa. A troop of chacma baboons wades across a narrow stream. But an eight-month-old infant named Chobe is left behind. She frantically paces the shore and calls out. The others ignore her as they move through the cold water without her.

Because the baboons' territory is flooded for half of the year, they must cross water all day. They move from island to island to find food and to escape predators such as lions and leopards.

1 DANGEROUS CROSSING

To cross the stream, bigger kid baboons hitch a ride with one of their parents, climbing onto the adult's back. Chobe usually gets a lift across the water with her dad, but today he's gone on ahead. So she has to figure out a way to get across the water and keep up with her troop. A young baboon cannot survive alone in the wild.

2 CAUGHT IN THE CURRENT

Chobe begins to wade into the cold stream. The water quickly becomes too deep for her, so she starts to swim clumsily. Midway, the strong current drags her downstream, farther from the shore. Her screams turn to gurgles as she starts to swallow water.

4 STAYING SAFE WITH DAD

Baboons have to learn to survive on their own, and sometimes that involves dangerous lessons. Chobe got a taste of what it's like to be an independent member of the troop. She decides she isn't quite ready to be a grown-up yet ... so she makes sure to find her father and hop onto his back at the next water crossing.

3 COMFORT AFTER A CLOSE CALL

Chobe's tiring fast, but just then, her feet find a shallow bank in the stream and she races out of the water. She sits on the shore, shivering. Her mother soon arrives, holds her close, and grooms her. Grooming is a great form of comfort for baboons. In no time, Chobe is running around with the other young baboons.

BIZARRE Insects

Check out some of the strangest bugs on Earth!

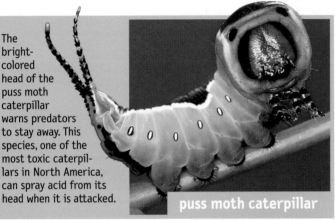

The bright-colored head of the puss moth caterpillar warns predators to stay away. This species, one of the most toxic caterpillars in North America, can spray acid from its head when it is attacked.

puss moth caterpillar

walking leaf

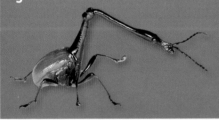

This flat, green insect is a master of disguise: It's common to mistake this bug for an actual leaf, thanks to its large, feathery wings. This clever camouflage provides protection from potential predators.

giraffe-necked weevil

No surprise, this bug gets its name from its extra-long neck. The males have longer necks than females do, which they use to fight other males for mating rights.

thorn bugs

One tiny thorn bug may not be a match for a bigger predator, but when grouped together on a branch, these spiky bugs create a prickly pack no bird wants a bite of!

spiny katydid

This katydid is covered in sharper-than-knives spikes. If a predator attacks, this species springs into action, defending itself by jabbing an enemy with its spiny legs and arms.

cockchafer beetle

The wild, feathery antennae on the male cockchafer may be cool to look at, but they're also helpful tools. They enable the bug to sniff for food and feel out its surrounding environment.

acorn weevil

The acorn weevil's hollow nose is longer than its body, and perfect for drilling through the shells of acorns. A female will feast on the nut by sucking up its rich, fatty liquid, and then lay her eggs in the acorn.

pink grasshopper

Though most grasshoppers are green or brown, some—like this pink nymph—are much brighter. Pink grasshoppers are rare, most likely because they are easy for predators to spot.

man-faced stinkbug

There are more than 4,500 species of stinkbugs world-wide, including this brilliant yellow species, whose shield-shaped body displays a unique pattern resembling a tribal mask. Like all stinkbugs, this species secretes a foul-smelling liquid from scent glands between its legs when it feels threatened.

rhinoceros beetle

Ounce for ounce, this insect, which gets its name from the hornlike structure on the male's head, is considered one of the world's strongest creatures. It is capable of carrying up to 850 times its own body weight.

5 COOL THINGS ABOUT Butterflies

MONARCH PUPA

2 Butterflies are nature's magicians.

Butterflies begin life as caterpillars. Once grown, the caterpillar becomes a pupa. Protected by a cocoon, the pupa transforms into a butterfly, a process called metamorphosis.

ZEBRA SWALLOWTAIL

1 Some butterflies start out smelly.

Not all butterflies stink, but the caterpillar of the zebra swallowtail butterfly sure does! Its nasty odor helps keep it safe from hungry animals.

3 Butterflies taste WITH THEIR "FEET."

Butterflies have chemical receptors on their legs, similar to taste buds, that allow them to taste the sweetness of a peach just by standing on it.

4 MANY butterflies ARE poisonous.

The monarch, for example, eats only poisonous milkweed plants, making both the caterpillar and the adult butterfly a dangerous snack for predators.

5 Some are winged tricksters.

OWL BUTTERFLY

Owl butterflies startle predators with huge "eyes" on their wings. The false eyes divert an attacker's attention, giving the butterfly time for a hasty escape.

Bet You Didn't Know

8 surprising facts about spiders

1 Golden silk orb-weaver spiders vibrate their webs to distract predators.

2 Black widow spiders are more venomous than rattlesnakes.

3 After a large meal, a tarantula may not eat for a month.

4 Crab spiders change color to blend in with their surroundings.

5 There are more than 37,000 species of spiders.

6 A spider eats about 2,000 insects a year.

7 The oldest known spider fossils are more than 300 million years old.

8 A pound (.45 kg) of spider silk could stretch around the Equator.

Does Your Pet L♥ve You?

More scientists are beginning to agree with what most pet owners already believe: Pets do love the people in their lives. Decide for yourself!

Rescue Dog ♡

When two-year-old Daisy Smith wandered from her family's yard one day, she was lucky to have her family's Labrador retriever, Thunder, tagging along. After 13 hours, a search party finally found the little girl (right) sitting by a river a mile and a half (2.4 km) from her home, with Thunder by her side. There's no doubt that this hero dog loves his Daisy!

Fire Cat

Boo Boo the cat is living proof that animals are capable of unselfish love. One night, as Frances Morris and her husband were asleep in their bed, Boo Boo began meowing and howling. Sleepily, Morris tried to calm Boo Boo, but the cat kept meowing. Fully awake, Morris realized the bedroom was filling with smoke. The kitchen was on fire! Instead of escaping outside, Boo Boo had run upstairs to warn the Morrises, and everyone escaped safely.

Funny Bunny

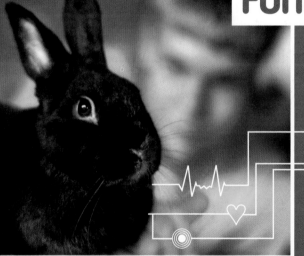

Who needs jokes when you have a bunny? That's what 13-year-old Kenny Clessas discovered when his pet rabbit, Killer, got him giggling after a bad day. Noticing Kenny crying, Killer started head-butting and running circles around the boy. Kenny just had to laugh!

How affectionate is your pet?

1

When you arrive at home, your dog ...

a hides under the couch.

b barely looks up from its nap.

c runs to greet you.

2

Whenever you sit down on a chair or the floor, your cat ...

a leaves the room.

b watches you from afar.

c cuddles up on your lap, purring.

3

If you reach into the cage, your gerbil ...

a digs into its wood chips to hide.

b backs away unless coaxed with a treat.

c jumps onto your hand eagerly.

IF YOUR ANSWER IS **a**, your pet plays it cool. It decides when it's cuddle time. **b**, your pet thinks you're its buddy. It likes you to be around. **c**, your pet is head over heels in love with you. It would do anything to be close to you.

A PUZZLE FOR YOUR POOCH

Difficulty Level:
Easy

Active Time Needed:
15 minutes

DISCOVER HOW FAST YOUR DOG LEARNS

Your new puppy wants a bit of your pizza. He tries sitting at your feet and whining. No deal. He paws at your knee and gets pushed away. Then he notices that your baby sister dropped some on the floor. Score! Tomorrow night, he'll head straight for the baby's chair. That's learning. You can test your dog's ability to learn by giving him this puzzle and seeing if he can solve it faster with practice.

YOU NEED

- **9 bite-size treats**
- **3 tennis balls**
- **muffin tin**
- **stopwatch or clock**
- **pencil and paper**

INSTRUCTIONS

1 Set three treats into different holes in the muffin tin. Show the muffin tin to your dog to get him interested.

2 Place a tennis ball on top of each treat and set the muffin tin on the floor.

3 Start timing. Record how long it takes your dog to uncover all three treats.

4 Repeat the procedure and record how long it takes him to find all the treats a second time.

5 Give him one more round and record the time for his third attempt.

6 Compare the three times. If your dog was faster on his second and third tries, it shows that he learned how to extract the treats quickly.

Whenever a dog does something and gets a reward, he is more likely to do it again. Psychologists call this conditioning. The problem is, dogs are in constant motion. It takes a lot of work to teach them which move is being rewarded. You can almost imagine your dog's thoughts the first time you reward him for a trick, "Oh, I wagged my tail. Is that why I got the treat? I sneezed. Did that do it? Maybe she gave me a treat because I wiggled my ears." Gradually, your dog will realize which action earns the treat.

Treat puzzles work similarly. Spot smells the treat and knows it's there. He may try several ways to get it out: nudging with his nose, pushing with his paw, and looking at you to see if you'll get it for him. With enough practice, he'll figure out the best way to get the treat, and soon he'll be gulping them down.

TIP
If the ball sinks all the way into the muffin tin opening, it may be difficult for your dog to move the ball. Try using a muffin tin with slightly narrower openings or a thick treat that will elevate the ball a little.

Check out the book!

20 CUTEST ANIMALS OF 2020

From furry bobcats to smiling geckos, there's no shortage of cute creatures on Earth. Here's NG Kids' roundup of cuddly critters that are sure to make you say *awww*.

1 GET UP, STAND UP

A group of meerkats stands at attention by its burrow. Extremely family-oriented, meerkat "mobs" spend a lot of time playing together in a tight-knit group. The furry family may look sweet, but if confronted, they will stand together, arching their backs, raising their hair, and hissing.

2 CLOSE-UP

This young wombat is definitely not camera shy! Native to Australia, these marsupials are about the size of a jelly bean at birth and stay in their mom's pouch for several months before venturing out, where they'll spend most of their days burrowing underground tunnels.

3 TRUNK SHOW

Get out of these elephants' way! African elephants can weigh some 200 pounds (91 kg) at birth; by adulthood, they can top the scales at more than seven tons (6.4 t). The world's largest land mammal also has a big appetite, eating more than 300 pounds (136 kg) of grass, fruit, and leaves a day.

5 THINK PINK

Adult greater flamingos may be famous for their coral-colored hue, but their chicks look a lot different—at first. Born with gray or white feathers, it takes two to three years for a young flamingo's pink feathers to show.

4 SPOT ON

This cuddly-looking bobcat may have one of the finest fur coats in the animal world, but it's not all about looking good. The spotted fur helps North America's most common wild cat blend in with many habitats. Those ear tufts? Bobcats may twitch them to communicate with other bobcats.

6

BEAR-Y HUNGRY

In the fall, this brown bear cub will start packing on about three pounds (1.4 kg) a day to prepare for its deep winter sleep. Those pounds of fat are what the bear will live on while snoozing. Luckily, Mom is an expert at sniffing out a meal in their northwestern U.S. habitat and can detect food from 18 miles (29 km) away.

7

HANGING OUT

This young raccoon might be an expert climber—many raccoons spend their first few months living in a nest in a tree hole. As adults, raccoons rely more on their sense of touch than on their senses of sight and smell to find meals such as frogs, bird eggs, insects, and even snakes.

8

UP A TREE

This baby orangutan may have figured out the best part of life in the trees: just hanging out! Orangutans spend up to 95 percent of their time high up in trees on the Southeast Asia islands of Borneo and Sumatra. They sleep, eat, and play in nests that are big enough for a 10-year-old kid to stretch out in.

9 RAD REPTILE

The gentle leopard gecko is famous for its spots as well as for its urine, which comes out as tiny crystals. Its calm nature and long life span—it can live up to 20 years if treated well—make this gecko a very popular pet.

ALL EARS

Nobody sports a birthday suit better than a baby aardvark. Born pink and wrinkly, this big baby slurps milk but will gobble thousands of ants a night when it's older. An African native, the aardvark's name means "earth pig" in one South African language. It has donkey ears, a kangaroo tail, and a piggy nose, but it's actually a distant relation to the elephant.

10

FLYING LEAP

11

Caracals may not have wings, but they can sure fly! This small wild cat, native to Africa and the Middle East, has strong hind legs that allow it to jump more than six feet (2 m) in the air—the height of a tall adult human.

12
HANGING ON
This 10-month-old gorilla keeps a tight hold on a bamboo pole in Volcanoes National Park in Rwanda, Africa. Gorillas are born with a powerful grip, which allows them to hang on to their moms for transport—and, of course, to climb.

BLENDING IN
Hares, beware! This critter may look adorable, but it could be your enemy. Silent and sneaky, the ermine can pounce on prey that's larger than it is, such as an arctic hare. The stealthy stalker gets help from its changing coat, which is white during winter and brown in spring and summer—perfect camouflage.

13

14
STARTING SMALL
Coyote pups may be tiny at first, but they eventually grow to be the size of medium dogs. They're cared for from birth by both parents, who give their offspring an early start on hunting by bringing live mice to their den for stalking practice.

WHAT A HOOT!
Why, hello there! A Eurasian pygmy owl peers out of a tree in a forest in Sweden. These tiny owls—which grow to be about the size of a robin—are small enough to squeeze into tree holes made by woodpeckers, where they build their nests.

15

SMILEY SQUID

Say cheese? It may look like this piglet squid is smiling, but in reality this deepwater dweller isn't quite hamming for the camera. Rather, the squid's friendly "face" is the result of tentacles and unusual skin patterns, which form the shape of an adorable mug topped by a mop of curly hair.

16

18

TALL TALE

Talk about a grand entrance: A baby giraffe falls about six feet (1.8 m) from its mom during birth before hitting the ground. But the bumpy landing doesn't stop the little guys from getting a jump start on life—they're usually up on their hooves and walking at just an hour old.

17

JUST LION AROUND

A mother Galápagos sea lion lounges around with her pup. These animals share a tight bond: Although baby sea lions usually learn to swim by the time they're two weeks old, they stick to their mothers' sides for a few years before venturing out on their own.

BADGE OF HONOR

What's black and white and striped all over? An American badger, of course! This species is easily recognized by the telltale white stripe, which runs from the tip of their noses all the way to the back of their heads. But it's the badgers' black cheek patches—called "badges"—that give them their name.

19

HOP TO IT

Native to tropical Amazon forests, this frog's see-through skin helps it hide high in the trees. Sunlight shines right through the frog and provides camouflage. When it's time to lay its eggs, a glass frog deposits tiny white eggs onto a leaf above a stream. When the tadpoles emerge, they slip off the leaf and splash into the water below.

20

Prehistoric TIMELINE

HUMANS HAVE WALKED on Earth for some 200,000 years, a mere blip in the planet's 4.5-billion-year history. A lot has happened during that time. Earth formed, and oxygen levels rose in the millions of years of the Precambrian time. The productive Paleozoic era gave rise to hard-shelled organisms, vertebrates, amphibians, and reptiles.

Dinosaurs ruled Earth in the mighty Mesozoic. And 65 million years after dinosaurs became extinct, modern humans emerged in the Cenozoic era. From the first tiny mollusks to the dinosaur giants of the Jurassic and beyond, Earth has seen a lot of transformation.

THE PRECAMBRIAN TIME

4.5 billion to 542 million years ago

- Earth (and other planets) formed from gas and dust left over from a giant cloud that collapsed to form the sun. The giant cloud's collapse was triggered when nearby stars exploded.
- Low levels of oxygen made Earth a suffocating place.
- Early life-forms appeared.

THE PALEOZOIC ERA

542 million to 252 million years ago

- The first insects and other animals appeared on land.
- 450 million years ago (m.y.a.), the ancestors of sharks began to swim in the oceans.
- 430 m.y.a., plants began to take root on land.
- More than 360 m.y.a., amphibians emerged from the water.
- Slowly, the major landmasses began to come together, creating Pangaea, a single supercontinent.
- By 300 m.y.a., reptiles had begun to dominate the land.

What Killed the Dinosaurs?

It's a mystery that's boggled the minds of scientists for centuries: What happened to the dinosaurs? While various theories have bounced around, a recent study confirms that the most likely culprit is an asteroid or comet that created a giant crater. Researchers say that the impact set off a series of natural disasters like tsunamis, earthquakes, and temperature swings that plagued the dinosaurs' ecosystem and disrupted their food chain. This, paired with intense volcanic eruptions that caused drastic climate changes, is thought to be why half of the world's species—including the dinosaurs—died in a mass extinction.

DINO TIMES

THE MESOZOIC ERA

251 million to 65 million years ago

The Mesozoic era, or the age of the reptiles, consisted of three consecutive time periods (shown below). This is when the first dinosaurs began to appear. They would reign supreme for more than 150 million years.

TRIASSIC PERIOD

251 million to 201 million years ago

- Appearance of the first mammals. They were rodent-size.
- The first dinosaur appeared.
- Ferns were the dominant plants on land.
- The giant supercontinent of Pangaea began breaking up toward the end of the Triassic.

JURASSIC PERIOD

201 million to 145 million years ago

- Giant dinosaurs dominated the land.
- Pangaea continued its breakup, and oceans formed in the spaces between the drifting landmasses, allowing sea life, including sharks and marine crocodiles, to thrive.
- Conifer trees spread across the land.

CRETACEOUS PERIOD

145 million to 66 million years ago

- The modern continents developed.
- The largest dinosaurs developed.
- Flowering plants spread across the landscape.
- Mammals flourished, and giant pterosaurs ruled the skies over small birds.
- Temperatures grew more extreme. Dinosaurs lived in deserts, swamps, and forests from the Antarctic to the Arctic.

THE CENOZOIC ERA—TERTIARY PERIOD

65 million to 2.6 million years ago

- Following the dinosaur extinction, mammals rose as the dominant species.
- Birds continued to flourish.
- Volcanic activity was widespread.
- Temperatures began to cool, eventually ending in an ice age.
- The period ended with land bridges forming, which allowed plants and animals to spread to new areas.

DINO Classification

Classifying dinosaurs and all other living things can be a complicated matter, so scientists have devised a system to help with the process. Dinosaurs are put into groups based on a very large range of characteristics.

Scientists put dinosaurs into two major groups: the bird-hipped ornithischians and the lizard-hipped saurischians.

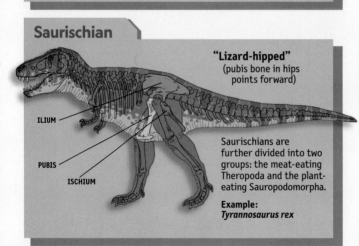

Ornithischian

"Bird-hipped"
(pubis bone in hips points backward)

ILIUM

PUBIS

ISCHIUM

Ornithischians have the same-shaped pubis as birds of today, but today's birds are actually more closely related to the saurischians.

Example: *Styracosaurus*

Saurischian

"Lizard-hipped"
(pubis bone in hips points forward)

ILIUM

PUBIS

ISCHIUM

Saurischians are further divided into two groups: the meat-eating Theropoda and the plant-eating Sauropodomorpha.

Example: *Tyrannosaurus rex*

Within these two main divisions, dinosaurs are then separated into orders and then families, such as Stegosauria. Like other members of the Stegosauria, *Stegosaurus* had spines and plates along the back, neck, and tail.

THE FIERCE *ALLOSAURUS* HAD NEARLY **70 TEETH.**

CORYTHO-SAURUS **LIVED IN BIG HERDS LIKE MODERN BUFFALO.**

BRACHIO-SAURUS **WAS TALLER THAN TWO GIRAFFES.**

THE *SPINOSAURUS* ATE SHARKS.

3 NEWLY DISCOVERED DINOS

Humans have been searching for—and discovering—dinosaur remains for hundreds of years. In that time, at least 1,000 species of dinos have been found all over the world, and thousands more may still be out there waiting to be unearthed. Recent discoveries include *Borealopelta markmitchelli*. Found in western Canada, the plant-eating armored dinosaur is so well preserved that paleontologists have discovered remnants of its skin.

1 *Borealopelta markmitchelli* (Ornithischian)

Named After: Mark Mitchell, the man who chipped the rock away from the fossil

Length: 18 feet (5.5 m)

Time Range: Cretaceous

Where: Alberta, Canada

2 *Mansourasaurus shahinae* (Saurischian)

Named After: Mansoura University in Egypt

Length: 33 feet (10 m)

Time Range: Late Cretaceous

Where: Egypt

3 *Diluvicursor pickeringi* (Ornithischian)

Named After: Australian paleontologist David Pickering

Length: 7.5 feet (2.3 m)

Time Range: Cretaceous

Where: Australian-Antarctic rift valley

DINO DEFENSES

Scientists don't know for sure whether plant-eating dinos used their amazing attributes to battle their carnivorous cousins, but these herbivores were armed with some pretty wicked ways they could have used to defend themselves.

ARMOR: *GASTONIA*

(GAS-TONE-EE-AH)

Prickly *Gastonia* was covered in heavy, defensive armor. To protect it from the strong jaws of meat-eaters it had four horns on its head, thick layers of bone shielding its brain, rows of spikes sticking out from its back, and a tail with triangular blades running along each side.

SPIKES: *KENTROSAURUS*

(KEN-TROH-SORE-US)

Stand back! This cousin of *Stegosaurus* had paired spikes along its tail, which it could swing at attackers with great speed. One paleontologist estimated that *Kentrosaurus* could have swung its treacherous tail fast enough to shatter bones!

CLUB TAILZ:
ANKYLOSAURUS
(AN-KYE-LOH-SORE-US)

Steer clear! *Ankylosaurus* possessed a heavy, knobby tail that it could have used to whack attackers. It may not have totally protected the tanklike late Cretaceous dino from a determined *T. rex*, but a serious swing could have generated enough force to do some real damage to its rival reptile.

WHIP TAIL:
DIPLODOCUS
(DIH-PLOD-UH-KUS)

Some scientists think this late Jurassic giant's tail—about half the length of its 90-foot (27-m) body—could have been used like a whip and swished at high speeds, creating a loud noise that would send potential predators running.

HORNS:
TRICERATOPS
(TRI-SER-UH-TOPS)

There's no evidence *Triceratops* ever used its horns to combat late Cretaceous snack-craving carnivores. But scientists do believe the famous three-horned creature used its frills and horns in battle with other members of its species.

Dynamite DINO AWARDS

Spiky body armor. Razor-sharp teeth. Unimaginable strength. No doubt, all dinos are cool. But whether they were the biggest, the fiercest, or the biggest-brained of the bunch, some stand out more than others. Here are seven of the most amazing dinos ever discovered.

Supersize Appetite

Big Brain

Cool Camo

Scientists think that **Tyrannosaurus rex** could gulp down 500 pounds (227 kg) of meat at a time—that's like eating 2,000 hamburger patties in one bite!

Troodon, a meat-eater the size of a man, had a brain as big as an avocado pit—relatively large for a dinosaur of its small stature. Because of its big brain, scientists think Troodon may have been the smartest dino and as intelligent as modern birds.

The birdlike **Sinornithosaurus** had feathers similar to those of modern birds. It may have also had reddish brown, yellow, and black coloring that kept this turkey-size raptor camouflaged as it hunted in the forest.

Heavy-weight

The heaviest of all dinosaurs, *Argentinosaurus* is believed to have weighed 220,000 pounds (99,790 kg)—more than 15 elephants.

Built for Speed

Ornithomimids, a group of dinosaurs that resembled ostriches, would have given the world's fastest man a run for his money. Some of these long-limbed, toothless meat-eaters are thought to have clocked speeds of 50 miles an hour (80 km/h).

Pint-Size Predator

Microraptor zhaoianus, the smallest meat-eating dinosaur, measured just 16 inches (40 cm) tall. With long toe tips for grasping branches, it's thought to be closely related to today's birds.

Super Spines

Known as the "spine lizard," *Spinosaurus* had huge spines sticking out of its back, some taller than a fourth grader! Weighing up to 22 tons (20 t), it may have been the biggest meat-eating dinosaur.

71

QUIZ WHIZ

Explore just how much you know about animals with this quiz!

Write your answers on a piece of paper. Then check them below.

1 Sea otters are related to _____.
- a. skunks
- b. dolphins
- c. sloths
- d. narwhals

2 One of the red-eyed tree frog's calls sounds like a _____.
- a. car horn
- b. baby rattle
- c. guitar
- d. cricket

3 **True or false?** A margay's ankle can rotate all the way around to face backward.

4 Which dinosaur feature is believed to have been used for defense?
- a. knobby tail
- b. horns and frills
- c. thick layer of bone
- d. all of the above

5 Which is not a characteristic of birds?
- a. They lay eggs.
- b. They breathe with lungs.
- c. They are cold-blooded.
- d. They have feathers and wings.

Not **STUMPED** yet? Check out the *NATIONAL GEOGRAPHIC KIDS QUIZ WHIZ* collection for more crazy **ANIMAL** questions!

ANSWERS: 1. a; 2. b; 3. True; 4. d; 5. c

HOMEWORK HELP

Wildly Good Animal Reports

Seahorse

Your teacher wants a written report on the seahorse. Not to worry. Use these organizational tools so you can stay afloat while writing a report.

STEPS TO SUCCESS: Your report will follow the format of a descriptive or expository essay (see p. 199 for "How to Write a Perfect Essay") and should consist of a main idea, followed by supporting details and a conclusion. Use this basic structure for each paragraph as well as the whole report, and you'll be on the right track.

1. Introduction

State your **main idea.**

Seahorses are fascinating fishes with many unique characteristics.

2. Body

Provide **supporting points** for your main idea.

Seahorses are very small fishes.
Seahorses are named for their head shape.
Seahorses display behavior that is rare among almost all other animals on Earth.

Then **expand** on those points with further description, explanation, or discussion.

Seahorses are very small fishes.
Seahorses are about the size of an M&M at birth, and most adult seahorses would fit in a teacup.
Seahorses are named for their head shape.
With long, tubelike snouts, seahorses are named for their resemblance to horses.
A group of seahorses is called a herd.
Seahorses display behavior that is rare among almost all other animals on Earth.
Unlike most other fish, seahorses stay with one mate their entire lives. They are also among the only species in which dads, not moms, give birth to the babies.

3. Conclusion

Wrap it up with a **summary** of your whole paper.

Because of their unique shape and unusual behavior, seahorses are among the most fascinating and easily distinguishable animals in the ocean.

KEY INFORMATION

Here are some things you should consider including in your report:

What does your animal look like?
To what other species is it related?
How does it move?
Where does it live?
What does it eat?
What are its predators?
How long does it live?
Is it endangered?
Why do you find it interesting?

SEPARATE FACT FROM FICTION: Your animal may have been featured in a movie or in myths and legends. Compare and contrast how the animal has been portrayed with how it behaves in reality. For example, penguins can't dance the way they do in *Happy Feet.*

PROOFREAD AND REVISE: As with any great essay, when you're finished, check for misspellings, grammatical mistakes, and punctuation errors. It often helps to have someone else proofread your work, too, as he or she may catch things you have missed. Also, look for ways to make your sentences and paragraphs even better. Add more descriptive language, choosing just the right verbs, adverbs, and adjectives to make your writing come alive.

BE CREATIVE: Use visual aids to make your report come to life. Include an animal photo file with interesting images found in magazines or printed from websites. Or draw your own! You can also build a miniature animal habitat diorama. Use creativity to help communicate your passion for the subject.

THE FINAL RESULT: Put it all together in one final, polished draft. Make it neat and clean, and remember to cite your references.

SCIENCE and TECHNOLOGY

It's a bird, it's a plane, it's a ... driverless air taxi? Volocopter 2X, still in the prototype stage, can transport two passengers. The 18-rotor drone aircraft is being tested in Dubai.

EARTH EXPLORER
Meet Kakani Katija!

This National Geographic emerging explorer blends biology and math to create cool tools.

K akani Katija loved science and math growing up, so she thought she would be an astronaut one day. But after discovering she had a passion for bio-engineering—the combination of engineering and biology—she decided to dive into an even deeper area: the ocean.

Today, Kakani develops instruments to enable exploration of previously hard-to-reach areas, like far below the ocean's surface. At the Monterey Bay Aquarium Research Institute (MBARI), Kakani created a tool called DeepPIV (short for Particle Image Velocimetry) that measures tiny plastic particles called microplastics thousands of meters underwater—and the animals that eat them.

"The tool uses laser illumination to see how these animals consume plastics," she says of DeepPIV, which is attached to a submersible robot that can travel 2.5 miles (4,000 m) below the ocean's surface. "Many people assume that the plastic problem is constrained to the surface of the ocean. What we discovered is that there are microplastics in the deepest parts, even on the ocean floor, and there are animals ingesting them."

By continuing to develop better observational tools and techniques, Kakani can arm biologists and other experts with more knowledge about what's going on in the deep sea. She hopes this will trigger change that can ultimately improve the condition of our oceans—and the entire planet.

"It's hard to come up with the best solutions if you don't know what the problem is," says Kakani. "As bio-engineers, we use technology to find new ways to approach a problem, and help others fix it."

MICROPLASTICS

8 million tons (7.2 million t) of trash wind up in the ocean each year.

" I was always enamored by the search for life in outer planets. And then I realized that there is a lot of life in our oceans that we knew almost nothing about. That story is just beginning. "

KAKANI OPERATING DEEPPIV

It took about four years for Kakani and her team to design, build, and finally use the DeepPIV tool.

INSPECTING A FISHING NET FOUND IN THE OCEAN

CALL TO ACTION!

Want to get into bioengineering? Better start crunching some numbers. "Math is the foundation of any bio-engineering career," says Kakani. "Our focus is on finding solutions." To do your part in reducing the amount of plastics that DeepPIV finds in the ocean, a good place to start is by using reusable straws instead of plastic ones. Encourage your friends and family to do the same!

COOL INVENTIONS

FLOATING ISLAND

You'd *want* to be stranded on this island. Modeled after a large species of lily pad that drifts down the Amazon River, the Lilypad floating ecopolis is designed to float on the ocean. This human-made habitat would feature homes and shops structured around a lagoon that could collect rain for drinking water. Fueled in part by wind and solar power, the island concept could provide up to 50,000 residents with an eco-friendly home—and the ultimate oceanfront view.

PART OF THE ISLAND HABITAT DIPS UNDERWATER.

GLOVES GIVE CONCERT

These gloves hit the right notes. Sensors inside the fingertips detect when you press on a hard surface and send a signal to a speaker to produce the same musical notes created by hitting piano keys. Tap out a tune with your hands side by side. Then move your mitts away from each other and drum your fingers again. The sensors can tell that your digits have moved, and they signal the speaker to play different notes—same as if you moved your hands in different directions on an actual piano. That rocks!

TAP YOUR FINGERS!

ROBOT FOLDS LAUNDRY

Doing laundry is no longer such a chore with FoldiMate, a robot that folds clean clothes. All you have to do is clip garments to hangers on the machine's exterior. The hangers, attached to a conveyor belt, rotate downward, pulling articles of clothing one at a time into a slot. Inside the robot, an electronic arm plucks each garment from its hanger and lays it on a platform. Here, more arms fold and dispense the item. Soon your laundry's done—case *clothed*.

BEFORE

AFTER

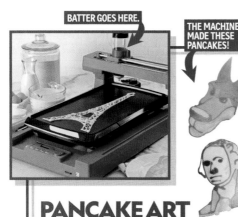

BATTER GOES HERE.

THE MACHINE MADE THESE PANCAKES!

PANCAKE ART

Create art with pancake mix! The PancakeBot produces flapjacks shaped as the Eiffel Tower, George Washington, Scooby-Doo, and more. First, use the PancakeBot computer program to trace over a design with the drawing tool. The movements are translated into step-by-step instructions for the PancakeBot to follow. Now just pour batter into the machine. The bot's electronic nozzle will squeeze the mixture onto a heated griddle below, shifting as it follows the directions to create the flapjack formation. The result? Pancakes that look *almost* too good to eat.

RAIN ALERT!

UMBRELLA PREDICTS WEATHER

Getting caught in the rain is no fun. That's where the Oombrella comes in. This umbrella's handle contains a device that measures temperature, air pressure, and humidity to predict exactly when it's going to rain. Connecting wirelessly to your phone, it alerts you about 15 minutes before the first drops fall. And don't worry about accidentally leaving this gear at a friend's house once the skies clear. The Oombrella pings your phone if you're more than 130 feet (40 m) away from it. That's one unforgettable umbrella.

SPACE GLIDER

The Perlan 2 plane will sweep you 17 miles (27 km) off the ground to the edge of space—and it doesn't even have an engine, jets, or propellers. What the two-passenger glider *does* have is an 84-foot (26-m) wingspan, about the length of two school buses. To take off, this lightweight craft is connected by cable to another plane and towed 10,000 feet (3,050 m) into the air. Then it's released over mountainous regions where extra-strong air currents buoy the plane under its large wings and carry the craft 90,000 feet (27,500 m) high. Here, data is collected on the atmosphere before pilots use the glider's air brakes to descend. Glide on!

PILOT

FUTURE WORLD:

The year is 2070 and it's time to get dressed for school. You step in front of a large video mirror that projects different clothes on you. After you decide on your favorite T-shirt, a robot fetches your outfit. No time is lost trying to find matching socks! Chores? What chores? Get ready for a whole new home life.

STAY CONNECTED

Whether your future home is an urban skyscraper or an underwater pod, all buildings will one day be connected via a central communications hub. Want to check out a *T. rex* skeleton at a faraway museum? You can virtually connect to it just as though you were checking it out in person. But you're not just seeing something miles away. Connect to a beach house's balcony and smell the salt water and feel the breeze. Buildings might also share information about incoming weather and emergencies to keep you safe.

CUSTOM COMFORT

Soon, your house may give you a personal welcome home. No need for keys—sensors scan your body and open the door. Walk into the living room, and the lighting adjusts to your preferred setting. Thirsty? A glass of water pops up on the counter. Before bed, you enter the bathroom and say, "Shower, please." The water starts flowing at exactly the temperature you want.

ON LOCATION

Your room has a spectacular view of the ocean ... because your house is suspended above it. New technologies will allow us to build our homes in unusual spots. In the future, "floating" structures elevated by supporting poles above water or other hard-to-access spots (think mountain peaks) will be more common as cities become more crowded. And this won't be limited to dry land on Earth. That means one day, your family could even live in space!

Homes

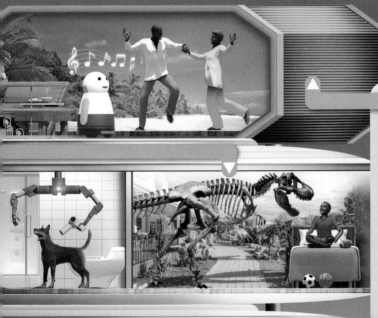

ON THE GO

Homes of the future will always be on the move. Walls will be capable of expanding and contracting, and houses will rotate with the sun's movements to conserve energy. Buildings will also be capable of changing size depending on who's inside. Grandparents could "move in" by attaching a modular section to the front, back, or top of the house.

BRING ON THE BOTS

While you were outside playing with your friends, your house robot did the laundry, vacuumed, and cleaned the bathroom. Meanwhile a drone just delivered groceries for the home-bot to put away. Minutes later, lunch is ready. The service is great ... but how will you earn your allowance? Instead of taking out the garbage or setting the table, you'll earn money by helping clean and maintain the robots.

FUTURE WORLD:

How do you get to the store in the year 2060? It's raining, so you decide not to take the drone. Instead you ride in your driverless cube car.

"The sky's no longer the limit in terms of where transportation is headed," says Tom Kurfess, a mechanical engineering professor at the Georgia Institute of Technology. Take a peek at these wild rides of the future.

GOING UP ... WAY UP!

The space elevator doors open—welcome to the space station lobby. It's possible that people will one day ride a space elevator from Earth to a space station that orbits our planet from 22,370 miles (36,000 km) above. The elevator will carry passengers and cargo into space without burning huge amounts of fuel, unlike today's rockets. Aboard the station, travelers might stay in a hotel room with a truly out-of-this-world view. Then those heading to, say, Mars, can transfer to a spaceship to continue their journey.

NO DRIVER NEEDED

You exit your high-rise apartment balcony into your own private glass elevator, take a seat, and say your destination. The elevator car descends 205 floors to street level before detaching from the building and moving to the street. It's now a cube-shaped car. Another cube carrying your friends is nearby; the vehicles connect while in motion, transforming into one bigger car. The cube drops you off at school and parks itself. According to Tommaso Gecchelin, founder of NEXT Future Transportation, driverless cars will work together to end traffic jams and improve safety.

Transportation

POWER PLANE

Passenger planes will still be around in the future—they'll just travel *much* faster. Today flying 6,850 miles (11,025 km) from New York City to Beijing, China, takes about 14 hours. But thanks to future technological advancements such as sleeker, more lightweight aircraft, a passenger plane could make the same trip in just under two hours.

FLOWN BY DRONE

"One day soon drones and robots will deliver our meals," Gecchelin says. But further into the future, helicopter-size drones could also deliver *people*. Some experts even think that cargo drones will be able to lift small houses from a city and carry them to scenic vacation spots.

TOTALLY TUBULAR

Your friend invites you to her birthday party. It's today—and across the country. No prob. You can tube it from the West Coast to the East Coast in just two hours. You sit in a capsule that looks like a train without rails. *Whoosh!* The capsule's sucked into a vacuum tube. Like a bullet train, the capsule uses magnets to fly forward in the tube without friction or resistance. The result: a smooth, fast ride that never slows down below 750 miles an hour (1,200 km/h).

WHAT IS LIFE?

This seems like such an easy question to answer. Everybody knows that singing birds are alive and rocks are not. But when we start studying bacteria and other microscopic creatures, things get more complicated.

SO WHAT EXACTLY IS LIFE?

Most scientists agree that something is alive if it can do the following: reproduce; grow in size to become more complex in structure; take in nutrients to survive; give off waste products; and respond to external stimuli, such as increased sunlight or changes in temperature.

KINDS OF LIFE

Biologists classify living organisms by how they get their energy. Organisms such as algae, green plants, and some bacteria use sunlight as an energy source. Animals (like humans), fungi, and some Archaea use chemicals to provide energy. When we eat food, chemical reactions within our digestive system turn our food into fuel.

Living things inhabit land, sea, and air. In fact, life also thrives deep beneath the oceans, embedded in rocks miles below Earth's crust, in ice, and in other extreme environments. The life-forms that thrive in these challenging environments are called extremophiles. Some of these draw directly upon the chemicals surrounding them for energy. Since these are very different forms of life than what we're used to, we may not think of them as alive, but they are.

HOW IT ALL WORKS

To try and understand how a living organism works, it helps to look at one example of its simplest form—the single-celled bacterium called *Streptococcus*. There are many kinds of these tiny organisms, and some are responsible for human illnesses. What makes us sick or uncomfortable are the toxins the bacteria give off in our bodies.

A single *Streptococcus* bacterium is so small that at least 500 of them could fit on the dot above this letter *i*. These bacteria are some of the simplest forms of life we know. They have no moving parts, no lungs, no brain, no heart, no liver, and no leaves or fruit. Yet this life-form reproduces. It grows in size by producing long chain structures, takes in nutrients, and gives off waste products. This tiny life-form is alive, just as you are alive.

What makes something alive is a question scientists grapple with when they study viruses, such as the ones that cause the common cold and smallpox. They can grow and reproduce within host cells, such as those that make up your body. Because viruses lack cells and cannot metabolize nutrients for energy or reproduce without a host, scientists ask if they are indeed alive. And don't go looking for them without a strong microscope— viruses are a hundred times smaller than bacteria.

Scientists think life began on Earth some 4.1 to 3.9 billion years ago, but no fossils exist from that time. The earliest fossils ever found are from the primitive life that existed 3.6 billion years ago. Other life-forms, some of which are shown below, soon followed. Scientists continue to study how life evolved on Earth and whether it is possible that life exists on other planets.

MICROSCOPIC ORGANISMS

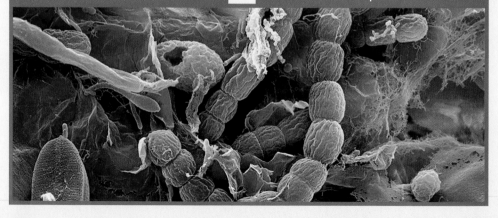

The Three Domains of Life

Biologists divide all living organisms into three domains: Bacteria, Archaea, and Eukarya. Archaean and Bacterial cells do not have nuclei, but they are so different from each other that they belong to different domains. Since human cells have a nucleus, humans belong to the Eukarya domain.

1 BACTERIA

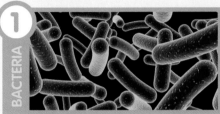

DOMAIN BACTERIA: These single-celled microorganisms are found almost everywhere in the world. Bacteria are small and do not have nuclei. They can be shaped like rods, spirals, or spheres. Some of them are helpful to humans, and some are harmful.

2 ARCHAEA

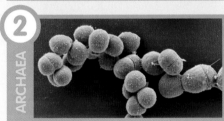

DOMAIN ARCHAEA: These single-celled microorganisms are often found in extremely hostile environments. Like Bacteria, Archaea do not have nuclei, but they have some genes in common with Eukarya. For this reason, scientists think the Archaea living today most closely resemble the earliest forms of life on Earth.

3 EUKARYA

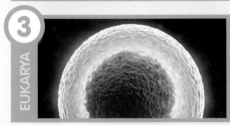

DOMAIN EUKARYA: This diverse group of life-forms is more complicated than Bacteria and Archaea, as Eukarya have one or more cells with nuclei. These are the tiny cells that make up your whole body. Eukarya are divided into four groups: fungi, protists, plants, and animals.

WHAT IS A DOMAIN? Scientifically speaking, a domain is a major taxonomic division into which natural objects are classified (see p. 26 for "What Is Taxonomy?").

FYI

FUNGI

KINGDOM FUNGI (about 100,000 species): Mainly multicellular organisms, fungi cannot make their own food. Mushrooms and yeast are fungi.

PROTISTS

PROTISTS (about 250,000 species): Once considered a kingdom, this group is a "grab bag" that includes unicellular and multicellular organisms of great variety.

PLANTS

KINGDOM PLANTAE (about 400,000 species): Plants are multicellular, and many can make their own food using photosynthesis (see p. 86 for "Photosynthesis").

ANIMALS

KINGDOM ANIMALIA (about 1,000,000 species): Most animals, which are multicellular, have their own organ systems. Animals do not make their own food.

HOW DOES YOUR GARDEN GROW?

The plant kingdom is about 400,000 species strong, growing all over the world: on top of mountains, in the sea, in frigid temperatures—everywhere. Without plants, life on Earth would not be able to survive. Plants provide food and oxygen for animals and humans.

Three characteristics make plants distinct:

1. Most have chlorophyll (a green pigment that makes photosynthesis work and turns sunlight into energy), while some are parasitic. These plants don't make their own food—they take it from other plants.
2. They cannot change their location on their own.
3. Their cell walls are made from a stiff material called cellulose.

Photosynthesis

Plants are lucky—most don't have to hunt or shop for food. Most use the sun to produce their own food. In a process called photosynthesis, a plant's chloroplast (the part of the plant where the chemical chlorophyll is located) captures the sun's energy and combines it with carbon dioxide from the air and nutrient-rich water from the ground to produce a sugar called glucose. Plants burn the glucose for energy to help them grow. As a waste product, plants emit oxygen, which humans and other animals need to breathe. When we breathe, we exhale carbon dioxide, which the plants then use for more photosynthesis—it's all a big, finely tuned system. So the next time you pass a lonely houseplant, give it thanks for helping you live.

Make a TERRARIUM

COLLECT MATERIALS FROM THE GREAT OUTDOORS

so you can enjoy nature when you're back inside. A terrarium is a great way to experiment with plants on a miniature level.

SUPPLY LIST

- Fishbowl or jar
- Activated charcoal
- Potting soil
- A variety of plants (miniature ferns or spider moss) or seeds (such as sweet alyssum or wheatgrass)
- Bits of nature from the outdoors, such as leaves, twigs, and mosses

STEPS

1. Wash and dry a large glass bowl or jar. (An old fishbowl works well.)
2. Fill the bottom—about 1 inch (2.5 cm) high—with stones you have collected from your nature hikes.
3. Using a shovel or spoon, add several inches of potting soil mixed with activated charcoal bits.
4. If you are using potted plants, dig a little hole in the soil for the roots and place the plants in. Pack extra soil around the plants. Add water until the soil is moist. (If you're using seeds, press them into the soil and moisten.)
5. Add sheet moss on top of the soil around the plants.
6. Now the fun part! Add a few decorative bits of nature—a small pinecone, a special rock, or a little figurine. Keep your terrarium in a well-lit place, and don't forget to add a little water when the soil looks dry.

Time: about 30 minutes

fun fact

Mosses grow in damp environments and are home to a little creature called a moss piglet! Moss piglets, also known as water bears, have eight legs and grow up to about .06 inch (1.5 mm) in length.

Bet You Didn't Know!

10 facts about the

1 **Brain cells** live longer than all of the other cells in your body.

2 **The more you concentrate,** the less you blink.

3 Your **teeth** are **harder** than your **bones.**

4 **Some people can hear their eyeballs** moving.

5 It is **not possible** to tickle yourself.

6 You can buy **fake eyebrows** and **eyelashes** made out of **real hair.**

human body

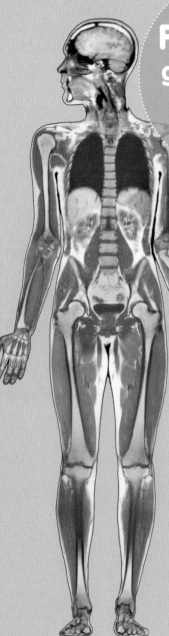

7

Fingernails grow **faster** than **toenails.**

8

Your heart beats about **100,000 times** each day.

9

Your foot is about the **same length** as the distance between your **elbow and wrist.**

10

The saliva you produce in your lifetime could fill nearly **30,000** water bottles.

89

MUSCLE POWER

With its strong bones and flexible joints, your skeleton is built to be on the go.

But without muscles, it won't go anywhere! You need muscle power to make your body walk, run, skip, rub your nose, or even just sit up without toppling over.

The muscles that do these jobs are called skeletal muscles. You have about 650 of them, and you can control what they do. Sometimes, it takes a lot of skeletal muscles to make even a simple move. Your tongue alone contains eight muscles!

You also have muscles that work without your having to do a thing. Most of these muscles are called smooth muscles. Sheets of smooth muscle line your blood vessels, throat, stomach, intestines, lungs, and other organs. They are hard at work keeping your blood circulating and your food digesting while you're busy doing other things. And there's also that mighty muscle, your heart. It pumps thanks to cardiac muscles, which are found only in the heart.

THE HIBERNATION MYSTERY

Very sick people often lie in bed for a long time as they recover. This lack of exercise weakens muscles—a process called "muscle atrophy." Preventing atrophy may be possible someday thanks to researchers who study hibernating animals.

Bears, for example, spend winter sleeping but do not suffer severe atrophy. When they wake up in spring, they're as strong as—well, bears! Scientists are studying the muscles and blood of bears, ground squirrels, and other hibernators to find out how they stay in shape while sleeping. The answers may one day help people suffering from muscle atrophy when they're sick or in the hospital for a long time.

Bet You Didn't Know!

Some of your body's strongest muscles aren't in your arms or legs. They're in your jaws! These strong muscles are called the masseters. They help you chew by closing your lower jaw. Clenching your teeth will make your masseters bulge so you can feel them.

BODY ELECTRIC

The nerve signal that tells your muscles to move is super fast! It zooms at 250 miles an hour (402 km/h), as fast as the fastest race car.

Your body is just humming with electricity.

Nerve cells from head to toe speak to each other through electrical signals. The electrical signals zap down each nerve cell and, when they get to the end, jump across a tiny gap called a synapse (see photo, right). How does the signal jump across the gap?

The nerve produces special chemicals that can flow across the gap to the next cell. There, a new electrical charge travels down the next nerve. Messages jump from neuron to neuron in a chain of electrical-chemical-electrical-chemical signals until they reach their destination.

Because nerves don't actually touch, they can change the path of their signals easily. They can make new connections and break old ones. This is how your brain learns and stores new information.

Bet You Didn't Know!

A reflex is a nerve message that doesn't go through your brain. When you touch a hot stove, for example, a sensory neuron picks up the message ("Hot!") and passes it to a motor neuron in your spinal cord. The motor neuron then sends a message to your hand, telling it to move ("Quick!").

BUNDLE OF NERVES

A 1.2-inch (3-cm) section of your brain stem (called the medulla oblongata) controls some of your body's most important functions, such as breathing and heart rate. Amazingly, it also contains your body's motor and sensory nerves and is where nerves from the left and right sides of your body cross each other on their journey toward your cerebrum.

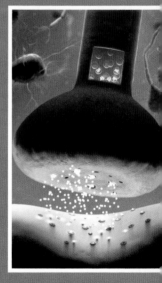

SENSORY NERVES pull in information from nerve endings in your eyes, ears, skin, hands, and other parts of your body and then send this information to your brain.

MOTOR NERVES send messages from your brain to your muscles, telling them to contract, to run, or to walk.

LOOK OUT!

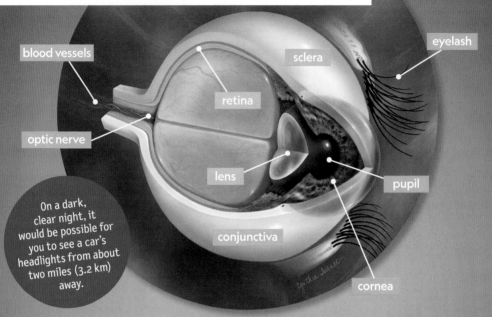

blood vessels

sclera

eyelash

retina

optic nerve

lens

pupil

conjunctiva

cornea

On a dark, clear night, it would be possible for you to see a car's headlights from about two miles (3.2 km) away.

Your eyes are two of the most amazing organs in your body.

These small, squishy, fluid-filled balls have almost three-quarters of your body's sensory receptors. They're like two supersmart cameras, but more complex.

So how do you see the world around you? It begins when you open the protective cover of your eyelid and let in the light. Light enters your eye through the window of your cornea and passes through the aqueous humor, a watery fluid that nourishes the eye tissue. It enters the black circle in the iris (the colored part of your eye), called the pupil. Because people need to be able to see in both bright and low light, muscles in the iris automatically make the pupil smaller when the light is strong and wider when the light is dim. Light then travels to the lens, whose muscles adjust it to be able to see objects both near and far. Then the light goes through the vitreous humor (a clear jellylike substance) to the retina. The retina, a layer of about 126 million light-sensitive cells, lines the back of your eyeball. When these cells absorb the light, they transform it into electrical signals that are sent along the optic nerve to the brain. The brain then makes sense of what you are seeing.

A TOPSY-TURVY WORLD

Turn this over in your mind: You're looking at the world topsy-turvy, and you don't even know it. Like a camera lens, your lens focuses light, creates an image, and turns it upside down. Yep, when your lens focuses light inside your eye, it flips the image so it lands on your retina upside down. But, your brain knows to flip the image automatically to match your reality. But what if your reality suddenly changed? A well-known experiment in the mid-20th century in which a person wore special light-inverting goggles showed that his brain actually adjusted to the new, inverted world by eventually seeing the reversed view as normal! It is thought that newborns see the world upside down for a short while, until their brains learn how to turn things right-side up.

CAMERA LENS

AWESOME
OPTICAL ILLUSIONS

Ready to work your brain and show your visual alertness?
Ponder these puzzling pictures to see what you see!

WHICH CIRCLE IS **BIGGER?**

Both of these circle clusters have an orange circle surrounded by purple ones. But which orange circle is bigger? The answer may surprise you: neither! The two orange circles are the same size. The one on the right may appear bigger because it's surrounded by purple circles that are smaller than it is. The one on the left seems smaller because it's surrounded by purple circles that are larger than it is.

RABBIT **OR** DUCK?

It's a duck! Or is it a rabbit? Can you see it both ways? A recent study using this illusion suggests that the more easily people can switch back and forth between the two images, the more creative they are.

SPINNING CIRCLES

Do you see all the spinning circles? Don't look too long, or you might get dizzy! This illusion plays with your peripheral vision (vision from the sides of your eyes, not the middle). Sometimes when you look out the sides of your eyes, you see movement where really there are only patterns.

THE INVADERS ARE COMING!

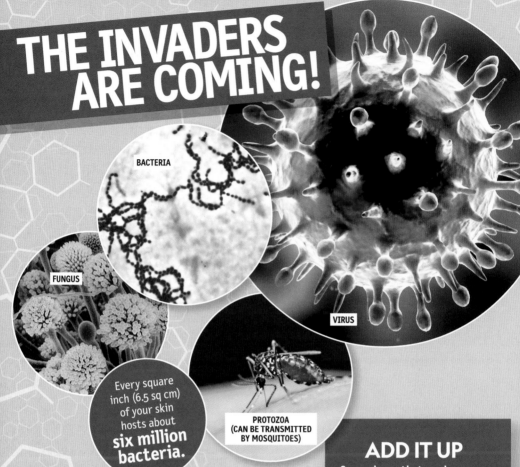

BACTERIA

FUNGUS

VIRUS

Every square inch (6.5 sq cm) of your skin hosts about **six million bacteria.**

PROTOZOA (CAN BE TRANSMITTED BY MOSQUITOES)

Some microorganisms (tiny living things) can make your body sick. They are too small to see with the naked eye. These creatures—bacteria, viruses, fungi, and protozoa—are what you may know as germs.

Bacteria are microscopic organisms that live nearly everywhere on Earth, including on and in the human body. "Good" bacteria help sour digestive systems work properly. Harmful bacteria can cause ailments, including ear infections and strep throat.

A virus, like a cold or the flu, needs to live inside another living thing (a host) to survive; then it can grow and multiply throughout the host's body.

Fungi get their food from the plants, animals, or people they live on. Some fungi can get on your body and cause skin diseases such as ringworm.

Protozoa are single-celled organisms that can spread disease to humans through contaminated water and dirty living conditions. Protozoa can cause infections such as malaria, which occurs when a person is bitten by an infected mosquito.

ADD IT UP

So you know that you have bacteria on your skin and in your body. But do you know how many? One hundred trillion— that's 100,000,000,000,000! Most are harmless and some are pretty friendly, keeping more dangerous bacteria at bay, protecting you from some skin infections, and helping your cuts heal.

GERM **SHOWDOWN**

Scientists in Wales studied three greeting styles to determine which was the cleanest. Find out which one has the upper hand.

HANDSHAKE

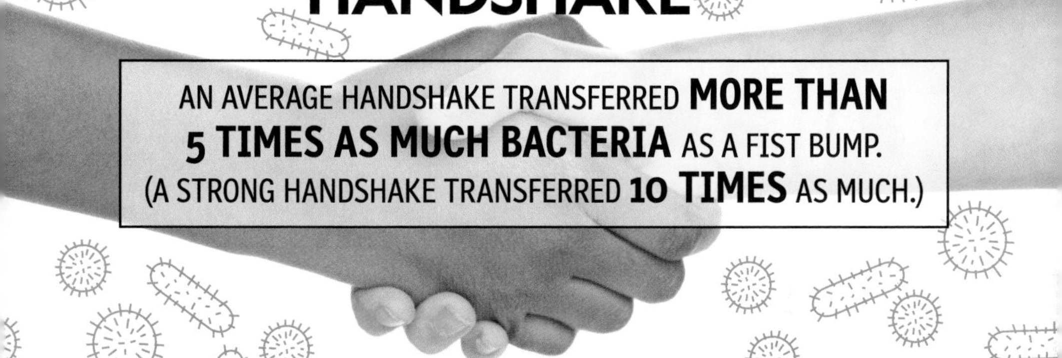

AN AVERAGE HANDSHAKE TRANSFERRED **MORE THAN 5 TIMES AS MUCH BACTERIA** AS A FIST BUMP. (A STRONG HANDSHAKE TRANSFERRED **10 TIMES** AS MUCH.)

HIGH FIVE

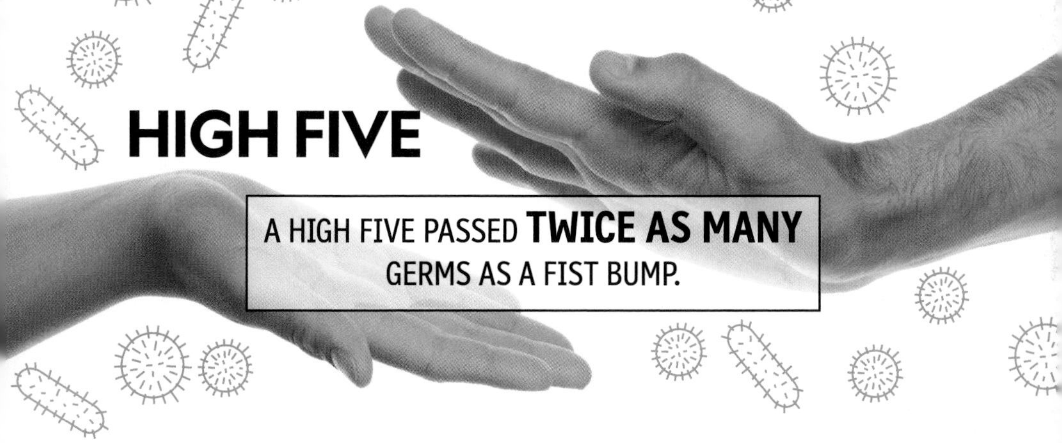

A HIGH FIVE PASSED **TWICE AS MANY** GERMS AS A FIST BUMP.

FIST BUMP

WINNER:

FIST BUMPS HAVE THE **LEAST SKIN-TO-SKIN CONTACT** OF THE GREETINGS, WHICH MAKES IT LESS LIKELY FOR MICROBES TO JUMP **FROM ONE HAND TO ANOTHER.**

WHAT DIED?

CONCEPTS
decomposition, microbiology, decay, organic materials, bacteria, insects, corpse fauna

HOW LONG IT TAKES
two to four days, possibly longer in cold weather

WHAT YOU NEED
food samples
containers
outdoor thermometer
magnifying lens
dissecting microscope
bug identification guides
optional: camera, smartphone, or video camera

f you leave food out, SOMETHING will come to live on it or lay eggs on it. In this observation, discover what arrives to make the most of your leftovers.

What comes to get food that's left out?

96

WHAT TO DO

DAY ONE:

1 WORK IN AN OPEN-AIR area, compost heap, or compost bin—a place that is open to bugs but not birds or other animals. Ask an adult to help you choose a location.

2 SET UP FOUR containers with a small sample of food inside each. If you want, these samples can represent the four food groups: vegetable/fruit, meat/fish, bread/grains, and milk/dairy.

DAYS TWO TO FOUR:

3 KEEP A CAREFUL record of what you observe through your senses. Each day, record the temperature in the area where your samples are. Note whether you can see signs that bugs or other creatures have been attracted to your samples, including any film or mold that forms. You may want to photograph the samples every day to compare them.

4 EVERY ONE OR TWO days (decide which interval you want to study), remove the samples from the containers to examine them with a magnifying lens and microscope. Count, try to identify, and sketch the bugs and other life-forms that colonize each sample. Add descriptions to your notes, including sensory observations: texture, color, and smell—but not taste!

WHAT TO EXPECT?
You may see mold, biofilm or scum, bugs, worms, flies, and so on.

WHAT'S GOING ON?
Nature abhors a vacuum. If there is food, something will come to eat it.

OUR TRY

We put out duplicate food—chicken broth, blackberry jam, and cat food—every other day for six days. We set out the food in the yard, in a cat carrier with a brick on top, but that didn't stop coyotes from pulling it apart and getting the food on the second night. After that we replaced the food and kept the cat carrier in the garage, where flies could still get to it. After we opened it to see what we had and examine it with the microscope, we dumped the cat carrier near the compost heap—and later, we had a glorious infestation of beetles.

QUESTION THIS!

- What would happen to this food if nothing were able to reach it?

- What would happen to this food if you let more time pass?

QUIZ WHIZ

Discover your tech-savvy smarts by taking this quiz!

Write your answers on a piece of paper. Then check them below.

1 How many plant species are there on Earth?
- **a.** 400,000
- **b.** 40,000
- **c.** 4,000
- **d.** 400

2 **True or false?** Some of your body's strongest muscles are in your jaw.

3 Microscopic organisms that live in moss are also known as _____.
- **a.** moss monsters
- **b.** moss piglets
- **c.** moss monkeys
- **d.** moss cows

4 **True or false?** Scientists think life began on Earth about 1 million years ago.

5 An architect has designed a conceptual floating island shaped like which object?
- **a.** a lotus flower
- **b.** a UFO
- **c.** a lily pad
- **d.** a roller coaster

Not **STUMPED** yet? Check out the *NATIONAL GEOGRAPHIC KIDS QUIZ WHIZ* collection for more crazy **TECHNOLOGY** questions!

ANSWERS:
1. a; 2. True; 3. b; 4. False. Experts think life began about four billion years ago; 5. c

HOMEWORK HELP

This Is How It's Done!

Sometimes, the most complicated problems are solved with step-by-step directions. These "how-to" instructions are also known as a process analysis essay. While scientists and engineers use this tool to program robots and write computer code, you also use process analysis every day, from following a recipe to putting together a new toy or gadget. Here's how to write a basic process analysis essay.

Step 1: Choose Your Topic Sentence

Pick a clear and concise topic sentence that describes what you're writing about. Be sure to explain to the reader why the task is important—and how many steps there are to complete it.

Step 2: List Materials

Do you need specific ingredients or equipment to complete your process? Mention these right away so the readers will have all they need to do this activity.

Step 3: Write Your Directions

Your directions should be clear and easy to follow. Assume that you are explaining the process for the first time, and define any unfamiliar terms. List your steps in the exact order the reader will need to follow to complete the activity. Try to keep your essay limited to no more than six steps.

Step 4: Restate Your Main Idea

Your closing idea should revisit your topic sentence, drawing a conclusion relating to the importance of the subject.

EXAMPLE OF A PROCESS ANALYSIS ESSAY

Downloading an app is a simple way to enhance your tablet. Today, I'd like to show you how to search for and add an app to your tablet. First, you will need a tablet with the ability to access the internet. You'll also want to ask a parent for permission before you download anything onto your tablet. Next, select the specific app you're seeking by going to the app store on your tablet and entering the app's name into the search bar. Once you find the app you're seeking, select "download" and wait for the app to load. When you see that the app has fully loaded, tap on the icon and you will be able to access it. Now you can enjoy your app and have more fun with your tablet.

GOING GREEN

An artist's rendering offers a glimpse of the world's first forest city—scheduled for completion in 2020—along the Liujiang River in southern China. Buildings will be covered in thousands of trees and plants.

EARTH EXPLORER
Meet **Katey Walter Anthony!**

This aquatic ecologist and National Geographic explorer is tapping into new research on global warming.

Katey Walter Anthony remembers the first time she saw the bubbles. One day, while walking across a frozen lake in Siberia, she looked down and saw clusters of gas trapped beneath the thick, dark ice. "It looked like the starry night sky," Katey recalls.

But these weren't your average air bubbles. As Katey soon discovered, the bubbles were actually methane, a potent greenhouse gas that contributes to global warming. So how does the methane get under the ice? It comes from permafrost, the frozen ground that once covered the entire Arctic, including the bottom of ancient lakes that Katey studies. As the permafrost thaws from solid, frozen ground to looser soil and mud with Earth's rising temperatures, it can release carbon. Microbes in the soil turn the carbon into methane. In the summer, the gas rises up from the bottom of the lake, through the lake's surface, and enters the atmosphere. In the winter, it gets stuck under the frozen surface, creating those beautiful bubbles.

The way Katey determines whether the bubbles are methane is, well, pretty lit. "We tap holes into the ice and light a match," she says. "If there's methane and it mixes with oxygen, you'll get fireballs up to the trees."

As she's looked for methane in some 250 ancient lakes throughout Alaska and Russia, Katey has uncovered preserved woolly mammoth tusks and rhino bones. And she's also dug up proof that the methane being released from the melting permafrost is a source of climate change that many experts haven't recognized.

"Right now, if you look at the models of climate change, none of them include methane from thawing permafrost at the bottom of lakes as a source," says Katey. "We believe that the release of these gases intensifies global warming. It's a big part of the climate change story."

Siberian lakes have the potential to release an estimated 50 billion tons (45.4 billion t) of methane—10 times more methane than the atmosphere holds right now.

FROZEN METHANE BUBBLES

"All that carbon was locked up safely in the permafrost freezer for tens of thousands of years. Now the freezer door is opening, releasing the carbon into Arctic lake bottoms, where microbes convert it to methane."

Katey's team has studied 42,000-year-old methane gas.

KATEY CHECKING BUBBLES FOR METHANE

CALL TO ACTION!

"My wish for all kids is that you go out and explore nature," says Katey. "Be curious, study the world around you. And maybe that will help you one day make decisions that will help save the planet." You can also do your part to fight climate change through simple steps at home like recycling, powering down your electronics when you're not using them, and trying not to waste food.

103

Trapped by TRASH!

VICTIM: SKUNK
TRASH: YOGURT CONTAINER
PROBLEM: HEAD STUCK

A HOMEOWNER finds a writhing baby skunk in her recycling bin. The skunk has a plastic yogurt container over his head. When the animal tries to push the container off, it won't budge. He claws at his head, struggling to free himself, then tumbles out of the uncovered bin. The panicked little skunk can't see a thing and begins to suffocate.

A PHONE CALL to Wildlife in Crisis, an animal rescue organization in nearby Weston, Connecticut, brings help. Director Dara Reid dispatches caretaker Anna Clark to the woman's home. She wraps the skunk in a towel and then gently tugs the container until the exhausted creature is finally free.

BUT HE'S NOT SAFE. There is no sign of the animal's mother, and this baby skunk is far too young to survive on his own. Wildlife in Crisis feeds him milk and wet cat food until his teeth grow in, and then adds natural foods like berries and worms to his diet. About four months later he's released into the wild.

Animals get trapped every day by the things people carelessly discard. Here are stories of lucky animals that have tangled with trash—and escaped.

VICTIM: SEA LION
TRASH: FISHING LINE
PROBLEM: MOUTH TRAPPED

The sea lion prowls for food off the California shore, sticking his nose in places where fish might hide. When his whiskers snag on some fishing line, he tries to shake it off. But the strong material tangles, wraps around his snout and neck, and eventually traps his mouth shut.

Someone notices the distressed animal and informs the Marine Mammal Center in nearby Sausalito. When the sea lion reappears in a bay, the center's rescue team speeds to the scene. The feisty sea lion eludes them for nearly three weeks.

The worried rescue team sedates him with darts while he rests on a dock. After he becomes sleepy, the team rushes the 260-pound (118-kg) mammal to the center to cut the fishing line, treat his wounds, and feed him. The sea lion eats 100 pounds (45 kg) of herring and is then set free. Hopefully now he steers clear of trash.

FISHING LINE

VICTIM: BALD EAGLE
TRASH: STRING
PROBLEM: WING TANGLED

A young bald eagle is in trouble. When her parents searched for sticks to build the nest, they also found balloon string, fishing line, and other trash. Now the young eagle is tangled in the debris and falls from the nest. The bird hangs four feet (1.2 m) above the ground, breaking her wing in the process.

Dara Reid of Wildlife in Crisis comes to the rescue. She cuts down the suspended eagle and rushes her to the rescue facility. After removing the trash, Reid aligns the bird's broken wing and immobilizes it by bandaging the wing against the eagle's body.

Following 14 months of TLC, the bald eagle is taken to a field. With a helpful heave from Reid, the eagle flaps hard, circles above, and then re-enters the wild—with a perfectly healed wing.

GETTING BETTER

FLYING AGAIN

A GLOBAL RACE TO ZERO WASTE

BOTH SWEDEN (MAIN PHOTO) AND SINGAPORE (INSET) ARE WORLDWIDE LEADERS IN RECYCLING AND WASTE REDUCTION.

It's an ambitious goal, but one that some countries hope to achieve in less than 10 years. The aim? Zero waste, meaning every single piece of trash will be reused or composted. The idea may seem impossible, but several spots are coming close.

Take Sweden, for example. Less than one percent of the country's household garbage ends up in landfills. Rather, the Swedes recycle nearly everything—some 1.5 billion bottles and cans annually—and the rest winds up at waste-to-energy plants to produce electricity. The program is so successful that Sweden actually imports trash from other places, such as the United

DUBAI—HOME TO THE FAMOUS PALM JUMEIRAH ISLAND—IS AIMING TO GO WASTE-FREE BY 2030.

Kingdom, Norway, and Ireland, to keep up the rapid pace of its incinerators.

Other places narrowing in on zero waste? The Himalayan country of Bhutan is shooting for that status by 2030, while Singapore and Dubai have announced similar timelines. In the United States, individual cities like San Francisco and New York have also declared their dedication to going zero waste. The U.S. National Park Service, as well as major corporations like Lego and Nike, are also making big moves toward creating zero waste—all in an effort to make this world a cleaner place.

So what's the secret to zero waste? It's all about enforcing the rules of reducing, reusing, and recycling. In Sweden, for example, recycling stations must be no more than 984 feet (300 m) from any residential area. And in Bhutan—which is aspiring to become the world's first nation to have an all-organic farming system—composting from food scraps is the norm. Simple practices like these, as well as educating the public on the problems stemming from too much trash, can lead to major changes. And, perhaps, zero waste around the world one day.

FROM FILTH TO FASHION

Order up! One creative company called Garbage Gone Glam made this dress out of diner menus. Other things they've made? A cocktail dress out of playing cards and a ball gown out of old magazines!

HOW SOME TRASH TRAVELS FROM THE RECYCLING CENTER TO THE RUNWAYS—AND EVEN TO YOUR CLOSET.

A hat made out of an old soccer ball brings new meaning to the term "header."

This eco-friendly bag is made from 365 recycled computer keyboard keys.

This head-piece, made from recycled corrugated cardboard, is hard to top!

LEVI STRAUSS & CO. MAKES JEANS OUT OF OLD COTTON T-SHIRTS.

This bow tie made out of an old aluminum can is both fashion-forward and eco-friendly.

Pollution
Cleaning Up Our Act

So what's the big deal about a little dirt on the planet? Pollution can affect animals, plants, and people. In fact, some studies show that more people die every year from diseases linked to air pollution than from car accidents. And right now nearly one billion of the world's people don't have access to clean drinking water.

A LITTLE POLLUTION = BIG PROBLEMS

You can probably clean your room in a couple of hours. (At least we hope you can!) But you can't shove air and water pollution under your bed or cram them into the closet. Once released into the environment, pollution—whether it's oil leaking from a boat or chemicals spewing from a factory's smokestack—can have a lasting environmental impact.

KEEP IT CLEAN

It's easy to blame things like big factories for pollution problems. But some of the mess comes from everyday activities. Exhaust fumes from cars and garbage in landfills can seriously trash Earth's health. We all need to pitch in and do some housecleaning. It may mean bicycling more and riding in cars less. Or not dumping water-polluting oil or household cleaners down the drain. Look at it this way: Just as with your room, it's always better not to let Earth get messed up in the first place.

kids vs. PLASTIC

Part of the PLANET **OR** PLASTIC? initiative

A straw stuck in a sea turtle's nostril. A seahorse swimming along with its tail curled around a cotton swab. Sea birds washing up on sandy shores, entangled in plastic bags. Sadly, we do not have to look too far to see how animals are directly impacted by the staggering amount of plastic piling up on our planet. We've created more than 6.9 billion tons (6.3 billion t) of plastic waste, with only a small percentage landing in recycling bins. The rest of it lingers in landfills and winds up in our oceans. In fact, 700 species of animals are threatened because of ocean waste—and among seabirds, a whopping 90 percent eat plastic trash, according to a study. But as scary as these stats are, we can do something about them. Experts say it all starts with reducing the amount of plastic we use, including options for reusable containers or those made with marine biodegradable components. You can also pledge to do your part to reduce the plastic problem by visiting kids.nationalgeographic.com/explore/nature/kids-vs-plastic. Together, we can work to cut back on plastic and protect our planet—and everything on it.

Declining Biodiversity

Saving All Creatures, Great and Small

Green sea turtle

Earth is home to a huge mix of plants and animals—millions and possibly billions of species—and scientists have officially identified and named only about 1.9 million so far! Scientists call this healthy mix biodiversity.

THE BALANCING ACT

The bad news is that half of the planet's plant and animal species may be on the path to extinction, mainly because of human activity. People cut down trees, build roads and houses, pollute rivers, overfish, and overhunt. The good news is that many people care. Scientists and volunteers race against the clock every day, working to save wildlife before time runs out. By building birdhouses, planting trees, and following the rules for hunting and fishing, you can be a positive force for preserving biodiversity, too. Every time you do something to help a species survive, you help our planet to thrive.

Habitats Threatened

Living on the Edge

Jaguar

Even though tropical rain forests cover only about 7 percent of the planet's total land surface, they are home to half of all known species of plants and animals. Because people cut down so many trees for lumber and firewood and clear so much land for farms, hundreds of thousands of acres of rain forest disappear every year.

SHARING THE LAND

Wetlands are also important feeding and breeding grounds. People have drained many wetlands, turning them into farm fields or sites for industries. More than half the world's wetlands have disappeared within the past century, squeezing wildlife out. Balancing the needs of humans and animals is the key to lessening habitat destruction.

WORLD ENERGY & MINERALS

Almost everything people do—from cooking to powering the International Space Station—requires energy. But energy comes in different forms. Traditional energy sources, still used by many people in the developing world, include burning dried animal dung and wood. Industrialized countries and urban centers around the world rely on coal, oil, and natural gas—called fossil fuels because they formed from decayed plant and animal material accumulated from long ago. Fossil fuel deposits, either in the ground or under the ocean floor, are unevenly distributed on Earth, and only some countries can afford to buy them. Fossil fuels are also not renewable, meaning they will run out one day. And unless we find other ways to create energy, we'll be stuck. Without energy we won't be able to drive cars, use lights, or send emails to friends.

TAKING A TOLL

Environmentally speaking, burning fossil fuels isn't necessarily the best choice, either: Carbon dioxide from the burning of fossil fuels, as well as other emissions, are contributing to global warming. Concerned scientists are looking at new ways to harness renewable, alternative sources of energy, such as water, wind, and sun.

HIGH VOLTAGE

It seems like we use electricity for everything—from TVs and cell phones to air conditioners and computers. In fact, power plants generate 3.7 times more electrical power than they did just 40 years ago. How they do this can differ around the world. Is it from burning coal or taming the energy in moving water? Here's the global breakdown.

5% OTHER, SUCH AS GEOTHERMAL, SOLAR, WIND, HEAT, ETC.

5% OIL

10.9% NUCLEAR

16.2% HYDRO POWER

40.4% COAL

22.5% NATURAL GAS

Electricity travels at the speed of light— about 186,000 miles a second (299,340 km/s).

Climate CHANGE

POLAR BEAR ON A PIECE OF MELTING ICEBERG

Rising Temperatures, Explained

Fact: The world is getting warmer.
Earth's surface temperature has been increasing. In the past 50 years, our planet has warmed twice as fast as in the 50 years before that. This is the direct effect of climate change, which refers not only to the increase in Earth's average temperature (known as global warming), but also to the long-term effects on winds, rain, and ocean currents. Global warming is the reason glaciers and polar ice sheets are melting—resulting in rising sea levels and shrinking habitats. This makes survival for some animals a big challenge. Warming also means more flooding along the coasts and drought for inland areas.

Why are temperatures climbing?
Some of the recent climate changes can be tied to natural causes—such as changes in the sun's intensity, the unusually warm ocean currents

SCIENTISTS ARE CONCERNED THAT GREENLAND'S ICE SHEET HAS BEGUN TO MELT IN SUMMER. BIRTHDAY CANYON, SHOWN HERE, WAS CARVED BY MELTWATER.

of El Niño, and volcanic activity—but human activities are a major factor as well.

Everyday activities that require burning fossil fuels, such as driving gasoline-powered cars, contribute to global warming. These activities produce greenhouse gases, which enter the atmosphere and trap heat. At the current rate, Earth's global average temperature is projected to rise between 1.8 and 11.5°F (1 and 6.4°C) by the year 2100, and it will get even warmer after that. And as the climate continues to warm, it will unfortunately continue to affect the environment and our society in many ways.

FUNKY JUNK ART

Try This!

Who knew recycling could be so much fun? Check out these ideas for turning junk into awesome art.

Bottle Cap Snake

ASK FOR A PARENT'S HELP AND PERMISSION BEFORE YOU START THESE PROJECTS.

YOU WILL NEED
- 30–50 BOTTLE CAPS
- HAMMER
- AWL
- BOARD (TO HAMMER ON)
- PLASTIC-COATED WIRE
- CRAFT GLUE
- SELF-HARDENING CLAY
- 1 CORK
- 2 PUSHPINS

Create a College

Cut up magazines or the Sunday comics and glue the pictures onto construction paper to make a funny collage.

WHAT TO DO

Work with a parent to punch a hole in the center of each bottle cap using a hammer and awl. Do this on a board that is resting on a sturdy surface. Cut a piece of wire that is slightly longer than you want your snake to be. Tie a knot at one end of the wire. String all the bottle caps on the wire with the tops facing the open end of the wire. Knot the other end of the wire and cut off the excess. Glue a piece of clay to the snake's tail end and twist it into a tail shape. Glue a piece of clay to the opposite end of the snake. Create an indentation with the cork. Let the clay dry. Glue the cork into the clay. Once dry, press pushpins into the cork for eyes and some wire into the end of the cork for the tongue. Glue a piece of clay to the cork tip.

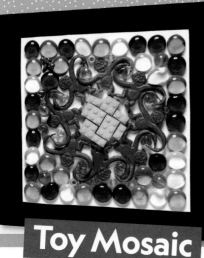

Toy Mosaic

YOU WILL NEED
- OLD TOYS, COLORED GLASS, STONES, BUTTONS, SHELLS, OR OTHER SMALL ITEMS
- THICK WHITE POSTER BOARD
- CRAFT GLUE
- THICK BLACK POSTER BOARD

WHAT TO DO

Collect small decorative items (see suggestions above) from around your house. Sketch a pattern for your collage on a piece of white poster board. Glue all of the pieces on top of the pattern. Let the glue dry. Cut a piece of heavy black poster board that is two inches (5 cm) wider on all sides than the white poster board. Center the white piece on the black one and glue it in place. Let the glue dry, then put your masterpiece on display for everyone to see.

Hang Your Name

Find the letters of your name in old posters or catalogs and cut them out. Glue the letters to cardboard that's covered with paper. Tape your nameplate to your bedroom door.

10 WAYS YOU CAN GO GREEN!

WANT TO DO YOUR PART TO SAVE THE PLANET? HERE ARE 10 THINGS TO TRY TODAY!

1 Use rechargeable batteries, and recycle them when they die to keep harmful metals from entering the environment.

2 Never litter. Trash tossed carelessly outside often winds up in storm drains, which empty into rivers and streams that eventually flow to the oceans.

3 Plant a deciduous (leafy) tree that loses its leaves in the fall on the south side of your home. When it grows tall, its shade will cool your house in the summer. After its leaves fall, sunlight will help warm your house in winter.

4 Reuse or recycle plastic bags. When one ton (0.9 t) of plastic bags is reused or recycled, the energy equivalent of 11 barrels of oil is saved!

5 Donate your old clothes and toys to reduce waste.

6 Take shorter showers to save water.

7 Switch off the light every time you leave a room.

8 Participate in cleanup days at your school or at a park—or organize one on your own.

9 Place your desk next to a window and use natural light instead of a lamp.

10 Have a drippy faucet at home? Ask your parents to replace the washer inside it to save water.

QUIZ WHIZ

What's your eco-friendly IQ? Find out with this quiz!

Write your answers on a piece of paper. Then check them below.

1 **True or false?** The country of Sweden recycles some 1.5 billion bottles and cans annually.

2 **What does global warming cause?**
a. rising sea levels   c. melting glaciers
b. shrinking animal habitats   d. all of the above

3 **Electricity travels at about the same rate as what?**
a. sound
b. light
c. Wi-Fi
d. a sloth

4 **True or false?** Hundreds of thousands of acres of rain forest disappear every year.

5 **700 species of animals are severely threatened because of _____ waste.**
a. ocean
b. food
c. electronic
d. paper

Not **STUMPED** yet? Check out the *NATIONAL GEOGRAPHIC KIDS QUIZ WHIZ* collection for more crazy **ENVIRONMENT** questions

ANSWERS: 1. True ; 2. d ; 3. b ; 4. True; 5. a

HOMEWORK HELP

Write a Letter That Gets Results

Knowing how to write a good letter is a useful skill. It will come in handy anytime you want to persuade someone to understand your point of view. Whether you're emailing your congressperson or writing a letter for a school project or to your grandma, a great letter will help you get your message across. Most important, a well-written letter leaves a good impression.

CHECK OUT THE EXAMPLE BELOW FOR THE ELEMENTS OF A GOOD LETTER.

Your address

Date

Salutation
Always use "Dear" followed by the person's name; use Mr., Mrs., Ms., or Dr. as appropriate.

Introductory paragraph
Give the reason you're writing the letter.

Body
The longest part of the letter, which provides evidence that supports your position. Be persuasive!

Closing paragraph
Sum up your argument.

Complimentary closing
Sign off with "Sincerely" or "Thank you."

Your signature

Abby Jones
1204 Green Street
Los Angeles, CA 90045

April 22, 2020

Dear Ms. School Superintendent,

I am writing to you about how much excess energy our school uses and to offer a solution.

Every day, we leave the computers on in the classroom. The TVs are plugged in all the time, and the lights are on all day. All of this adds up to a lot of wasted energy, which is not only harmful for the Earth, as it increases the amount of harmful greenhouse gas emissions into the environment, but is also costly to the school. In fact, I read that schools spend more on energy bills than on computers and textbooks combined!

I am suggesting that we start an Energy Patrol to monitor the use of lighting, air-conditioning, heating, and other energy systems within our school. My idea is to have a group of students dedicated to figuring out ways we can cut back on our energy use in the school. We can do room checks, provide reminders to students and teachers to turn off lights and computers, replace old lightbulbs with energy-efficient products, and even reward the classrooms that do the most to save energy.

Above all, I think our school could help the environment tremendously by cutting back on how much energy we use. Let's see an Energy Patrol at our school soon. Thank you.

Sincerely,

Abby Jones

Abby Jones

COMPLIMENTARY CLOSINGS

Sincerely, Sincerely yours, Thank you, Regards, Best wishes, Respectfully,

Inca dancers perform in traditional dress in the Cusco region of Peru.

CULTURE
CONNECTION

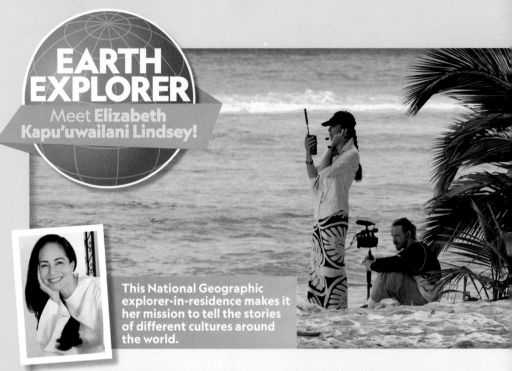

EARTH EXPLORER

Meet **Elizabeth Kapu'uwailani Lindsey!**

This National Geographic explorer-in-residence makes it her mission to tell the stories of different cultures around the world.

As a little girl growing up in Hawaii, Elizabeth Kapu'uwailani Lindsey watched her elders—the older women who looked after her—pay close attention to signs in nature to gain a better understanding of the world around them. "They didn't rely on their smartphones to tell them the weather forecast," she explains. "Instead, they watched the clouds, felt the winds, and looked at the color of the sky. The simple task of observing what's going on around you can teach you so much."

Today, Elizabeth is an anthropologist who travels the world to study indigenous—or native—people who still follow ancient traditions, like the adults she grew up with. Her purpose? To keep these cultures from vanishing.

"Their cultures are often misunderstood and forced to blend into mainstream society," she says. "Instead, why not learn more about them and understand that they are just a part of our planet?"

Elizabeth has spent time with Southeast Asian sea nomads and with native people of New Zealand, Peru, China, Micronesia, and India, among others. She has also studied wayfinding—or the native science of navigating without tools, most recently featured in the movie *Moana*.

"Wayfinders don't use maps," Elizabeth explains. "They look at everything from ocean waves to the flight patterns of birds to get to where they need to go. Their approach is that if you gather enough information from the world around you, you essentially find your way home."

Elizabeth is hoping to discover a complete story of the peoples of the world, with each culture representing a chapter.

"We are alive at an age when there are still elders whose wisdom is available," she says. "I look for the lessons we can learn from their ancient wisdom and knowledge. This way, we can be sure their voices are heard for many more years to come. If one voice is missing, the story is incomplete."

There are at least 8 different languages spoken in Micronesia, a country in the Pacific Ocean.

WOMEN SINGING AND DANCING IN MICRONESIA

" Wayfinders look at nature to know where they are. The underbellies of the clouds are like mirrors and reflect colors. When you're on the ocean and you can see the palest color of green in the clouds, you know you're getting close to land. Little clues help them find their way. "

BOATS OF THE MOKEN TRIBE IN SOUTHERN THAILAND

Maui, the famous demigod from the movie *Moana*, is based on a legend from traditional Polynesian stories passed down from generation to generation.

CALL TO ACTION!

Be curious! Seek out information about traditions in your own family and learn their importance. Talk to your parents, grandparents, aunts, and uncles about what makes your family's history unique. Gather as many details as you can and share them. That way you can carry on traditions from one generation to another.

CELEBRATIONS

1 CHINESE NEW YEAR
January 25
Also called Lunar New Year, this holiday marks the new year according to the lunar calendar. Families celebrate with parades, feasts, and fireworks. Young people may receive gifts of money in red envelopes.

2 HOLI
March 9
This festival in India celebrates spring and marks the triumph of good over evil. People cover one another with powdered paint, called *gulal*, and douse one another with buckets of colored water.

3 NYEPI
March 25
A national day of silence, this Hindu holiday marks Lunar New Year in Bali, Indonesia, and encourages meditation and reflection. Those who follow traditional customs do not talk, use electricity, travel, or eat for 24 hours.

4 QINGMING FESTIVAL
April 4
Also known as Grave Sweeping Day, this Chinese celebration calls on people to return to the graves of their deceased loved ones. There, they tidy up the graves, as well as light firecrackers, burn fake money, and leave food as an offering to the spirits.

5 EASTER
April 12
A Christian holiday that honors the resurrection of Jesus Christ, Easter is celebrated by giving baskets filled with gifts, decorated eggs, or candy to children.

6 VESAK DAY
April or May, date varies by country
Buddhists around the world observe Buddha's birthday with rituals including chanting and prayer, candlelight processions, and meditation.

7 RAMADAN AND EID AL-FITR
April 23*–May 24**
A Muslim holiday, Ramadan is a month long, ending in the Eid al-Fitr celebration. Observers fast during this month—eating only after sunset. People pray for forgiveness and hope to purify themselves through observance.

8 BERMUDA DAY
May 29
The first day of the year that Bermudians take a dip in the ocean. It is also traditionally the first day on which Bermuda shorts are worn as business attire. To celebrate the holiday, there is a parade in Hamilton, and a road race from the west end of the island into Hamilton.

9 ST. JOHN'S NIGHT
June 23
In Poland, people celebrate the longest day of the year—also known as the summer solstice—with rituals including bonfires, floating flower wreaths down a stream, and releasing thousands of paper lanterns into the night sky.

10 BORYEONG MUD FESTIVAL
July
During the Boryeong Mud Festival in South Korea, people swim, slide, and wrestle in the mud, then kick back and relax to music and fireworks.

*Begins at sundown.
**Dates may vary slightly by location.

Around the World

11 LA TOMATINA
August 26
Close to 250,000 pounds (113,000 kg) of tomatoes are hurled during this annual event in the Spanish town of Buñol. The festivities involve more than 20,000 people, making this one of the world's largest food fights.

12 MASSKARA FESTIVAL
October
Celebrated in Bacolod, Philippines, this relatively young holiday was established in 1980 to promote happiness. People dance in the streets wearing colorful costumes and smiley-face masks.

13 ROSH HASHANAH
September 18*–20
A Jewish holiday marking the beginning of a new year on the Hebrew calendar. Celebrations include prayer, ritual foods, and a day of rest.

14 HANUKKAH
December 10*–18
This Jewish holiday is eight days long. It commemorates the rededication of the Temple in Jerusalem. Hanukkah celebrations include the lighting of menorah candles for eight days and the exchange of gifts.

15 CHRISTMAS DAY
December 25

A Christian holiday marking the birth of Jesus Christ, Christmas is usually celebrated by decorating trees, exchanging presents, and having festive gatherings.

2020 CALENDAR

JANUARY

S	M	T	W	T	F	S
			1	2	3	4
5	6	7	8	9	10	11
12	13	14	15	16	17	18
19	20	21	22	23	24	25
26	27	28	29	30	31	

FEBRUARY

S	M	T	W	T	F	S
						1
2	3	4	5	6	7	8
9	10	11	12	13	14	15
16	17	18	19	20	21	22
23	24	25	26	27	28	29

MARCH

S	M	T	W	T	F	S
1	2	3	4	5	6	7
8	9	10	11	12	13	14
15	16	17	18	19	20	21
22	23	24	25	26	27	28
29	30	31				

APRIL

S	M	T	W	T	F	S
			1	2	3	4
5	6	7	8	9	10	11
12	13	14	15	16	17	18
19	20	21	22	23	24	25
26	27	28	29	30		

MAY

S	M	T	W	T	F	S
					1	2
3	4	5	6	7	8	9
10	11	12	13	14	15	16
17	18	19	20	21	22	23
24	25	26	27	28	29	30
31						

JUNE

S	M	T	W	T	F	S
	1	2	3	4	5	6
7	8	9	10	11	12	13
14	15	16	17	18	19	20
21	22	23	24	25	26	27
28	29	30				

JULY

S	M	T	W	T	F	S
			1	2	3	4
5	6	7	8	9	10	11
12	13	14	15	16	17	18
19	20	21	22	23	24	25
26	27	28	29	30	31	

AUGUST

S	M	T	W	T	F	S
						1
2	3	4	5	6	7	8
9	10	11	12	13	14	15
16	17	18	19	20	21	22
23	24	25	26	27	28	29
30	31					

SEPTEMBER

S	M	T	W	T	F	S
		1	2	3	4	5
6	7	8	9	10	11	12
13	14	15	16	17	18	19
20	21	22	23	24	25	26
27	28	29	30			

OCTOBER

S	M	T	W	T	F	S
				1	2	3
4	5	6	7	8	9	10
11	12	13	14	15	16	17
18	19	20	21	22	23	24
25	26	27	28	29	30	31

NOVEMBER

S	M	T	W	T	F	S
1	2	3	4	5	6	7
8	9	10	11	12	13	14
15	16	17	18	19	20	21
22	23	24	25	26	27	28
29	30					

DECEMBER

S	M	T	W	T	F	S
		1	2	3	4	5
6	7	8	9	10	11	12
13	14	15	16	17	18	19
20	21	22	23	24	25	26
27	28	29	30	31		

DIWALI

FLAMES FROM OIL LAMPS flicker as families gather together to share music, food, and gifts in the spirit of Diwali, often called the Festival of Lights. This Hindu holiday, celebrating the triumph of good over evil and the lifting of spiritual darkness, is actually a series of festivals: Each of the five days of Diwali honors a different tradition. Diwali customs include cleaning and decorating houses and wearing new clothes.

Women in Chandigarh, India, light lamps on the eve of Diwali.

Carnival celebration in Salvador, Brazil

CARNIVAL

COLORFUL COSTUMES, festive music, parades, and parties for days—sounds fun, huh? One of the biggest bashes around the world, Carnival originated as a way for Catholics to mark the last days before Lent, the period of fasting before Easter. Thousands of partyers also take to the streets each spring, especially in the Caribbean country of Trinidad and Tobago and throughout South America. The hottest place to celebrate at Carnival time? Salvador, Brazil, considered one of the biggest street parties on the planet!

What's Your Chinese Horoscope?
Locate your birth year to find out.

In Chinese astrology the zodiac runs on a 12-year cycle, based on the lunar calendar. Each year corresponds to one of 12 animals, each representing one of 12 personality types. Read on to find out which animal year you were born in and what that might say about you.

RAT
1972, '84, '96, 2008, '20
Say cheese! You're attractive, charming, and creative. When you get mad, you can have really sharp teeth!

HORSE
1966, '78, '90, 2002, '14
Being happy is your "mane" goal. And while you're smart and hardworking, your teacher may ride you for talking too much.

OX
1973, '85, '97, 2009, '21
You're smart, patient, and as strong as an ... well, you know what. Though you're a leader, you never brag.

SHEEP
1967, '79, '91, 2003, '15
Gentle as a lamb, you're also artistic, compassionate, and wise. You're often shy.

TIGER
1974, '86, '98, 2010
You may be a nice person, but no one should ever enter your room without asking—you might attack!

MONKEY
1968, '80, '92, 2004, '16
No "monkey see, monkey do" for you. You're a clever problem-solver with an excellent memory.

RABBIT
1975, '87, '99, 2011
Your ambition and talent make you jump at opportunity. You also keep your ears open for gossip.

ROOSTER
1969, '81, '93, 2005, '17
You crow about your adventures, but inside you're really shy. You're thoughtful, capable, brave, and talented.

DRAGON
1976, '88, 2000, '12
You're on fire! Health, energy, honesty, and bravery make you a living legend.

DOG
1970, '82, '94, 2006, '18
Often the leader of the pack, you're loyal and honest. You can also keep a secret.

SNAKE
1977, '89, 2001, '13
You may not speak often, but you're very smart. You always seem to have a stash of cash.

PIG
1971, '83, '95, 2007, '19
Even though you're courageous, honest, and kind, you never hog all the attention.

HALLOWEEN PET PARADE

What spell can I cast to get some oats and hay?

DISGUISED AS HARRY POTTER, RAMSEY THE HORSE MAKES MAGIC.

Stop in the name of the paw, er, law!

COREY THE DACHSHUND IS ARRESTING IN HIS WILD WEST SHERIFF GARB.

I am one classy kitty.

ELROY THE CAT SHOWS SOME STYLE DRESSED AS THE MAD HATTER FROM ALICE'S ADVENTURES IN WONDERLAND.

I'm ready to say "I do" to a chew toy and a belly rub.

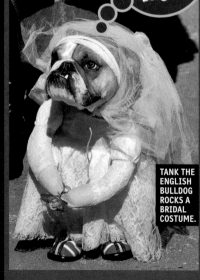

TANK THE ENGLISH BULLDOG ROCKS A BRIDAL COSTUME.

Cool Carvings

Show your pumpkin's true personality with these wacky designs. Use a child-safe carving tool or ask an adult for help.

Express Yourself!

Let your jack-o'-lantern tell the world how it feels with emoticon smileys. It'll make your friends LOL!

Ahoy, Matey!

Pumpkins can wear costumes, too. Hats, inexpensive jewelry, and other accessories can create a pirate, cowboy, or even a baseball player.

Spell It Out

Who says a jack-o'-lantern needs a face? Carve spooky messages into your pumpkins instead.

Stack 'Em Up

Build a snowman by placing the biggest pumpkin at the bottom and the smallest one on top. Slant the knife when you cut off the tops, creating a ledge to support another pumpkin.

CREATE THE **PERFECT** DESIGN

Before you start cutting, sketch your design on white paper. Tape the paper to your pumpkin where you want the design to be. Punch along the lines of the sketch with a pin, poking through the paper and into the pumpkin. Then carve along the dotted lines you've made on the pumpkin.

125

CHEW ON THIS

TACOS!

The word "taco" hasn't always been on restaurant menus. In the 18th century, "tacos" were charges of gunpowder wrapped in paper used by Mexican miners. The wrap concept stuck when cooks started calling tortillas stuffed with meat and beans "tacos." Chow down on more filling facts.

People in the United States spend more money on **SALSA** than on ketchup.

Made from avocado, **GUACAMOLE** comes from the Aztec word *ahuacamolli* (ah-wah-kah-MOH-lee), or avocado sauce.

Natural **CHEDDAR CHEESE** has an almost white color. The bright orange color you see in grocery store cheddar comes from food coloring.

One type of **BLACK BEAN** tastes like mushrooms.

Crunchy corn **TACO** shells have been in U.S. cookbooks only since 1939. But soft tortillas have been around since the 13th century.

MAKE YOUR OWN TACOS

Tacos are crunchy sandwiches—the tortilla is like the bread, which you can stuff with anything you want! Get a parent's help to create a yummy taco.

1 Warm a skillet over medium heat. Cook 1½ pounds (680 g) ground beef or turkey for 6 to 8 minutes.

2 Add 1 teaspoon (2 g) cumin and ¾ teaspoon (4 g) salt. Stir occasionally for 2 to 3 minutes.

3 Fill 8 taco shells with the meat and top with diced avocado, sour cream, black beans, and salsa.

4 Sprinkle with cheddar cheese.

PIZZA!

Pizza may have originated 2,000 years ago when the ancient Greeks prepared round, flat breads covered with oil, herbs, and spices. In 1830, chefs in Naples, Italy, cooked their crust in an oven lined with rocks from a nearby volcano. Some say that could have been the first pizzeria. The restaurant is still open today. Gobble up these other tasty tidbits.

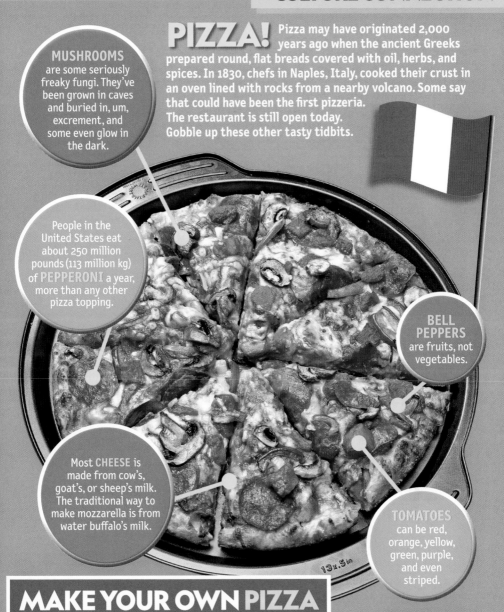

MUSHROOMS are some seriously freaky fungi. They've been grown in caves and buried in, um, excrement, and some even glow in the dark.

People in the United States eat about 250 million pounds (113 million kg) of **PEPPERONI** a year, more than any other pizza topping.

BELL PEPPERS are fruits, not vegetables.

Most **CHEESE** is made from cow's, goat's, or sheep's milk. The traditional way to make mozzarella is from water buffalo's milk.

TOMATOES can be red, orange, yellow, green, purple, and even striped.

13 x 5 in

MAKE YOUR OWN PIZZA

Created in Naples, Italy, the Margherita pizza represents the colors in the Italian flag: red tomatoes, green basil, and white cheese. Get a parent's help to make your own Margherita pizza, or use toppings like mushrooms and bell peppers to make a new tasty creation!

1 Bake premade pizza dough at 450°F (232°C) for about 5 minutes. Brush the crust lightly with olive oil.

2 Top dough with 4 or 5 thin tomato slices, and a pinch each of dried oregano, salt, and pepper. Sprinkle 1 cup (125 g) shredded mozzarella on top.

3 Bake until golden for 10 to 12 minutes. Sprinkle ½ cup (20 g) chopped fresh basil over the top.

MONEY AROUND THE WORLD!

Jordan's HALF-DINAR COIN has seven sides.

ACCORDING to some **PEOPLE, CANADA'S $100 BANKNOTE** gives off the scent of **MAPLE SYRUP.**

A British businessman created his own currency —named the **PUFFIN**— for an island he owned off of England.

IN FEBRUARY 2015 SCUBA **DIVERS OFF ISRAEL FOUND OVER 2,600 GOLD COINS** DATING BACK AS FAR AS THE 9TH CENTURY.

A **20,000**-PESO **BANKNOTE FROM CHILE CONTAINS INK THAT CHANGES COLOR WHEN TILTED.**

The **INCA called gold "THE SWEAT OF THE SUN"** and silver **"THE TEARS OF THE MOON."**

3-CENT COINS CIRCULATED IN THE **UNITED STATES** FROM **1851** TO **1889.**

IN 2002, A MAN OPENED A FAKE BANK AND TOOK IN **$650,000** BEFORE HE WAS CAUGHT.

I knew I should've tried a fake ATM instead.

COINS CREATED IN **1616** FOR WHAT IS NOW **BERMUDA** WERE NICKNAMED **"HOGGIES"** BECAUSE THEY PICTURED **HOGS.**

A 1913 U.S. LIBERTY HEAD NICKEL—ONE OF THE ONLY FIVE IN EXISTENCE— **SOLD AT** AUCTION FOR MORE THAN **$3.1 MILLION.**

THE PHRASE **"BRING HOME THE BACON"** STARTED AFTER A 12TH-CENTURY PRIEST REWARDED A MARRIED COUPLE WITH A SIDE OF BACON.

A BRITISH ARTIST MADE A DRESS OUT OF USED **BANKNOTES** FROM AROUND THE **WORLD.**

MONEY TIP! WHEN YOU GET YOUR ALLOWANCE OR A CASH GIFT, BREAK IT INTO **SMALLER BILLS.** ONLY SPEND HALF AND STASH THE REST IN YOUR **PIGGY BANK.**

CRAFTS AROUND THE GLOBE

Try This!

Try these fun activities inspired by different cultures

Ask for a parent's help and permission before you start these projects.

FUN FACT
Trolls are part of Norway's folklore. Legend has it that these creatures of the dark turn to stone if they're caught in the sun.

TROLL DOLLS

YOU WILL NEED
- GLUE
- FELT AND/OR FABRIC
- SMALL PLASTIC BOTTLE SUCH AS A SPICE JAR
- FAKE FUR
- GOOGLY EYES
- DECORATIONS SUCH AS YARN, STICKERS, AND PAPER CUTOUTS

WHAT TO DO
Decide what characters you want to make and pick out the materials you need at a craft store. Glue felt around the bottle where the face will go. Glue the fake fur along the top edge of the felt so it stands up straight. Then glue on the fabric "clothing," googly eyes, and your choice of decorations and accessories. Be sure to let each layer dry before adding the next layer of material.

FUN FACT
Navajo Indians create sandpaintings as part of healing ceremonies and other rituals.

SANDPAINTING

YOU WILL NEED
- CANVAS BOARD OR FOAM BOARD
- GLUE
- COLORED SAND (AVAILABLE IN CRAFT STORES)
- PENCIL AND BLACK MARKER

WHAT TO DO
Sketch your design on the board in pencil. When you are happy with the sketch, outline it with the marker. Starting at the top, cover a small area with glue and then one color of sand. Make sure you don't get glue and sand on the marker lines. Shake excess sand back into the container and let the glue dry. Repeat using different colors for different areas. Dry overnight.

FUN FACT
Japanese tie-dye, or *shibori*, is more than 1,000 years old. Peasants used the technique to brighten up old clothes. Tie-dye was also fashionable among royalty.

TIE-DYED T-SHIRT

YOU WILL NEED
- WHITE, 100% COTTON T-SHIRT (PREWASHED)
- RUBBER BANDS
- LARGE POT
- HOT WATER
- FABRIC DYE (ANY COLOR)
- LARGE BUCKET
- TONGS
- WATER- AND HEAT-SAFE RUBBER GLOVES

CAUTION! Dye can stain anything, even the sink. Cover your work area with plastic and read the cleaning instructions on the dye package. Always wear rubber gloves.

WHAT TO DO
1. Dampen the T-shirt. For a random pattern, twist and scrunch the fabric, using rubber bands to hold the T-shirt in that position. For a circular pattern like the one at right, grab part of the T-shirt and squeeze it into a long, skinny shape. Tie several equally spaced rubber bands around the fabric. Each rubber band will form a circle.

2. Ask a parent to boil water in the large pot. Using the measurements on the dye package, ask your parent to pour the hot water into a bucket and stir in the dye.

3. Dunk the shirt into the water with the tongs and stir constantly for about 10 to 15 minutes. (The T-shirt appears slightly darker when it's wet.)

4. Rinse the shirt under cold water. Then remove the rubber bands and rinse until the water runs clear. Dry in a clothes dryer to help set the color.

15 Ways to Say Hello

1. ARMENIAN: **Barev**
2. DUTCH: **Goedendag**
3. FINNISH: **Hei**
4. FRENCH: **Bonjour**
5. GREEK: **Yia sou**
6. HEBREW: **Shalom**
7. HINDI: **Namaste**
8. ICELANDIC: **Halló**
9. ITALIAN: **Ciao**
10. MANDARIN: **Ni hao**
11. RUSSIAN: **Privyet**
12. SPANISH: **Hola**
13. SWAHILI: **Jambo**
14. TURKISH: **Merhaba**
15. WELSH: **Helô**

LANGUAGES IN PERIL

TODAY, there are more than 7,000 languages spoken on Earth. But by 2100, more than half of those may disappear. In fact, experts say one language dies every two weeks, due to the increasing dominance of larger languages, such as English, Spanish, and Mandarin. So what can be done to keep dialects from disappearing? Efforts like National Geographic's Enduring Voices Project have been created to track and document the world's most threatened indigenous languages, such as Tofa, spoken only by people in Siberia, and Magati Ke, from Aboriginal Australia. The hope is to preserve these languages—and the cultures they belong to.

10 LEADING LANGUAGES

Approximate population of first-language speakers (in millions)

1. Chinese*	1,299
2. Spanish	442
3. English	378
4. Arabic	315
5. Hindi	260
6. Bengali	243
7. Portuguese	223
8. Russian	154
9. Japanese	122
10. Punjabi	93

Some languages have only a few hundred speakers, while Chinese has nearly 1.3 billion native speakers worldwide. That's about triple the next largest group of language speakers. Colonial expansion, trade, and migration account for the spread of the other most widely spoken languages. With growing use of the internet, English is becoming the language of the technology age.

*Includes all forms of the language.

Bet You Didn't Know!

6 fun language facts

1 The **most commonly** used letters in the English language are **E, T, A,** and **O.**

2 The **Russian** word for **"RED"** also means **"beautiful."**

3 The **longest** word in English is **pneumonoul-tramicroscopic-silicovolcanoco-niosis,** a lung disease.

4 **Babies' cries** can sound **different** in various **languages.**

5 People in **Papua New Guinea** speak more than **840** languages.

6 The word **"taxi"** means the same thing in English, German, French, Swedish, Spanish, and Portuguese.

MYTHOLOGY

GREEK

EGYPTIAN

The ancient Greeks believed that many gods and goddesses ruled the universe. According to this mythology, the Olympians lived high atop Greece's Mount Olympus. Each of these 12 principal gods and goddesses had a unique personality that corresponded to particular aspects of life, such as love or death.

Egyptian mythology is based on a creation myth that tells of an egg that appeared on the ocean. When the egg hatched, out came Ra, the sun god. As a result, ancient Egyptians became worshippers of the sun and of the nine original deities, most of whom were the children and grandchildren of Ra.

THE OLYMPIANS

Aphrodite was the goddess of love and beauty.

Apollo, Zeus's son, was the god of the sun, music, and healing. Artemis was his twin.

Ares, Zeus's son, was the god of war.

Artemis, Zeus's daughter and Apollo's twin, was the goddess of the hunt and of childbirth.

Athena, born from the forehead of Zeus, was the goddess of wisdom and crafts.

Demeter was the goddess of fertility and nature.

Hades, Zeus's brother, was the god of the underworld and the dead.

Hephaestus, the son of Hera, was the god of fire.

Hera, the wife and older sister of Zeus, was the goddess of women and marriage.

Hermes, Zeus's son, was the messenger of the gods.

Poseidon, the brother of Zeus, was the god of the sea and earthquakes.

Zeus was the most powerful of the gods and the top Olympian. He wielded a thunderbolt and was the god of the sky and thunder.

THE NINE DEITIES

Geb, son of Shu and Tefnut, was the god of the earth.

Isis (Ast), daughter of Geb and Nut, was the goddess of fertility and motherhood.

Nephthys (Nebet-Hut), daughter of Geb and Nut, was protector of the dead.

Nut, daughter of Shu and Tefnut, was the goddess of the sky.

Osiris (Usir), son of Geb and Nut, was the god of the afterlife.

Ra (Re), the sun god, is generally viewed as the creator. He represents life and health.

Seth (Set), son of Geb and Nut, was the god of the desert and chaos.

Shu, son of Ra, was the god of air.

Tefnut, daughter of Ra, was the goddess of rain.

All cultures around the world have unique legends and traditions that have been passed down over generations. Many myths refer to gods or supernatural heroes who are responsible for occurrences in the world. For example, Norse mythology tells of the red-bearded Thor, the god of thunder, who is responsible for creating lightning and thunderstorms. And many creation myths, especially those from some of North America's native cultures, tell of an earth-diver represented as an animal that brings a piece of sand or mud up from the deep sea. From this tiny piece of earth, the entire world takes shape.

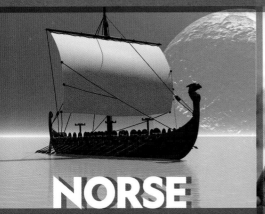

NORSE

ROMAN

Norse mythology originated in Scandinavia, in northern Europe. It was complete with gods and goddesses who lived in a heavenly place called Asgard that could be reached only by crossing a rainbow bridge.

While Norse mythology is lesser known, we use it every day. Most days of the week are named after Norse gods, including some of these major deities.

NORSE GODS

Balder was the god of light and beauty.

Freya was the goddess of love, beauty, and fertility.

Frigg, for whom Friday was named, was the queen of Asgard. She was the goddess of marriage, motherhood, and the home.

Heimdall was the watchman of the rainbow bridge and the guardian of the gods.

Hel, the daughter of Loki, was the goddess of death.

Loki, a shape-shifter, was a trickster who helped the gods—and caused them problems.

Skadi was the goddess of winter and of the hunt. She is often represented as "The Snow Queen."

Thor, for whom Thursday was named, was the god of thunder and lightning.

Tyr, for whom Tuesday was named, was the god of the sky and war.

Wodan, for whom Wednesday was named, was the god of war, wisdom, death, and magic.

Much of Roman mythology was adopted from Greek mythology, but the Romans also developed a lot of original myths as well. The gods of Roman mythology lived everywhere, and each had a role to play. There were thousands of Roman gods, but here are a few of the stars of Roman myths.

ANCIENT ROMAN GODS

Ceres was the goddess of the harvest and motherly love.

Diana, daughter of Jupiter, was the goddess of hunting and the moon.

Juno, Jupiter's wife, was the goddess of women and fertility.

Jupiter, the patron of Rome and master of the gods, was the god of the sky.

Mars, the son of Jupiter and Juno, was the god of war.

Mercury, the son of Jupiter, was the messenger of the gods and the god of travelers.

Minerva was the goddess of wisdom, learning, and the arts and crafts.

Neptune, the brother of Jupiter, was the god of the sea.

Venus was the goddess of love and beauty.

Vesta was the goddess of fire and the hearth. She was one of the most important of the Roman deities.

World Religions

Around the world, religion takes many forms. Some belief systems, such as Christianity, Islam, and Judaism, are monotheistic, meaning that followers believe in just one supreme being. Others, like Hinduism, Shintoism, and most native belief systems, are polytheistic, meaning that many of their followers believe in multiple gods.

All of the major religions have their origins in Asia, but they have spread around the world. Christianity, with the largest number of followers, has three divisions—Roman Catholic, Eastern Orthodox, and Protestant. Islam, with about one-fifth of all believers, has two main divisions—Sunni and Shiite. Hinduism and Buddhism account for almost another one-fifth of believers. Judaism, dating back some 4,000 years, has more than 13 million followers, less than one percent of all believers.

CHRISTIANITY

Based on the teachings of Jesus Christ, a Jew born some 2,000 years ago in the area of modern-day Israel, Christianity has spread worldwide and actively seeks converts. Followers in Switzerland (above) participate in an Easter season procession with lanterns and crosses.

BUDDHISM

Founded about 2,400 years ago in northern India by the Hindu prince Gautama Buddha, Buddhism spread throughout East and Southeast Asia. Buddhist temples have statues, such as the Mihintale Buddha (above) in Sri Lanka.

HINDUISM

Dating back more than 4,000 years, Hinduism is practiced mainly in India. Hindus follow sacred texts known as the Vedas and believe in reincarnation. During the festival of Navratri, which honors the goddess Durga, the Garba dance is performed (above).

Technology Meets Tradition

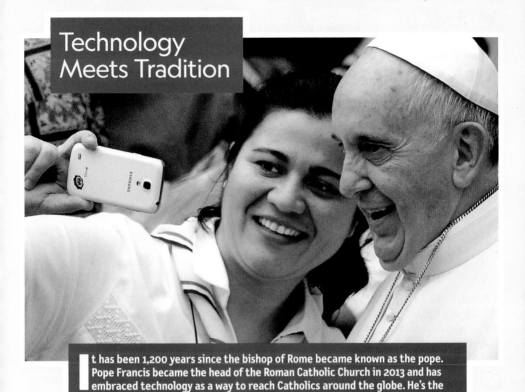

It has been 1,200 years since the bishop of Rome became known as the pope. Pope Francis became the head of the Roman Catholic Church in 2013 and has embraced technology as a way to reach Catholics around the globe. He's the first pope to pose for a selfie and has more than 34 million Twitter followers.

ISLAM

Muslims believe that the Koran, Islam's sacred book, records the words of Allah (God) as revealed to the Prophet Muhammad beginning around A.D. 610. Believers (above) circle the Kaaba in the Haram Mosque in Mecca, Saudi Arabia, the spiritual center of the faith.

JUDAISM

The traditions, laws, and beliefs of Judaism date back to Abraham (the Patriarch) and the Torah (the first five books of the Old Testament). Followers pray before the Western Wall (above), which stands below Islam's Dome of the Rock in Jerusalem.

QUIZ WHIZ

How vast is your knowledge about the world around you? Quiz yourself!

Write your answers on a piece of paper. Then check them below.

1 The word _____ means the same thing in English, German, French, Swedish, Spanish, and Portuguese.
a. "hello"
b. "goodbye"
c. "taxi"
d. "banana"

2 Today, there are more than _____ languages spoken on Earth.
a. 70
b. 700
c. 7,000
d. 70,000

3 A British artist made a dress out of _____ from around the world.
a. gum wrappers
b. postcards
c. newspapers
d. banknotes

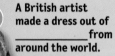

4 _____ is a Hindu holiday often called the Festival of Lights.

5 True or false? Bell peppers are fruits, not vegetables.

Not **STUMPED** yet? Check out the *NATIONAL GEOGRAPHIC KIDS QUIZ WHIZ* collection for more crazy **CULTURE** questions!

ANSWERS: 1. c; 2. c; 3. d; 4. Diwali; 5. True

HOMEWORK HELP

Explore a New Culture

STAMPS OF BRAZIL

CURRENCY AND COINS OF BRAZIL

THE FLAG OF BRAZIL

YOU'RE A STUDENT, but you're also a citizen of the world. Writing a report on a foreign nation or your own country is a great way to better understand and appreciate how different people live. Pick the country of your ancestors, one that's been in the news, or one that you'd like to visit someday.

Passport to Success

A country report follows the format of an expository essay because you're "exposing" information about the country you choose.

The following step-by-step tips will help you with this monumental task.

1 **RESEARCH.** Gathering information is the most important step in writing a good country report. Look to internet sources, encyclopedias, books, magazine and newspaper articles, and other sources to find important and interesting details about your subject.

2 **ORGANIZE YOUR NOTES.** Put the information you gathered into a rough outline. For example, sort everything you found about the country's system of government, climate, etc.

3 **WRITE IT UP.** Follow the basic structure of good writing: introduction, body, and conclusion. Remember that each paragraph should have a topic sentence that is then supported by facts and details. Incorporate the information from your notes, but make sure it's in your own words. And make your writing flow with good transitions and descriptive language.

4 **ADD VISUALS.** Include maps, diagrams, photos, and other visual aids.

5 **PROOFREAD AND REVISE.** Correct any mistakes, and polish your language. Do your best!

6 **CITE YOUR SOURCES.** Be sure to keep a record of your sources.

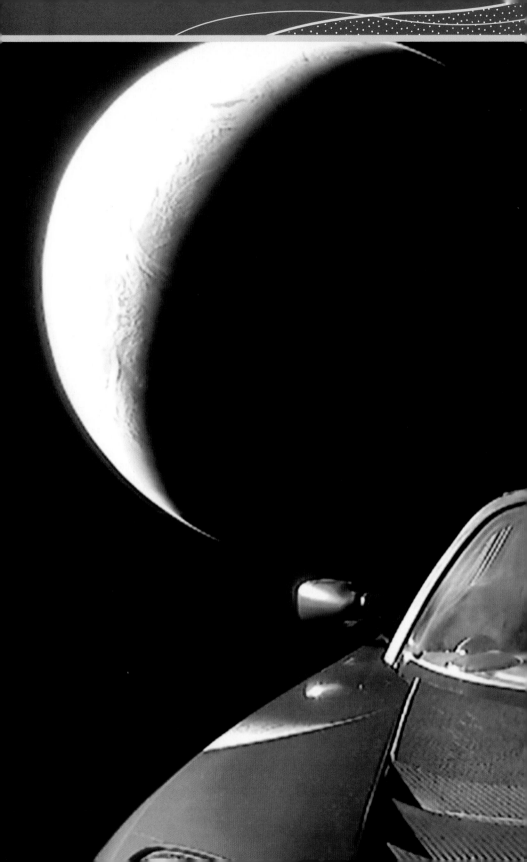

SPACE and EARTH

A Tesla roadster launched from a Falcon Heavy rocket heads around Mars with a dummy driver named "Starman" at the wheel. The Falcon Heavy—considered the world's most powerful rocket—is being tested by the company SpaceX.

EARTH EXPLORER

Meet **Christine Chen**!

This National Geographic young explorer studies ancient lakes to predict future climate change.

Just call Christine Chen a climate detective! As a geologist and climate scientist, she is on the hunt for clues about ancient climate change to piece together a puzzle that may reveal what Earth's future may look like.

So where do Christine's clues come from? She heads to ancient lake basins in places such as the Mojave Desert in California, U.S.A., and the Andes Mountains in South America. Because these specific locations are landlocked, their ancient lakes were once filled exclusively by rainfall. Over time, as the climate shifted and these landscapes went from lush and green to dry and arid, the lakes dried up—leaving behind a rocky landscape and fossilized remains of algae reefs called tufa, which Christine collects samples of and studies.

"My goal is to determine the ages of many tufa samples so that I can begin to build a broad picture of the history of lake level changes in the western United States and the central Andes," she says. "Perhaps we'll be able to see how rainfall patterns shifted in response to past abrupt climate changes thousands of years ago."

This bigger picture, says Christine, can teach us about current climate change, including how rainfall patterns may shift as Earth's temperature rises.

"One of the biggest questions climate scientists still have is how rainfall patterns will change and reorganize in response to our rapidly warming planet," says Christine. "Will places that are already dry continue to get drier? Since water availability plays a big role in determining where people and animals can live, knowing how rainfall will change now and in the future is important."

Christine has collected tufa samples dating back to 25,000 years ago.

THE CENTRAL ANDES MOUNTAINS WHERE CHRISTINE DOES RESEARCH

" Like an archaeologist recovering artifacts from ancient human civilizations to reconstruct their history, I hunt for clues left behind by these ancient climates and try to piece together a picture of what these old climates were like. "

A CLOSE-UP LOOK AT TUFA

Some tufa towers are as a high as a three-story building.

CALL TO ACTION!

To follow Christine's rockin' career path, head to a museum to check out geology exhibits, read about local geology at your library, or simply go outside and research the rocks in your neighborhood. "Learn more about what story they capture about the history of Earth," Christine says. "Each rock on Earth has an interesting story to tell."

CHRISTINE WORKING IN THE AUSTRALIAN OUTBACK

A Universe of Galaxies

5 COOL FACTS TO RECORD

When astronauts first journeyed beyond Earth's orbit in 1968, they looked back to their home planet. The big-picture view of our place in space changed the astronauts' lives—and perhaps humanity. If you could leave the universe and similarly look back, what would you see? Remarkably, scientists are mapping this massive area. They see ... bubbles. Not literal soap bubbles, of course, but a structure that looks like of a pan full of them. Like bubble walls, thin surfaces curve around empty spaces in an elegantly simple structure. Zoom in to see that these surfaces are groups of galaxies. Zoom in further to find one galaxy, with an ordinary star—our sun—orbited by an ordinary planet—Earth. How extraordinary.

DIGITAL TRAVELER!

Take a simulated flight through our universe, thanks to the data collected by the Sloan Digital Sky Survey. Search the internet for "APOD flight through universe sdss." Sit back and enjoy the ride!

2 DARK MATTER

The universe holds a mysterious source of gravity that cannot be properly explained. This unseen matter—the ghostly dark ring in this composite Hubble telescope photo—seems to pull on galaxy clusters, drawing galaxies toward it. But what is this strange stuff? It's not giant black holes, planets, stars, or anti-matter. These would show themselves indirectly. For now, astronomers call this source of gravity "dark matter."

1 GALAXY CLUSTERS AND SUPERCLUSTERS

Gravity pulls things together—gas in stars, stars in galaxies. Galaxies gather, too, sometimes by the thousands, forming galaxy clusters and superclusters with tremendously superheated gas. This gas can be as hot as 180 million degrees Fahrenheit (100 million degrees Celsius), filling space between them. These clusters hide a secret. The gravity among the galaxies isn't enough to bring them together. The source of the extra gravity is a dark secret.

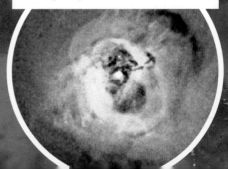

3 IT STARTED WHEN ...
The Big Bang

Long ago, the universe was compressed: It was hotter, smaller, denser than now, and completely uniform—almost. Extremely minor unevenness led to a powerful energy release that astronomers call the big bang. In a blip of time, the universe expanded tremendously. The first particles formed. Atoms, galaxies, forces, and light ... all developed from this. Today's great filaments (see fact 4) may be organized where those first uneven patches existed.

4 FILAMENTS AND SHEETS
Bubbles of space

What is the universe like at its grandest scale? The biggest big-picture view is jaw-dropping. Clusters and superclusters of galaxies—red and yellow areas in this illustration—along with dark matter, string together to form structures that are millions and billions of light-years long. These so-called walls, sheets, or filaments surround vast voids, or "bubbles," of nearly empty space—the blue areas. The universe has a structure, non-random and unexpected.

5 COLLISION ZONE

Saying that galaxies form clusters and superclusters is like saying two soccer teams simply meet. During a game, there's a lot of action and energy. Similarly, as clusters and superclusters form, there's lots going on—as evidenced by the super-high-energy x-rays that are detected (pink in this colorized image).

PLANETS

CERES

MARS

EARTH

VENUS

MERCURY

JUPITER

SUN

MERCURY
Average distance from the sun:
  35,980,000 miles (57,900,000 km)
Position from the sun in orbit: 1st
Equatorial diameter: 3,030 miles (4,878 km)
Length of day: 59 Earth days
Length of year: 88 Earth days
Surface temperatures: -300°F (-184°C)
  to 800°F (427°C)
Known moons: 0
Fun fact: Mercury is shrinking.

VENUS
Average distance from the sun:
  67,230,000 miles (108,200,000 km)
Position from the sun in orbit: 2nd
Equatorial diameter: 7,520 miles (12,100 km)
Length of day: 243 Earth days
Length of year: 224.7 Earth days
Average surface temperature: 864°F (462°C)
Known moons: 0
**Fun fact: Venus is covered in thick
  clouds that reflect a lot of
  light, making it the brightest
  planet in the night sky.**

EARTH
Average distance from the sun:
  93,000,000 miles (149,600,000 km)
Position from the sun in orbit: 3rd
Equatorial diameter: 7,900 miles (12,750 km)
Length of day: 24 hours
Length of year: 365 days
Surface temperatures: -126°F (-88°C)
  to 134°F (57°C)
Known moons: 1
**Fun fact: Earth is the only planet in
  our solar system with liquid water.**

MARS
Average distance from the sun:
  141,633,000 miles (227,936,000 km)
Position from the sun in orbit: 4th
Equatorial diameter: 4,221 miles (6,794 km)
Length of day: 25 Earth hours
Length of year: 1.9 Earth years
Surface temperatures: -270°F (-168°C)
  to 80°F (27°C)
Known moons: 2
**Fun fact: Deserts have been
  discovered on Mars.**

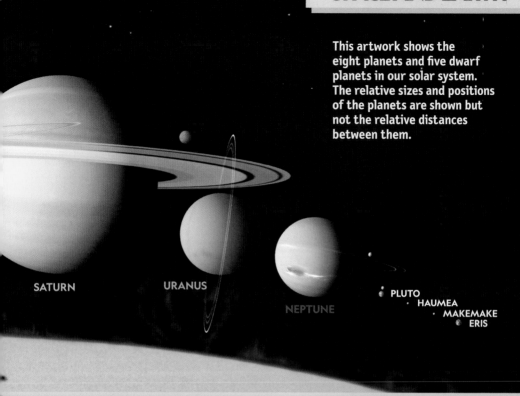

This artwork shows the eight planets and five dwarf planets in our solar system. The relative sizes and positions of the planets are shown but not the relative distances between them.

SATURN

URANUS

NEPTUNE

PLUTO
HAUMEA
MAKEMAKE
ERIS

JUPITER
Average distance from the sun:
   483,682,000 miles (778,412,000 km)
Position from the sun in orbit: 6th
Equatorial diameter: 88,840 miles (142,980 km)
Length of day: 9.9 Earth hours
Length of year: 11.9 Earth years
Average surface temperature: -235°F (-148°C)
Known moons: 79*
Fun fact: Jupiter has a magnetic field that's 19,000 stronger than Earth's.

SATURN
Average distance from the sun:
   890,800,000 miles (1,433,600,000 km)
Position from the sun in orbit: 7th
Equatorial diameter: 74,900 miles (120,540 km)
Length of day: 10.7 Earth hours
Length of year: 29.5 Earth years
Average surface temperature: -218°F (-139°C)
Known moons: 62*
Fun fact: You can't walk on Saturn because it doesn't have a solid surface.

*Includes provisional moons, which await confirmation and naming from the International Astronomical Union.

URANUS
Average distance from the sun:
   1,784,000,000 miles (2,871,000,000 km)
Position from the sun in orbit: 8th
Equatorial diameter: 31,760 miles (51,120 km)
Length of day: 17.2 Earth hours
Length of year: 84 Earth years
Average surface temperature: -323°F (-197°C)
Known moons: 27
Fun fact: It may rain diamonds on Uranus.

NEPTUNE
Average distance from the sun:
   2,795,000,000 miles (4,498,000,000 km)
Position from the sun in orbit: 9th
Equatorial diameter: 30,775 miles (49,528 km)
Length of day: 16 Earth hours
Length of year: 164.8 Earth years
Average surface temperature: -353°F (-214°C)
Known moons: 14*
Fun fact: It would take about 4,500 years to drive to Neptune.

For information about dwarf planets—Ceres, Pluto, Haumea, Makemake, and Eris—see p. 148.

DWARF PLANETS

Haumea

Eris

Pluto

Thanks to advanced technology, astronomers have been spotting many never-before-seen celestial bodies with their telescopes. One new discovery? A population of icy objects orbiting the sun beyond Pluto. The largest, like Pluto itself, are classified as dwarf planets. Smaller than the moon but still massive enough to pull themselves into a ball, dwarf planets nevertheless lack the gravitational "oomph" to clear their neighborhood of other sizable objects. So, while larger, more massive planets pretty much have their orbits to themselves, dwarf planets orbit the sun in swarms that include other dwarf planets as well as smaller chunks of rock or ice.

So far, astronomers have identified five dwarf planets: Ceres, Pluto, Haumea, Makemake, and Eris. There are also three newly discovered dwarf planets that will need additional study before they are named. Astronomers are observing hundreds of newly found objects in the frigid outer solar system. As time and technology advance, the family of known dwarf planets will surely continue to grow.

CERES
Position from the sun in orbit: 5th
Length of day: 9.1 Earth hours
Length of year: 4.6 Earth years
Known moons: 0

PLUTO
Position from the sun in orbit: 10th
Length of day: 6.4 Earth days
Length of year: 248 Earth years
Known moons: 5

HAUMEA
Position from the sun in orbit: 11th
Length of day: 3.9 Earth hours
Length of year: 282 Earth years
Known moons: 2

MAKEMAKE
Position from the sun in orbit: 12th
Length of day: 22.5 Earth hours
Length of year: 305 Earth years
Known moons: 1*

ERIS
Position from the sun in orbit: 13th
Length of day: 25.9 Earth hours
Length of year: 561 Earth years
Known moons: 1

*Includes provisional moons, which await confirmation and naming from the International Astronomical Union.

THE SEARCH FOR
PLANET NINE

IS A NEPTUNE-SIZE WORLD HIDDEN IN OUR SOLAR SYSTEM?

Way out in the farthest reaches of the solar system, a mysterious undiscovered planet could be orbiting through space. It's gigantic—almost four times the size of Earth. And it's so far away that it takes up to 20,000 years to orbit the sun. Astronomers have dubbed it Planet Nine, and they're searching the skies to find it.

FAR OUT

Scientists used to think the area beyond Neptune, known as the Kuiper (sounds like KY-pur) belt, was empty. But it turns out the Kuiper belt is home to icy, rocky objects; billions of comets; and a few dwarf planets such as Pluto. While observing the belt in 2014, astronomer Mike Brown and his research partner, Konstantin Batygin, saw something strange: The orbits of many of the smaller objects in the Kuiper belt were aligned. Weirder still, they never came closer to the sun than twice the distance to Neptune. It was like something was pulling them away. But what?

STRANGE SPACE

Brown and Batygin spent over a year trying to figure out the objects' odd behavior and could only come to one conclusion. "We were convinced another planet was out there," Brown says.

To find out if they were right, the pair created a computer model illustrating the objects. Then they plugged an imaginary planet into the model. The model showed that the

planet's gravity would pull on these icy objects, making them move in exactly the way they had moved in space. The pair also inferred that the planet would be roughly the size of Neptune. Like Neptune, it would likely be made of gas, and the temperature there would be a frigid minus 374.8°F (-226°C).

"It's hard to believe that we could miss something as big as Neptune!" Brown says. But the planet is really far away, about 56 billion miles (90 billion km) from Earth. If it exists, only two telescopes in the world are powerful enough to search vast areas of the sky for it efficiently—and until now, they haven't been looking for the planet.

THE HUNT IS ON

Brown and Batygin are convinced that their evidence proves that Planet Nine is hidden somewhere beyond the Kuiper belt. But Brown predicts the search will take at least a few years.

"There's this huge part of the solar system that we're only just beginning to learn about," says Brown.

OUR NEW SOLAR SYSTEM? Scientists aren't sure of Planet Nine's exact location, but they think it might lurk in the outer edges of our solar system, somewhere beyond Neptune.

SUN ▶

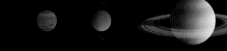

PLANET NINE   NEPTUNE   URANUS   SATURN   JUPITER   MARS EARTH VENUS MERCURY

Sky Calendar 2020

Jupiter

Leonid meteor shower

Supermoon

- **JANUARY 3–4**
  QUADRANTIDS METEOR SHOWER PEAK. Featuring up to 40 meteors an hour, it is the first meteor shower of every new year.

- **JANUARY 10**
  PENUMBRAL LUNAR ECLIPSE. Look for the moon to darken as it passes through Earth's penumbra—or partial shadow. Visible throughout most of Europe, western Australia, Asia, Africa, and the Indian Ocean. View three more eclipses on June 5 (most of Europe, Australia, Asia, Africa, and the Indian Ocean), July 5 (North and South America), and November 30 (North America, northeastern Asia, and the Pacific Ocean).

- **FEBRUARY 9**
  SUPERMOON, FULL MOON. The moon will be full and at a close approach to Earth, likely appearing bigger and brighter than usual. Look for three more supermoons on March 9, April 8, and May 7.

- **FEBRUARY 10**
  MERCURY AT GREATEST EASTERN ELONGATION. Visible low in the western sky just after sunset, Mercury will be at its highest point above the horizon.

- **MAY 6–7**
  ETA AQUARIDS METEOR SHOWER PEAK. View about 30 to 60 meteors an hour.

- **AUGUST 12–13**
  PERSEID METEOR SHOWER PEAK. One of the best! Up to 60 meteors an hour. Best viewing is in the direction of the constellation Perseus.

- **OCTOBER 13**
  MARS AT OPPOSITION. Grab a friend … and your camera! This is your best chance to view the red planet in 2020. Mars will appear bright in the sky and be visible throughout the night.

- **OCTOBER 21–22**
  ORIONID METEOR SHOWER PEAK. View up to 20 meteors an hour. Look toward the constellation Orion for the best show.

- **NOVEMBER 17–18**
  LEONID METEOR SHOWER PEAK. View up to 15 meteors an hour.

- **DECEMBER 13–14**
  GEMINID METEOR SHOWER PEAK. A spectacular show! Up to 120 multicolored meteors an hour.

- **DECEMBER 21**
  RARE CONJUNCTION OF JUPITER AND SATURN. Look for two bright planets in the western sky just after sunset. They will be so close they could appear as a double planet! The last time this rare event occurred was 2000.

  VARIOUS DATES THROUGHOUT 2020
  VIEW THE INTERNATIONAL SPACE STATION. Visit spotthestation.nasa.gov to find out when the ISS will be flying over your neighborhood.

  Dates may vary slightly depending on your location. Check with a local planetarium for the best viewing time in your area.

SUPER SUN!

THE SUN IS 99.8 PERCENT OF ALL THE MASS IN OUR SOLAR SYSTEM.

The SUN'S surface is about 10,000°F! (5500°C)

E ven from 93 million miles (150 million km) away, the sun's rays are powerful enough to provide the energy needed for life to flourish on Earth. This 4.6-billion-year-old star is the anchor of our solar system and accounts for more than 99 percent of the mass in the solar system. What else makes the sun so special? For starters, it's larger than one million Earths and is the biggest object in our solar system. The sun also converts about four million tons (3,628,739 t) of matter to energy every second, helping to make life possible here on Earth. Now that's *sun*-sational!

The SUN has HOLES in it.

Storms on the Sun!

Solar flares are 10 million times more powerful than a volcanic eruption on Earth.

With the help of specialized equipment, scientists have observed solar flares—or bursts of magnetic energy that explode from the sun's surface as a result of storms on the sun. Solar storms occur about 2,000 times every 11 years, or once every two days. Most solar storms are minor and do not impact Earth. But the fiercer the flare, the more we may potentially feel its effects, as it could disrupt power grids or interfere with GPS navigation systems. Solar storms can also trigger stronger-than-usual auroras, light shows that can be seen on Earth.

Some solar storms travel at speeds of **THREE MILLION MILES AN HOUR** (4.8 million km/h).

Solar storm

ROCK STARS

The world is full of rocks—some big, some small, some formed deep within the Earth, and some formed at the surface. While they may look similar, not all rocks are created equal. Look closely, and you'll see differences between every boulder, stone, and pebble. Here's more about the three top varieties of rocks.

Igneous

Named for the Greek word meaning "from fire," igneous rocks form when hot, molten liquid called magma cools. Pools of magma form deep underground and slowly work their way to the Earth's surface. If they make it all the way, the liquid rock erupts and is called lava. As the layers of lava build up, they form a mountain called a volcano. Typical igneous rocks include obsidian, basalt, and pumice, which is so chock-full of gas bubbles that it actually floats in water.

ANDESITE

GRANITE PORPHYRY

Metamorphic

Metamorphic rocks are the masters of change! These rocks were once igneous or sedimentary, but thanks to intense heat and pressure deep within the Earth, they have undergone a total transformation from their original form. These rocks never truly melt; instead, the heat twists and bends them until their shapes substantially change. Metamorphic rocks include slate as well as marble, which is used for buildings, monuments, and sculptures.

MICA SCHIST

BANDED GNEISS

Sedimentary

When wind, water, and ice constantly wear away and weather rocks, smaller pieces called sediment are left behind. These are sedimentary rocks, also known as gravel, sand, silt, and clay. As water flows downhill, it carries the sedimentary grains into lakes and oceans, where they get deposited. As the loose sediment piles up, the grains eventually get compacted or cemented back together again. The result is new sedimentary rock. Sandstone, gypsum, limestone, and shale are sedimentary rocks that have formed this way.

LIMESTONE

HALITE

A LOOK INSIDE

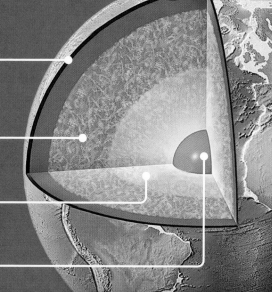

The **CRUST** includes tectonic plates, landmasses, and the ocean. Its average thickness varies from 5 to 25 miles (8 to 40 km).

The **MANTLE** is about 1,800 miles (2,897 km) of hot, thick, solid rock.

The **OUTER CORE** is liquid molten lava made mostly of iron and nickel.

The **INNER CORE** is a solid center made mostly of iron and nickel.

The distance from Earth's surface to its center is 3,963 miles (6,378 km) at the Equator. There are four layers: a thin, rigid crust; the rocky mantle; the outer core, which is a layer of molten iron; and finally the inner core, which is believed to be solid iron.

What would happen if Earth had rings like Saturn?

It's good that Earth *doesn't* have rings. Saturn's rings are made of countless pieces of rock and ice that can be as tiny as a grain of sand or as big as a house. If Earth had similar rings, they'd be positioned in a way that would block sunlight and cast a shadow over the Northern and Southern Hemispheres during each region's winter. (That's when the hemispheres are tilted away from the sun.) Both areas would be darker and colder at these times. With less light coming in, crops and plants that depend on the sun to survive the season might die out. No thanks!

153

It's a Rocky World!

ROCKS AND MINERALS can be found in a wide range of different environments. In addition to being useful materials, they also give scientists clues to how our world has changed over time.

GRANITE Plutonic igneous rock rich in quartz and feldspar. It is a hard rock used as a building stone and for monuments.

GYPSUM Sedimentary rock that forms from the evaporation of mineral-rich water.

FOSSILS IN SHALE Shale is a fine-grained sedimentary rock made from compacted mud. It often contains fossils of extinct organisms or plants, such as the fern at right.

SANDSTONE Sedimentary rock that forms when sand grains get cemented back together again.

BASALT The most common type of igneous rock, basalts form most of the Earth's crust under the ocean.

OLIVINE This group of greenish minerals is found mainly in dark-colored igneous rocks such as basalt, peridotite, and gabbro.

BERYL Commonly found in pegmatite and schist. Well-formed green beryl crystals are also known as emeralds.

TOURMALINE Commonly found in both igneous and metamorphic rocks.

SULFUR AND SALT CRYSTALS They give the crater of Dallol volcano in Ethiopia its unique color.

FELDSPAR Like quartz, feldspar can be found in all three major rock types.

NATIVE COPPER This soft metal forms with basalt in hydrothermal vents near volcanoes.

FLUORITE Most often found in igneous and metamorphic rocks.

A HOT TOPIC

WHAT GOES ON
INSIDE A STEAMING, BREWING VOLCANO?

If you could look inside a volcano, you'd see something that looks like a long pipe, called a conduit. It leads from inside the magma chamber under the crust up to a vent, or opening, at the top of the mountain. Some conduits have branches that shoot off to the side, called fissures.

When pressure builds from gases inside the volcano, the gases must find an escape, and they head up toward the surface! An eruption occurs when lava, gases, ash, and rocks explode out of the vent.

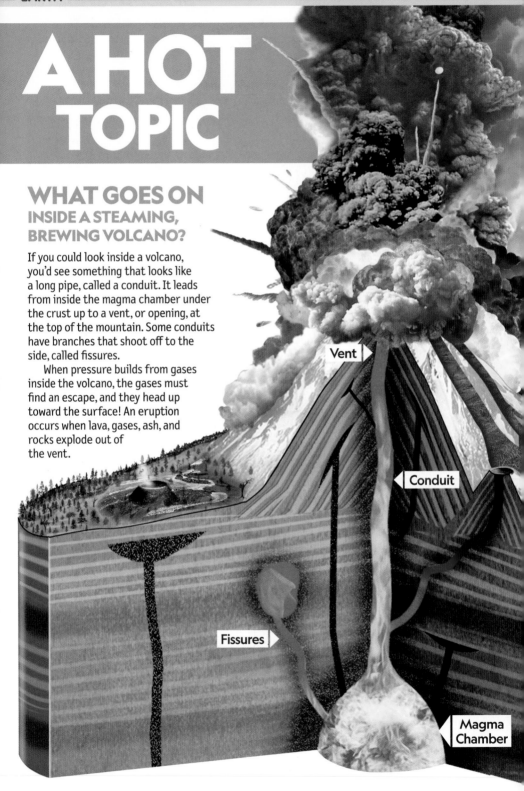

Vent

Conduit

Fissures

Magma Chamber

TYPES OF VOLCANOES

CINDER CONE VOLCANO
Eve's Cone, Canada

Cinder cone volcanoes look like an upside-down ice-cream cone. They spew out cinder and hot ash. Some of these volcanoes smoke and erupt for years at a time.

COMPOSITE VOLCANO
Licancábur, Chile

Composite volcanoes, or stratovolcanoes, form as lava, ash, and cinder from previous eruptions harden and build up over time. These volcanoes spit out pyroclastic flows, or thick explosions of hot ash that travel at hundreds of miles an hour.

SHIELD VOLCANO
Mauna Loa, Hawaii, U.S.A.

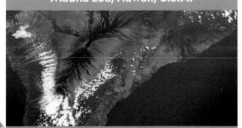

The gentle, broad slopes of a shield volcano look like an ancient warrior's shield. Its eruptions are often slower. Lava splatters and bubbles rather than shooting forcefully into the air.

LAVA DOME VOLCANO
Mount St. Helens, Washington, U.S.A.

Dome volcanoes have steep sides. Hardened lava often plugs the vent at the top of a dome volcano. Pressure builds beneath the surface until the top blows.

HOT SPOTS
Some volcanoes form at hot spots, or holes beneath Earth's crust in the middle of a tectonic plate. As lava pushes up through the hole and forms a volcanic island, the plate keeps moving. More volcanoes form as it moves. Some hot spots are big enough to create a chain of volcanic islands, such as the Hawaiian Islands.

COLLAPSE!
An erupting volcano can cause damage to itself! A caldera is a large bowl-like depression caused by the collapse of a magma chamber during an eruption. Crater Lake in Oregon, U.S.A., is a caldera that has filled with rainwater and snowfall.

FROZEN

A COLORFUL ICE CAVE LIES HIDDEN BENEATH A REMOTE RUSSIAN GLACIER.

RUSSIA

Kamchatka Peninsula

Bering Sea

Sea of Okhotsk

KAMCHATKA CAVE

PACIFIC OCEAN

RUSSIA

ASIA

NORTH AMERICA

PACIFIC OCEAN

The inside of Kamchatka (Kam-CHAT-kuh) Cave is full of cool shades of white and gray. That's because it's an ice cave—a 20-foot (6-m)-high, 30-foot (9-m)-wide passage that tunnels half a mile (0.8 km) through a glacier. But sometimes the cave's scenery is transformed. Its icy interior occasionally glows with a dazzling display of blue and violet lights. So what gives this cave its unique colors?

COLD HARD FACTS

The icy tunnel is tucked away in a remote valley on the Kamchatka Peninsula in Russia. But because it's a three-hour off-road drive from the nearest community, the cave was hidden from the world until 2012. That's when local hiking guide Denis Budkov and some fellow adventurers discovered the site.

The magical-looking cave is in a region known for a weird mix of volcanoes and glaciers.

That's why Kamchatka is sometimes called "the land of fire and ice." It's a combination of these two forces that created the cavern.

The first force in action: ice. Regular winter blizzards in the area created gigantic snow piles, which eventually became the many glaciers found on Kamchatka. "The weight of the snow from above squeezes ice crystals together," says Daniel McGrath, a glacier scientist with the U.S. Geological Survey. "Over long periods of time, these crystals combine to produce a glacier." Or, in this case, hundreds of glaciers.

But how did one of these glaciers become an ice cave? Blame the second force, fire—sort of. A nearby volcano-heated spring sends a steady stream of hot water down a mountainside that the glacier runs up against. Steam from this water seeped under the glacier and hollowed it out from the ground up, carving out the ice cave.

WORLD

Russia is the world's largest country. It covers about 11 percent of Earth's land.

THE ENTRANCE TO THE CAVE IS ONLY ACCESSIBLE TO EXPERIENCED HIKERS.

The Ural Mountains split Russia between two continents, Europe and Asia.

The country's Trans-Siberian Railway, the world's longest railroad, stretches from Europe to the Sea of Japan.

THIS IS A PERSON!

THE RED COLOR OF A FLARE REFLECTS OFF THE CAVE'S INTERIOR, GIVING AN EXPLORER A BETTER VIEW.

RAINBOW ROOF

The colors visible in the cave's ceiling are a result of sunlight streaming in through the cave's thin walls—or, at least, trying to. Snow and ice have something called a high albedo, meaning they reflect much of the sunlight that reaches their surface. But some shades of light are able to filter through water better than others. Red and yellow hues don't make it very far through the cave's icy ceiling, but blue and violet shades do.

MAJOR MELTDOWN

Some melting is natural for glaciers. Budkov has witnessed this meltdown in Kamchatka, where the area of the peninsula's visible glaciers has shrunk

TAKE A PEEK INTO KAMCHATKA CAVE'S ICY INTERIOR. The water in the cave's stream comes from a hot spring gushing from the nearby Mutnovsky volcano and winds about a half mile (0.8 km) until it dries up at the cave's end. Sunlight streaming into the cavern through the glacial ice that forms the "roof" of the cave creates spectacular light shows on the inside.

VOLCANO

ENTRANCE

OUTSIDE/ROOF INSIDE

CAVE EXIT THIS WAY!

STREAM

by about 24 percent since 2000. But even though Kamchatka Cave has melted a couple of times, it always reforms. "If it melts, it reappears the next year," Budkov says. Guess you could call it the comeback cave.

159

QUIZ WHIZ

Are your space and Earth smarts out of this world? Take this quiz!

Write your answers on a piece of paper. Then check them below.

1 **True or false?** There will be 14 supermoon sightings in 2020.

2 **What is Earth's outer core made of?**
a. mud
b. molten lava
c. minerals
d. marshmallows

3 **True or false?** The sun has holes in it.

4 **Which of the following is NOT a volcano?**
a. lava dome
b. composite
c. shield
d. sedimentary

5 _____ **is an example of metamorphic rock.**
a. Marble
b. Pumice
c. Brick
d. Limestone

Not **STUMPED** yet? Check out the _NATIONAL GEOGRAPHIC KIDS QUIZ WHIZ_ collection for more crazy **SPACE AND EARTH** questions!

ANSWERS:
1. False. There will be four supermoons in 2020; 2. b; 3. True; 4. d; 5. a

HOMEWORK HELP

ACE YOUR SCIENCE FAIR

You can learn a lot about science from books, but to really experience it firsthand, you need to get into the lab and "do" some science. Whether you're entering a science fair or just want to learn more on your own, there are many scientific projects you can do. So put on your goggles and lab coat, and start experimenting.

Most likely, the topic of the project will be up to you. So remember to choose something that is interesting to you.

THE BASIS OF ALL SCIENTIFIC INVESTIGATION AND DISCOVERY IS THE SCIENTIFIC METHOD. CONDUCT YOUR EXPERIMENT USING THESE STEPS:

Observation/Research—Ask a question or identify a problem.

Hypothesis—Once you've asked a question, do some thinking and come up with some possible answers.

Experimentation—How can you determine if your hypothesis is correct? You test it. You perform an experiment. Make sure the experiment you design will produce an answer to your question.

Analysis—Gather your results, and use a consistent process to carefully measure the results.

Conclusion—Do the results support your hypothesis?

Report Your Findings— Communicate your results in the form of a paper that summarizes your entire experiment.

Bonus!

Take your project one step further. Your school may have an annual science fair, but there are also local, state, regional, and national science fair competitions. Compete with other students for awards, prizes, and scholarships!

EXPERIMENT DESIGN
There are three types of experiments you can do.

MODEL KIT—a display, such as an "erupting volcano" model. Simple and to the point.

DEMONSTRATION—shows the scientific principles in action, such as a tornado in a wind tunnel.

INVESTIGATION—the home run of science projects, and just the type of project for science fairs. This kind demonstrates proper scientific experimentation and uses the scientific method to reveal answers to questions.

FUN  and GAMES

WHAT IN THE WORLD?

BACK TO NATURE

These photographs are close-up and faraway views of different textures in nature. On a separate sheet of paper, unscramble the letters to identify what's in each picture.

ANSWERS ON PAGE 338

UDM

_____

WOTDSRNIFS

_____

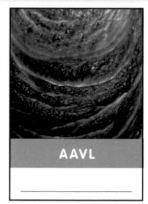

AAVL

_____

SMSO

_____

NSESOT

_____

LPMA AEFL

_____

ERTE KTURN

_____

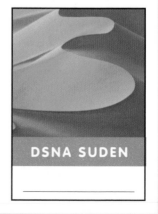

REIEGCB

_____

DSNA SUDEN

_____

FIND THE HIDDEN ANIMALS

Animals often blend in with their environments for protection. Find the animals listed below in the photographs. Write the letter of the correct photo on a separate sheet of paper.

ANSWERS ON PAGE 338

1. spider	_____
2. frog	_____
3. bald eagle	_____
4. fox	_____
5. jaguar	_____
6. viscacha*	_____

*HINT: A viscacha is a type of rodent that lives in South America.

SIGNS OF THE TIMES

Seeing isn't always believing. Two of these funny signs are not real. Can you figure out which two are fake?

ANSWER ON PAGE 338

1

212 Boring

SURFER X-ING

2

DUMP CLEAN DIRT HERE
SEE 910

3

45 TH PARALLEL
HALFWAY BETWEEN THE EQUATOR AND THE NORTH POLE

PASS WITH CARE

4

W 37 ST

5

NO NAME ST

6

SIGN NOT IN USE

7

SLIDE AREA

8

SMILE PLEASE

9

FUNNY FILL-IN

Ask a friend to give you words to fill in the blanks in this story and write them on a separate sheet of paper. Then read the story out loud and fill in the words for a laugh.

I was deep in the rain forest of _____ (country) with my friend _____ (famous person), searching for an ancient ruin called the Lost _____ (noun) of the _____ (animal). But just _____ (number) minutes into the journey, we realized we'd forgotten our _____ (type of insect) spray! A swarm of bugs were _____ (verb ending in -ing) us! We _____ (adverb ending in -ly) _____ (past-tense verb) through the trees and soon smacked into a(n) _____ (something hard). I pulled back some _____ (type of plant, plural) and couldn't believe my _____ (body part, plural). It was a part of the ruin—and we could hear _____ (sound ending in -ing) coming from inside! We peeked through a hole in the wall and saw a group of _____ (animal, plural). They were lounging on stone _____ (type of furniture, plural), snacking on _____ (favorite food, plural), and even swimming in a pool filled with _____ (liquid). I guess this ruin isn't really lost at all!

Play more Funny Fill-In!
natgeokids.com/ffi

167

STUMP
YOUR PARENTS

Answer the questions on a separate sheet of paper. If your parents can't answer these questions, maybe they should go to school instead of you!

ANSWERS ON PAGE 338

1 Where is the world's tallest building?
A. New York, New York
B. Chicago, Illinois
C. Moscow, Russia
D. Dubai, United Arab Emirates

2 More _____ live in New Zealand than people.
A. river otters
B. sheep
C. koalas
D. unicorns

3 Which rain forest animal is attracted to the gross-smelling flowers of the kapok tree?
A. snake
B. monkey
C. toucan
D. bat

4 About how many teeth will a shark lose in its lifetime?
A. 4,000
B. 23,000
C. 30,000
D. 120,000

5 In the virtual world of *Animal Jam*, which land is most similar to the Arctic on Earth?
A. Appondale
B. Mount Shiveer
C. Lost Temple of Zios
D. Crystal Sands

6 A dog's eye has how many eyelids?
A. 1
B. 2
C. 3
D. 422

7 The first space tourist to visit the International Space Station paid how much for a 10-day trip?
A. $20 million
B. $100 million
C. $1 billion
D. nothing

8 Match these Harry Potter characters with their pets.
A. Ron Weasley
B. Hermione Granger
C. Neville Longbottom
D. Hagrid
E. Dumbledore

1. Fawkes the phoenix
2. Trevor the toad
3. Fang the dog
4. Crookshanks the cat
5. Pigwidgeon the owl

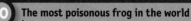

9 What type of bat can eat 600 mosquitoes in an hour?
A. little brown bat
B. big brown bat
C. leaf-nosed bat
D. fruit bat

10 The most poisonous frog in the world is _____.
A. the blue poison dart frog
B. the golden poison frog
C. the red-eyed tree frog
D. the American bullfrog

LAUGH OUT LOUD

"JOEY AND TEDDY
LOVE MY NEW HOODIE."

"HE CAN ONLY FIND
SEVEN OF HIS SHOES."

"PULL OVER, SPEEDY."

"IF YOU DON'T STOP PLAYING POSSUM,
YOU'RE GOING TO MISS THE SCHOOL BUS!"

"YOU SAY YOU'VE BEEN FEELING
RATHER JUMPY LATELY?"

"I WISH YOU WOULD EAT LIKE OTHER SEA OTTERS."

WHAT IN THE WORLD?

TRUE BLUE

These photographs show close-up and faraway views of things that are blue. On a separate sheet of paper, unscramble the letters to identify what's in each picture. Feeling blue? **ANSWERS ON PAGE 338**

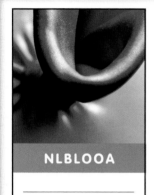

NLBLOOA

_____

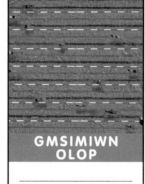

GMSIMIWN OLOP

_____

LEDERDI

_____

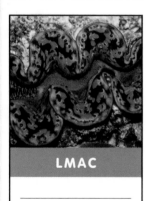

LMAC

_____

TBLRYUTEF

_____

AMAWC

_____

DMTAISU TSSAE

_____

EGPNSO

_____

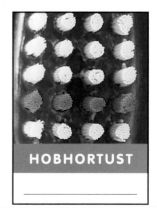

HOBHORTUST

_____

Just Joking

BLUE-WEBBED GLIDING FROG

KNOCK, KNOCK.

Who's there?
Cash.
Cash who?
No thanks.
I prefer peanuts.

How did **the lion** greet **the impala?**

Q

A "Pleased to eat you!"

Q **What** protects a **clown** from **the sun?**

A The bozone layer.

Q What do you call a shy lamb?

A Baaash-ful.

171

ARE YOU A GARBAGE GENIUS?

Hey! Don't throw away that doggie bag!

How much do you know about trash? Take this quiz and write your answers on a separate sheet of paper, to find out if you're a waste whiz. **ANSWERS ON PAGE 338**

1 TRUE OR FALSE?

Before the days of trash collectors and dumps, people used to throw their trash on the streets for animals to eat.

3 PICK ONE

What makes up the bulk of waste around the world?
A. newspapers
B. plastic
C. food scraps
D. yard trimmings

4 FILL IN THE BLANK

Some _____ zip(s) around at 20 times the speed of sound.
A. garbage trucks
B. motorized trash cans
C. space trash
D. trash robots

5 PICK ONE

Which creepy crawlers can help compost your food?
A. crickets
B. centipedes
C. spiders
D. worms

2 TRUE OR FALSE?

Old landfills are often turned into parks or green spaces.

Trash isn't just filthy— it's funny!

Here are some rubbish-themed riddles and jokes to try on your friends and family.

Q What has four wheels and flies?
A A garbage truck.

Q What did the waste collector say while digging through the trash?
A I'm down in the dumps today!

Check out this book!

THIS BOOK STINKS!

FIND THE HIDDEN ANIMALS

Animals often blend in with their environments for protection. Find each animal listed below in one of the pictures. Write the letter of the correct picture next to each animal's name.

ANSWERS ON PAGE 338

1. sea star _____
2. crab _____
3. arctic hare _____
4. owl _____
5. antelope _____
6. chameleon _____

FUNNY FILL-IN

Ask a friend to give you words to fill in the blanks in this story and write them on a separate sheet of paper. Then read the story out loud and fill in the words for a laugh.

My band, the Three _____ , finally got our big break. _____ was looking
                        animal, plural   male celebrity

for kids to star in his new show, "_____'s Got Talent." We grabbed our musical
                                    your hometown

_____ and filed into the auditorium, where _____ people were waiting to audition.
  noun, plural   large number

Finally it was my band's turn to perform. I took a(n) _____ breath, then we started to
                                                          adjective

play a rock 'n' _____ tune. _____ jammed on the _____ keyboard and
                  verb   relative's name   adjective

_____ _____ on the drums. Then it was time for my _____ solo.
 friend's name   past-tense verb   adjective

I went to hit a(n) _____ chord when my guitar flew out of my hands. I _____
                      adjective   past-tense verb

backward and grabbed it in midair, but I lost my balance, crashed into the drum set, and broke

the keyboard. I _____ off the stage and landed in the front row. Everyone was silent
                  past-tense verb

until _____ jumped to his feet and gave us a(n) _____ ovation.
       same celebrity   verb ending in -ing

"_____!" he yelled. "That was the best comedy routine I've seen so far. You're in!"
   silly word

FROM THE PAGES OF *QUIZ WHIZ*:

STUMP YOUR PARENTS

Answer the questions on a separate sheet of paper. If your parents can't answer these questions, maybe they should go to school instead of you!

ANSWERS ON PAGE 338

1 How many years can a macaw, a kind of parrot, live in the wild?
A. 5
C. 60
B. 20
D. 100

2 Each year, almost a million people travel to the Andes Mountains in Peru to see which cultural site?
A. Angkor Wat
C. Machu Picchu
B. Chichén Itzá
D. Stonehenge

3 Paper can be made from which of these materials?
A. panda droppings
B. hemp
C. wood
D. all of the above

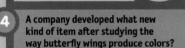

4 A company developed what new kind of item after studying the way butterfly wings produce colors?
A. color screens for electronic devices
B. color-changing helmets
C. tie-dyed sunglasses
D. holiday lights

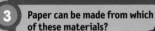

5 The tropical forest around the Lost Temple of Zios in the virtual world of *Animal Jam* would need long days and plenty of rain. If it were on Earth, where would it be found?
A. Arctic Circle
C. Great Barrier
B. Equator
Reef
D. South Pole

6 On the Indonesian island of Komodo, which large animals do Komodo dragons eat?
A. water buffalo
C. polar bear
B. blue whale
D. hippopotamus

7 If you were to make a rain forest ice cream, which flavors could you use?
A. lemon
B. banana
C. mango
D. all of the above

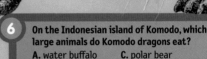

8 Which type of animal is Rikki-Tikki-Tavi from *The Jungle Book?*
A. goat
B. bear
C. mongoose
D. meerkat

9 In the Sagano Forest in Japan, bamboo grows at a rate of _____ a day.
A. 1 inch
B. 12 inches
C. 40 inches
D. 60 inches

10 Spider monkeys have a prehensile tail, meaning they can _____ with their tails.
A. shoot venom
B. grab branches
C. peel bananas
D. scratch their backs

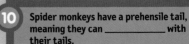

MOVIE MADNESS

It's chaos on this crazy movie set in Hollywood. Eleven things beginning with the letter C have gone missing. Find and write down on a separate sheet of paper the missing items in the scene so the show can go on.

ANSWERS ON PAGE 338

CRITTER CHAT

If wild animals used social media, what would they say? Follow this Galápagos tortoise's day as it updates its feed.

GALÁPAGOS TORTOISE

LIVES IN: Galápagos Islands, off the coast of Ecuador **SCREEN NAME:** SwellShell
FRIENDS:

TealToes
BLUE-FOOTED BOOBY

FrostyFur
HOARY BAT

LionAround
GALÁPAGOS SEA LION

START

11 a.m.

SwellShell — Boy, it's hot! Time to head up the "Tortoise Highway" to cooler ground for a few months. Thousands of tortoises made these tracks!

LionAround — You weigh, what, 500 pounds? How fast can you cruise with that big backpack?

SwellShell — My shell's actually pretty light—it's my legs that weigh so much! And it's not like I need to hustle to get food: I can go an entire year without eating or drinking.

FrostyFur — A year's nothing to **SwellShell**—he's at *least* a hundred years older than me. Do you even remember your birthday?

SwellShell — Nope! So I'll go ahead and celebrate today. Grass cake, anyone? 😊

2 p.m.

SwellShell — I feel like a mud bath. How's everyone else doing?

TealToes — I'm feeling blue.

LionAround — Can I snag you a fish? That always cheers me up.

TealToes — No—it's a good thing! I'm going to flash these baby blues around the beach and try to get a date!

LionAround — Looking good, TealToes! Just like me when I get out of the water.

6:30 p.m.

SwellShell — Sun's going down—time to find a patch of soil to snuggle down in. #PerfectDay

FrostyFur — Are you kidding? It's party o'clock! Nighttime is when I can really spread my wings.

TealToes — Admit it—you come out at night for the bugs. And hey, I got plenty. I surround my nesting area with dung, so lots of flies over here!

LionAround — That's *fowl*. Get it? You're a bird—you're fowl. 😎

WHAT IN THE WORLD?

SPACED OUT

These images show close-up and faraway views of things that are associated with outer space. Unscramble the letters to identify each picture. Seeing stars?

ANSWERS ON PAGE 338

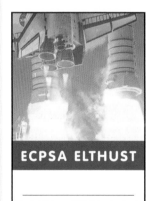

LAYAGX

_____

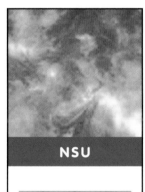

TUNRATOSA

_____

NOMO

_____

ECPSA ELTHUST

_____

NSU

_____

TMOEC

_____

RUANST

_____

RMSA REVRO

_____

IASEELTLT

_____

FUNNY FILL-IN

Ask a friend to give you words to fill in the blanks in this story and write them on a separate sheet of paper. Then read the story out loud and fill in the words for a laugh.

I've never been more _____ . My baseball team, the _____ _____ , was
         adjective   color   noun, plural

about to play the championship game. But Coach _____ announced that the official
              celebrity

rules had changed! First, every player would _____ _____ times before going
          verb   large number

to bat. We also had to wear our gloves on our _____ like _____
           body part, plural   article of clothing, plural

and run like a(n) _____ . Before Coach could explain more, the umpire shouted,
        animal

"_____ ball!" The umpire tossed me our new official bat, a(n) _____ . When
  verb   tool

the _____ threw the new official ball, a(n) _____ , it zoomed past
   type of job   fruit

me and _____ all over the catcher. After _____ tries, I finally hit the
   past-tense verb   large number

_____ all the way to _____ . I started _____ as fast as I could
 same fruit   faraway city   verb ending in -ing

until I slid into home base. This new game isn't so _____ after all.
                                    adjective

AWESOME
EXPLORATION

Wasfia Nazreen—Bangladeshi human rights activist and adventurer—paddles her canoe on the Columbia River Valley Wetlands, near Wilmer, British Columbia, Canada.

EARTH EXPLORER

Meet **Barrington Irving!**

This National Geographic emerging explorer dares kids to fly high.

Barrington Irving's soaring career hit high altitude when he was just 23 years old. That's when he set out to pilot a single-engine airplane on a trip spanning the globe. During that 97-day journey he navigated through thunderstorms, monsoons, snowstorms, and sandstorms—and eventually landed in the history books as the youngest person and the first African American to fly solo around the world.

Barrington's 2007 record has since been broken, but he has yet to stop inspiring kids around the globe to spread their wings and go after their own high-flying ambitions. As the "captain" of the Flying Classroom (flyingclassroom.com), Barrington visits students and shares his own experiences while offering real-life lessons in science, technology, engineering, and math (also known as STEM+).

"I use STEM+ in everything I do," says Irving, who has worked with middle school kids to create things like a car that goes from 0 to 60 miles an hour (96.6 km/h) in less than three seconds. "Kids can build anything!"

Barrington also believes kids can be anything, even if their dreams seem out of reach.

"I was always fascinated with planes as a kid but never thought I was smart enough to fly one," he says. "Then I randomly met an airline pilot named Capt. Gary Robinson. Interest turned into passion and I fell in love with aviation because someone believed in me."

Today, Irving hopes to pay it forward when it comes to supporting kids and getting them to believe in themselves.

"You have to have confidence," he says. "If you don't believe, no one else will. Confidence will always keep you going."

One trip around the world is about 30,000 miles (48,280 km) long.

IRVING READING NOTES FROM STUDENTS AS HE CROSSES THE EQUATOR

> " Always be willing to explore beyond what you don't know and can ever dream of. Never let anything limit you from soaring. See the world! "

During his 97-day trip around the world, Barrington made just 26 stops.

WORKING WITH THE INVASIVE CANE TOAD IN AUSTRALIA

CALL TO ACTION!

Want to fly the friendly skies one day? You can build your knowledge base right in your own bedroom. "Start with YouTube videos [about flying and pilots]," suggests Barrington. Or, you can ask your parents to put you in touch with a pilot or someone who works in aviation. "I remember when I started I simply picked up the phone and would call offices to have a discussion with professionals," says Irving.

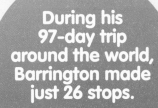

BARRINGTON AND CO-PILOT TOM

Meet Your Shark Bestie

Some sharks grow over 30,000 teeth in their lifetime.

YOU WON'T BELIEVE THESE PREDATOR PERSONALITIES.

While diving off the Bahama Islands, National Geographic photographer Brian Skerry noticed an oceanic whitetip shark swimming toward him. Soon the nine-foot (2.7-m)-long female was gently bumping her snout against Skerry's camera.

The shark's mouth was closed, so Skerry knew she wasn't trying to bite him. Instead, she just examined his photographic equipment like a curious kid. Skerry says this type of behavior shows that sharks have all sorts of personalities. And even individuals belonging to a species that's thought to be aggressive can have a major sweet side.

PERSONALITY POWER

Hiking in the Bahamas through a mangrove forest—a group of shrubs or trees that grow in coastal waters—Skerry arrived at a wild nursery for lemon shark pups in about a foot (0.3 m) of water. He put on his snorkel gear and scrambled onto his stomach to snap pics of the fish, watching as three shark pups swished closer to investigate. "Certain sharks are quicker to explore new things in their environment," Skerry says. Meaning some sharks are also super social, while others within the same species prefer their me time.

Different sharks within the same species thrive in different situations. Social lemon sharks may do better when food is plentiful because they'll share the grub with each other. But when food is scarce, the loner lemon sharks might thrive, since they don't divide their meals.

SUPERSIZE SHARK

On another diving trip, Skerry caught sight of a 14-foot (4.3-m)-long tiger shark in the Atlantic Ocean. Skerry admits to being nervous at first, but the shark just glided over him and actually allowed Skerry to touch her. The tiger shark, known as Emma, visited the dive site almost every day during Skerry's stay. "She was just a gentle giant," says Skerry.

Skerry hopes that by showing the different personalities of sharks, people will view them

SKERRY TOOK THIS PHOTO OF A LEMON SHARK PUP FROM THE WATERY FLOOR OF A MANGROVE FOREST.

More than 450 species of sharks exist, but at least 26 of them are endangered and at least 48 are vulnerable.

THIS PHOTO, TAKEN BY BRIAN SKERRY, SHOWS A DIVER INTERACTING WITH A TIGER SHARK OFF THE BAHAMA ISLANDS.

THE ULTIMATE BOOK OF SHARKS

Check out this book!

SKERRY READIES HIS CAMERA TO TAKE PHOTOS OF A SCHOOL OF CARIBBEAN REEF SHARKS.

less as scary animals and more as individuals that deserve our care and protection. Even if they do have a lot of teeth!

GUARDIANS OF THE SEA

Want to help keep coral reefs in good condition? Call in the sharks! Certain sharks eat animals that prey on herbivorous (or plant-eating) fish. Since herbivorous fish eat harmful algae that grow on the reefs, a break in that chain would be bad news for coral. Thank goodness for hungry sharks.

A REMORA FISH CATCHES A RIDE ON A TIGER SHARK OFF THE BAHAMA ISLANDS.

THE LOST SKULL

Bones found in a submerged Mexican cave give clues about the first Americans.

DIVER SUSAN BIRD CLEANS THE SKULL WITH A BRUSH.

A man once dived more than 900 feet (274 m) underwater without an oxygen supply.

caused by dropping sea levels and erosion. Over time, sea levels rose again and water flooded the cave, burying Naia for the next 12 millennia.

A LINK TO THE PAST

By examining the bones and other items found nearby like teeth, experts ran DNA tests to assess that Naia is a direct ancestor of present-day Native Americans. Naia's DNA also matches with people native to Siberia, a part of Russia. Scientists have long thought that ancient people from this region crossed to North America on land exposed between what is now Russia and Alaska during the last ice age. They were the first humans to inhabit the Americas, and Naia proves how far south they went.

Today, Naia's skull is in a lab. Researchers are still studying her skull to learn about early Americans, so she can continue to shed light on the past.

THE WATER IN WHICH NAIA WAS FOUND HELPED PRESERVE HER SKULL.

I n 2007, a team of scuba divers swimming off Mexico's Yucatán Peninsula came across an eerie, but exciting find. Deep within an underwater cave, in a chamber the size of two basketball courts, was the oldest complete human skeleton ever found in the Americas. These ancient remains held clues to ultimately reveal new things about the first people to live in North America.

A JAW-DROPPING FIND

Experts suspected that the remains belonged to a teenage girl who lived in the last ice age some 12,000 years ago. They named her Naia, after a sea creature in Greek myths, and assessed that she likely died after falling into a large hole

The Yucatán Peninsula has 2,500 Maya ruins.

Out of This World

SCIENTISTS SPEND EIGHT MONTHS IN ISOLATION TO MIMIC LIFE ON MARS

What's life like on Mars? A crew of researchers have a pretty good idea about living on the red planet after spending eight straight months in a Mars-like habitat. In an initiative run by the University of Hawaii and sponsored by NASA, the six scientists lived inside a vinyl dome below the summit of Hawaii's Mauna Loa volcano, meant to mimic the rugged, rocky terrain on Mars.

JUST LIKE THE REAL DEAL

Eating mostly freeze-dried and canned food, the crew conducted surveys and experiments while practicing protocols for an actual mission to Mars, including fixing equipment, mapping, and even growing fresh vegetables. Any communication with the outside world was on a 20-minute delay—the time it takes for signals to travel between Earth and Mars. And anytime they left the dome to do fieldwork outside, they'd put on their spacesuits, just like they'd need to do while on Mars.

HEAD GAMES

The experiment also tested the crew's ability to be mostly cut off from the rest of the world. While the six of them bonded by playing games like Pictionary and watching movies together, it's hard to avoid conflict while living in isolation. Making matters a bit more, well, stressful? Sharing a space about the size of a two-bedroom home—including two composting toilets and one shower—a similar setup to what astronauts would have on Mars. Throughout the eight-month experiment, the team worked on practicing open and honest communication to resolve conflict so they could better focus on completing their tasks.

MISSION ACCOMPLISHED

While the mock mission may seem out of this world, NASA says the experiment and others like it will help it better plan and prepare for an actual trip to Mars, which may be just a decade or two away.

BE A 2020 VISIONARY!

A lot has happened in the world since the first *National Geographic Kids Almanac* was published 10 years ago. We've discovered evidence of water on Mars, mass-produced electric cars for consumers, and tracked the DNA sequence of the human genome. Smartphones took off and tons of apps were invented. Selfies, makerspaces, and 3D printers came into fashion.

In the past decade, National Geographic explorers have also accomplished great things to further our mission to understand and protect the planet. They've helped establish important new marine sanctuaries and national parks to preserve animal habitats and biodiversity all over the globe. These adventurers have explored the deepest realms of the ocean, and uncovered the oldest human fossils and new dinosaur species to shed light on the past—and the future.

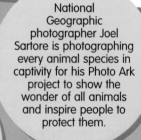

NATIONAL GEOGRAPHIC

PHOTO ARK
JOEL SARTORE

National Geographic photographer Joel Sartore is photographing every animal species in captivity for his Photo Ark project to show the wonder of all animals and inspire people to protect them.

A new species of human ancestor, called *Homo naledi,* was discovered by National Geographic Explorer Lee Berger and his team in a South African cave.

THIS YEAR'S CHALLENGE

To celebrate the Almanac's 10th anniversary, we invite you to be a 2020 Visionary. Think about the world 10 years from now, picture a positive change, invention, or discovery that you'd like to see happen, and share your vision with us. Focus on whatever you're interested in—animals, plants, people, places, science, medicine, technology, conservation. The sky's the limit! You don't have to be an expert on how to make your vision a reality. You just have to tell us what it is, how it would make the world better, and why it matters to you. Send us your visionary idea, and it could be featured in next year's Almanac!

Find inspiration and info on how to submit your entry at **natgeokids.com/almanac.**

LAST YEAR'S CHALLENGE

Save the Lions
Save the World

WINNER

NORA B., AGE 12, SEVERNA PARK, MARYLAND, U.S.A.

Check out the winner of last year's Lions Forever poster contest. We received more than 500 entries with amazing artwork and inspiring messages of conservation. Thanks to all the kids from around the world who entered and shared their interest in saving lions. See more entries at **natgeokids.com/almanac.**

RUNNERS-UP

LIONS ARE WORTH SAVING

(LEFT) MARIAM S., AGE 11, PRAIRIE VILLAGE, KANSAS, U.S.A.
(MIDDLE) SHABAD S., AGE 11, BOWIE, MARYLAND, U.S.A.
(RIGHT) LILAH P., AGE 10, ST. LOUIS, MISSOURI, U.S.A.

SEARCH-AND-RESCUE DOG

SKI PATROLLER IVAN MCGURK TRAINS SHAKA THE GOLDEN RETRIEVER TO FIND LOST SKIERS AFTER AVALANCHES.

Have no fear, superdog is here!

SHAKA TAKES A BREAK FROM TRAINING AS MCGURK LOOKS ON.

North Lake Tahoe, California, U.S.A.

Shaka the golden retriever digs in the snow. He's not pawing through the snow for fun, though—he's practicing to save lives. That's because Shaka is part of Squaw Dogs, a team of search-and-rescue dogs at the Squaw Valley Ski Resort. The animals assist their human handlers with finding lost skiers after avalanches.

Shaka's handler, ski patroller Ivan McGurk, says that though humans can use their eyes to look for injured skiers aboveground, they need help to find people under the snow. "Shaka's trained to search for humans using his nose," McGurk says. "I need his sense of smell to track down what I can't see."

When Shaka's not working, he's with his best friend, Kaya the Belgian Malinois, another Squaw Dog. And when they play something called "flying squirrel," look out! "Shaka runs at Kaya and leaps on her!" says Ben Stone, Kaya's handler. He saves lives *and* he can fly? Someone get this dog a cape.

HOW TO SURVIVE ...

A LION ATTACK

1 CATFIGHT
Lions usually avoid confrontations with people. But if one lunges toward you, swing a tree branch, throw rocks, even gouge its eyes. Fighting back may make it slink away like the Cowardly Lion.

2 DON'T TAKE IT "LION DOWN"
Never crouch, kneel, or play dead. The lion might think you're ready to become a Kid McNugget.

3 ACT LIKE A PRO WRESTLER
Lions go after weaker prey, so show it that you rule. Scream, snarl, and bare your teeth (even if you have braces). Come on stronger than The Rock in a smackdown.

4 STRENGTH IN NUMBERS
Lions prefer to attack solitary prey, so make sure you safari with plenty of friends. Don't let the lion divide and conquer—keep your pals close by at all times.

5 SEE YA LATER
See an escape route? Don't wait for a permission slip, Einstein! Slowly back away—but never turn tail and run. You just might avoid a major *cat*-astrophe.

QUICKSAND

1 NO MORE *SOUP-*ERSTITIONS
Quicksand isn't some bottom-less pit waiting to suck you in. It's a soupy mixture of sand and water found near riverbanks, shorelines, and marshes. It's rarely more than a few feet deep, though it can be deeper.

2 GO WITH THE FLOAT
Not that you'd want to, but quicksand is actually easier to float on than water. So lean back, place your arms straight out from your sides, and let the sopping sand support your weight.

3 YOU FLAIL, YOU FAIL
Don't kick or struggle. That creates a vacuum, which only pulls you down. Ignore the gritty goop squishing into your underpants and remain calm.

4 LEG LIFTS
Conquer the quicksand with a slow stand. As you're lying back with your arms out, carefully inch one leg, then the other, to the surface.

5 ROLL OVER!
When both legs are afloat, pretend you're performing a dog trick. Keeping your face out of the muck, gently roll over the quicksand until you're on solid ground.

awes8me
EXTREME SPORTS

CLIFF JUMPERS!

2 WINGING IT

At the World BASE Race, competitors soar from cliffs wearing wingsuits. Free-falling faster than a speeding train for about two minutes, the jumpers eventually pull a parachute to glide gently to the ground.

1 TAKE THE PLUNGE

Cannonball! A brave diver leaps off the La Quebrada Cliffs in Acapulco, Mexico. The height of the jump? Some 150 feet (45.7 m)—four times taller than most platform diving boards.

4 GO WITH THE FLOW

This sport is on fire. In ash boarding, you strap a wooden board onto your feet before shooting down the slope of an active volcano, reaching speeds up to 50 miles an hour (80.5 km/h).

3 CURVE APPEAL

Cars and motorcycles drive sideways along a wall in this dizzying display in India. Thanks to centripetal force, vehicles stay stuck to the wall as they loop around the curved course.

5 WHEELS UP

Rock 'n' roll! A free rider sails over a steep rock wall in Moab, Utah, U.S.A. In free riding, cyclists use obstacles in nature—like rock formations and twisty trails—to do daring tricks and stunts.

6 BALANCING ACT

No fear here: A daredevil tiptoes along a wire as she crosses between two cliffs in the Italian Alps. A stumble at this height would be like falling from the top of the Empire State Building.

7 THROWN FOR A LOOP

Stunt cyclist Danny MacAskill seems to defy gravity by riding around a 16-foot (4.9-m)-tall loop. Here, he's shown in a time-lapsed photo making a full circle before riding away on his bike.

8 BIG AIR

A snowboarder is flying high during the slopestyle event at the 2014 Winter Olympics in Sochi, Russia. Slopestyle competitors race down a mountain dotted with obstacles like ramps, which allow them to catch major air.

DUH! Don't try these tricks on your own.

PHOTO TIPS:
Getting Started

TAKING A PHOTO IS AS EASY AS PUSHING A BUTTON, but taking a good photo requires patience and a general understanding of how photography works. Whether you're using a low-end smartphone or a high-end digital camera, check out National Geographic photographer Annie Griffith's top tips and tricks for taking better pictures. With these expert pointers, you'll discover how to get the shot you want.

 TIP 1

Get Closer When You Photograph People

Remember, it's the face of a person that makes us love people pictures, not their shoes! So move in close and show that beautiful face!

 TIP 2

Take Time to Think About Your Composition

Composition is the way you place objects or people inside the frame. This is where you can be most creative. Remember, what is left OUT of the frame is as important as what is left in, so look carefully to see if anything in the shot will distract from your subject. If so, find a way to recompose, or rearrange, the photo so the distraction is left out.

 composition: the arrangement of the subject and its surroundings in a frame

TIP 3
Get Moving!

If you have taken lots of shots from one spot, try looking at the subject from another angle: above, behind, close up, far away. Professional photographers are moving all the time, always trying for a better shot.

TIP 4
Don't Photograph People in the Sun

Bright sun is usually the worst light for photographing people. The sun causes deep shadows and harsh light. Besides, everyone in the picture is usually squinting! It's much better to move your subjects to a shady spot where the light is softer.

TIP 5
Quality Not Quantity

It's far better to take fewer, more thoughtfully composed pictures, than it is to shoot like a maniac. It's not about how many pictures you take. It's about how cool those pictures are!

Check out the book!

197

QUIZ WHIZ

Discover just how much you know about exploration with this quiz!

Write your answers on a piece of paper. Then check them below.

1 More than _____ species of sharks exist.
- **a.** 45
- **b.** 260
- **c.** 450
- **d.** 700

2 **True or false?** It's easier to float on quicksand than water.

3 Which location has a rocky terrain that's similar to Mars?
- **a.** Chile
- **b.** Hawaii
- **c.** Mongolia
- **d.** Tunisia

4 Bright _____ is usually the worst light for photographing people.

5 In _____ boarding, you strap a wooden board to your feet and shoot down an active volcano.
- **a.** hot
- **b.** ash
- **c.** lava
- **d.** snow

Not **STUMPED** yet? Check out the *NATIONAL GEOGRAPHIC KIDS QUIZ WHIZ* collection for more crazy **EXPLORATION** questions!

ANSWERS: 1. c; 2. True 3. b; 4. sun; 5. b

HOMEWORK HELP

How to Write a Perfect Essay

Need to write an essay? Does the assignment feel as big as climbing Mount Everest? Fear not. You're up to the challenge! The following step-by-step tips will help you with this monumental task.

1 **BRAINSTORM.** Sometimes the subject matter of your essay is assigned to you, sometimes it's not. Either way, you have to decide what you want to say. Start by brainstorming some ideas, writing down any thoughts you have about the subject. Then read over everything you've come up with and consider which idea you think is the strongest. Ask yourself what you want to write about the most. Keep in mind the goal of your essay. Can you achieve the goal of the assignment with this topic? If so, you're good to go.

2 **WRITE A TOPIC SENTENCE.** This is the main idea of your essay, a statement of your thoughts on the subject. Again, consider the goal of your essay. Think of the topic sentence as an introduction that tells your reader what the rest of your essay will be about.

3 **OUTLINE YOUR IDEAS.** Once you have a good topic sentence, you then need to support that main idea with more detailed information, facts, thoughts, and examples. These supporting points answer one question about your topic sentence—"Why?" This is where research and perhaps more brainstorming come in. Then organize these points in the way you think makes the most sense, probably in order of importance. Now you have an outline for your essay.

4 **ON YOUR MARK, GET SET, WRITE!** Follow your outline, using each of your supporting points as the topic sentence of its own paragraph. Use descriptive words to get your ideas across to the reader. Go into detail, using specific information to tell your story or make your point. Stay on track, making sure that everything you include is somehow related to the main idea of your essay. Use transitions to make your writing flow.

5 **WRAP IT UP.** Finish your essay with a conclusion that summarizes your entire essay and restates your main idea.

6 **PROOFREAD AND REVISE.** Check for errors in spelling, capitalization, punctuation, and grammar. Look for ways to make your writing clear, understandable, and interesting. Use descriptive verbs, adjectives, or adverbs when possible. It also helps to have someone else read your work to point out things you might have missed. Then make the necessary corrections and changes in a second draft. Repeat this revision process once more to make your final draft as good as you can.

Lightning flashes above Monument Valley Navajo Tribal Park on the border of Arizona and Utah, U.S.A.

WONDERS of NATURE

EARTH EXPLORER
Meet Enric Sala!

This National Geographic explorer-in-residence is fighting to save the world's oceans, one fish at a time.

Picture this: You're diving off the coast of Costa Rica when you look up to see 200 hammerhead sharks swimming above you. Later, you slowly cruise through a school of some 100 whitetip reef sharks, before setting your gaze on a pod of giant whale sharks—all in the same pocket of the Pacific Ocean.

This is what Enric Sala, a National Geographic explorer-in-residence, experienced on a recent dive trip off Cocos Island, a national park about 330 miles (530 km) from Costa Rica's mainland. As a marine ecologist, Enric travels the world studying the world's oceans and working to save marine life.

As amazing as some of those trips are, Enric has seen things that turned his career into his passion. He has seen sharks pierced with rusty steel hooks, whales washed up on shores with their bellies full of plastic, and coral reefs dying off at an alarming rate.

"Humans are destroying ocean life because of too much fishing, pollution, and climate change," says Enric. "But if we protect the ocean, marine life can come back."

Through his Pristine Seas project, Enric is hoping to save the oceans. He and his team are setting up Marine Protected Areas (MPAs) throughout the world. Like national parks on land, these are safe spaces in the ocean where human activities, like fishing, are strictly regulated.

So far, the Pristine Seas project has helped to establish 19 marine reserves across the globe, in spots like Russia and Chile. Still, less than 5 percent of the world's oceans are officially protected. But Enric is hopeful that number will continue to increase as people become more and more aware of the desperate need to save the oceans—and everything in them.

"The ocean is vital to our survival as it gives us food, more than half of the oxygen we breathe, and many more wonderful things," says Enric.

About 70 percent of Earth's surface is covered with water.

RAINBOW WRASSES IN THE MEDITERRANEAN SEA

" In only three years, we can see already more fish than before. In ten years, the abundance of fish inside a protected area is, on average, six times greater than outside. Everything comes back. "

GREEN SEA TURTLE, COCOS ISLAND, COSTA RICA

The Mariana Trench, the deepest part of the ocean, is deeper than Mount Everest is tall.

CALL TO ACTION!

"Go in the ocean, swim, and snorkel. Or just go to any place where you can enjoy the natural world," says Enric. "Take a walk through a forest, explore a marsh, or run through a prairie. Spend time in nature and you'll fall in love with it."

TABUAERAN LAGOON, KIRIBATI

Weather and Climate

Weather is the condition of the atmosphere—temperature, wind, humidity, and precipitation—at a given place at a given time. Climate, however, is the average weather for a particular place over a long period of time. Different places on Earth have different climates, but climate is not a random occurrence. It is a pattern that is controlled by factors such as latitude, elevation, prevailing winds, the temperature of ocean currents, and location on land relative to water. Climate is generally constant, but evidence indicates that human activity is causing a change in its patterns.

WOW-WORTHY WEATHER

CANADIAN COLD SNAP: In December 2017, Toronto, Canada, cracked a 57-year-old weather record with temperatures dropping to minus 7.6°F (-22°C).

SEEING ORANGE: Dark orange snow sometimes falls on parts of Europe, the result of storms blowing dust from the Sahara into the atmosphere, where it mixes with the white stuff.

RECORD RAIN: A record-setting rainstorm soaked the Hawaiian island of Kauai in April 2018, with nearly 50 inches (127 cm) of rain falling in just one 24-hour period.

GLOBAL CLIMATE ZONES

Climatologists, people who study climate, have created different systems for classifying climates. One that is often used is called the Köppen system, which classifies climate zones according to precipitation, temperature, and vegetation. It has five major categories—Tropical, Dry, Temperate, Cold, and Polar—with a sixth category for locations where high elevations override other factors.

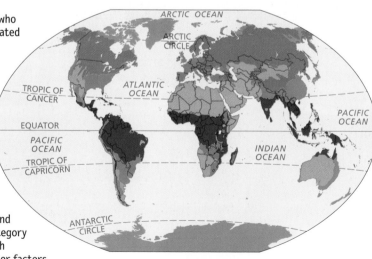

ARCTIC OCEAN
ARCTIC CIRCLE
ATLANTIC OCEAN
TROPIC OF CANCER
PACIFIC OCEAN
EQUATOR
PACIFIC OCEAN
TROPIC OF CAPRICORN
INDIAN OCEAN
ANTARCTIC CIRCLE

Climate
Tropical | Dry | Humid temperate | Humid cold | Polar

EXTREME CLIMATES

Talk about a temperature swing! The difference between the coldest place on Earth—east Antarctica—and the hottest—Death Valley, in Nevada and California, U.S.A.—is a whopping 270°F (150°C). Though they are both deserts, these two opposites are neck and neck in the race for world's most extreme climate.

HOT
DEATH VALLEY

CRAZY TEMPS	Hottest temperature ever recorded: **134°F** (57°C)
RAINFALL	Death Valley is the driest place in North America. The average yearly rainfall is about **2 inches (5 cm)**.
ELEVATION	At **282 feet (86 m) below sea level,** Death Valley is the lowest point in North America.
STEADY HEAT	In 2001, Death Valley experienced **160 consecutive days** of temperatures **100°F (38°C)** or hotter.

COLD
EAST ANTARCTIC PLATEAU

CRAZY TEMPS	Coldest temperature ever recorded: **-135.8°F** (-93°C)
RAINFALL	East Antarctica gets less than **2 inches (5 cm)** of precipitation in a year.
ELEVATION	The record low temperature was recorded just below the plateau's **13,000-foot (3,962-m)** ridge.
DARKNESS	During parts of winter, there is **24 hours** of darkness.

WATER CYCLE

Precipitation falls

Water storage in ice and snow

Water vapor condenses in clouds

Water filters into the ground

Meltwater and surface runoff

Freshwater storage

Evaporation

Groundwater discharge

Water storage in ocean

The amount of water on Earth is more or less constant— only the form changes. As the sun warms Earth's surface, liquid water is changed into water vapor in a process called **evaporation.** Water on the surface of plants' leaves turns into water vapor in a process called **transpiration.** As water vapor rises into the air, it cools and changes form again. This time, it becomes clouds in a process called **condensation.** Water droplets fall from the clouds as **precipitation,** which then travels as groundwater or runoff back to the lakes, rivers, and oceans, where the cycle (shown above) starts all over again.

To a meteorologist— a person who studies the weather— a "light rain" is less than 1/48 inch (0.5 mm). A "heavy rain" is more than 1/6 inch (4 mm).

You drink the same water as the dinosaurs! Earth has been recycling water for more than four billion years.

206

Types of Clouds

If you want a clue about the weather, look up at the clouds. They'll tell a lot about the condition of the air and what weather might be on the way. Clouds are made of both air and water. On fair days, warm air currents rise up and push against the water in clouds, keeping it from falling. But as the raindrops in a cloud get bigger, it's time to set them free. The bigger raindrops become too heavy for the air currents to hold up, and they fall to the ground.

4

3

1

2

How Much Does a Cloud Weigh?

A light, fluffy cumulus cloud typically weighs about 216,000 pounds (98,000 kg). That's about the weight of 18 elephants. A rain-soaked cumulonimbus cloud typically weighs 105.8 million pounds (48 million kg), or about the same as 9,000 elephants.

1 **STRATUS** These clouds make the sky look like a bowl of thick gray porridge. They hang low in the sky, blanketing the day in dreary darkness. Stratus clouds form when cold, moist air close to the ground moves over a region.

2 **CIRRUS** These wispy tufts of clouds are thin and hang high up in the atmosphere where the air is extremely cold. Cirrus clouds are made of tiny ice crystals.

3 **CUMULONIMBUS** These are the monster clouds. Rising air currents force fluffy cumulus clouds to swell and shoot upward, as much as 70,000 feet (21,000 m). When these clouds bump against the top of the troposphere, or the tropopause, they flatten out on top like tabletops.

4 **CUMULUS** These white, fluffy clouds make people sing, "Oh, what a beautiful morning!" They form low in the atmosphere and look like marshmallows. They often mix with large patches of blue sky. Formed when hot air rises, cumulus clouds usually disappear when the air cools at night.

HURRICANE
HAPPENINGS

A storm is coming! But is it a tropical cyclone, a hurricane, or a typhoon? These weather events go by different names depending on where they form and how fast their winds get. Strong tropical cyclones are called hurricanes in the Atlantic and parts of the Pacific Ocean; in the western Pacific they are called typhoons. But any way you look at it, these storms pack a punch.

1,380 MILES (2,221 km)

diameter of the most massive tropical cyclone ever recorded, 1979's Typhoon Tip

82°F (27.8°C)

water surface temperature necessary for a tropical cyclone to form

16.6

average number of tropical storms each year in the Northeast and Central Pacific Basins

10

number of Hurricane Sandy–related pictures uploaded every second to Instagram on October 29, 2012

31

number of days Hurricane John lasted in 1994

12.1
average number of tropical storms in the Atlantic Basin each year

254 MPH
(408 km/h)

strongest gust of storm wind ever recorded

12-25 MILES
(20–40 km)

diameter of a hurricane eye

HURRICANE NAMES FOR 2020

Hurricane names come from six official international lists. The names alternate between male and female. When a storm becomes a hurricane, a name from the list is used, in alphabetical order. Each list is reused every six years. A name "retires" if that hurricane caused a lot of damage or many deaths. Check out the names for 2020.

Arthur	Hanna	Omar
Bertha	Isaias	Paulette
Cristobal	Josephine	Rene
Dolly	Kyle	Sally
Edouard	Laura	Teddy
Fay	Marco	Vicky
Gonzalo	Nana	Wilfred

SCALE OF HURRICANE INTENSITY

CATEGORY	ONE	TWO	THREE	FOUR	FIVE
DAMAGE	Minimal	Moderate	Extensive	Extreme	Catastrophic
WINDS	74–95 mph (119–153 km/h)	96–110 mph (154–177 km/h)	111–129 mph (178–208 km/h)	130–156 mph (209–251 km/h)	157 mph or higher (252+ km/h)
(DAMAGE refers to wind and water damage combined.)					

209

HURRICANE!

With warnings of a major hurricane heading toward Puerto Rico, the territory's governor declared a state of emergency and ordered an evacuation. Those who stayed stocked up on food and water, and boarded up their windows.

But no one could quite prepare for Hurricane Maria, which hit Puerto Rico on September 20, 2017. With winds whipping up to 155 miles an hour (250 km/h), this Category 4 hurricane brought catastrophic winds, heavy rainfall, and devastation throughout the island. Rivers rose to epic heights, buildings were destroyed, and power was wiped out across nearly the entire island. An estimated 2,975 people died as a result of the storm, with hundreds of others injured. All told, Maria was Puerto Rico's worst ever natural disaster.

For months, thousands of people remained without power, cell service, or internet as electrical grids and utility towers were slowly repaired or replaced. The storm racked up some $90 billion in damage, making it one of the most costly hurricanes ever.

After receiving support from around the world, Puerto Rico has begun to recover. Six months after the storm took out a road through Puerto Rico's popular El Yunque rain forest, parts of the park reopened. It's a promising sign that life is returning to usual on this island.

EARTHQUAKE!

In the wee hours of Monday, February 26, 2018, life was quiet in Papua New Guinea. But at 3:44 a.m., a powerful 7.5 earthquake split the ground open and devastated the nation in an instant.

Roads became impassable. Homes crumbled to the ground. Landslides caused contamination of safe drinking water. The quake destroyed crops and vegetable gardens, cutting off the primary food sources for a significant percentage of Papua New Guinea's 8.3 million citizens. Significant aftershocks, which lasted into March, caused additional damage.

With thousands of people impacted—and a death toll of more than 100—humanitarian groups such as World Food Programme stepped in to supply food, medical care, and other much needed aid. Countries such as Australia and New Zealand committed funding as well as the use of their military planes.

While the recovery after a natural disaster never happens right away, these types of efforts are helping Papua New Guinea piece itself back together.

THE ENHANCED FUJITA SCALE

The Enhanced Fujita (EF) Scale, named after tornado expert T. Theodore Fujita, classifies tornadoes based on wind speed and the intensity of damage that they cause.

What is a tornado?

EF0
65–85 mph winds
(105–137 km/h)
Slight damage

EF1
86–110 mph winds
(138–177 km/h)
Moderate damage

EF2
111–135 mph winds
(178–217 km/h)
Substantial damage

EF3
136–165 mph winds
(218–266 km/h)
Severe damage

EF4
166–200 mph winds
(267–322 km/h)
Massive damage

EF5
More than 200 mph winds
(322+ km/h)
Catastrophic damage

TORNADOES, ALSO KNOWN AS TWISTERS, are funnels of rapidly rotating air that are created during a thunderstorm. With wind speeds of up to 300 miles an hour (483 km/h), tornadoes have the power to pick up and destroy everything in their path.

THIS ROTATING FUNNEL OF AIR, formed in a cumulus or cumulonimbus cloud, becomes a tornado if it touches the ground.

TORNADOES HAVE OCCURRED IN ALL 50 U.S. STATES AND ON EVERY CONTINENT EXCEPT ANTARCTICA.

Biomes

A BIOME, OFTEN CALLED A MAJOR LIFE ZONE, is one of the natural world's major communities where plants and animals adapt to their specific surroundings. Biomes are classified depending on the predominant vegetation, climate, and geography of a region. They can be divided into six major types: forest, freshwater, marine, desert, grassland, and tundra. Each biome consists of many ecosystems.

Biomes are extremely important. Balanced ecological relationships among biomes help to maintain the environment and life on Earth as we know it. For example, an increase in one species of plant, such as an invasive one, can cause a ripple effect throughout a whole biome.

FOREST

Forests occupy about one-third of Earth's land area. There are three major types of forests: tropical, temperate, and boreal (taiga). Forests are home to a diversity of plants, some of which may hold medicinal qualities for humans, as well as thousands of animal species, some still undiscovered. Forests can also absorb carbon dioxide, a greenhouse gas, and give off oxygen.

The rabbit-size royal antelope lives in West Africa's dense forests.

FRESHWATER

Most water on Earth is salty, but freshwater ecosystems—including lakes, ponds, wetlands, rivers, and streams—usually contain water with less than one percent salt concentration. The countless animal and plant species that live in freshwater biomes vary from continent to continent, but they include algae, frogs, turtles, fish, and the larvae of many insects.

The place where fresh and salt water meet is called an estuary.

MARINE

The marine biome covers almost three-fourths of Earth's surface, making it the largest habitat on our planet. Oceans make up the majority of the saltwater marine biome. Coral reefs are considered to be the most biodiverse of any of the biome habitats. The marine biome is home to more than one million plant and animal species.

Estimated to be up to 100,000 years old, sea grass growing in the Mediterranean Sea may be the oldest living thing on Earth.

DESERT

Covering about one-fifth of Earth's surface, deserts are places where precipitation is less than 10 inches (25 cm) per year. Although most deserts are hot, there are other kinds as well. The four major kinds of deserts are hot, semiarid, coastal, and cold. Far from being barren wastelands, deserts are biologically rich habitats.

Some sand dunes in the Sahara are tall enough to bury a 50-story building.

GRASSLAND

Biomes called grasslands are characterized by having grasses instead of large shrubs or trees. Grasslands generally have precipitation for only about half to three-fourths of the year. If it were more, they would become forests. Grasslands can be divided into two types: tropical (savannas) and temperate. Some of the world's largest land animals, such as elephants, live there.

Grasslands in North America are called prairies; in South America, they're called pampas.

TUNDRA

The coldest of all biomes, a tundra is characterized by an extremely cold climate, simple vegetation, little precipitation, poor nutrients, and a short growing season. There are two types of tundra: arctic and alpine. A tundra is home to few kinds of vegetation. Surprisingly, though, there are quite a few animal species that can survive the tundra's extremes, such as wolves, caribou, and even mosquitoes.

Formed 10,000 years ago, the arctic tundra is the world's youngest biome.

THE OC

PACIFIC OCEAN

STATS

Surface area
65,436,200 sq mi (169,479,000 sq km)

Portion of Earth's water area
47 percent

Greatest depth
**Challenger Deep
(in the Mariana Trench)
-36,070 ft (-10,994 m)**

Surface temperatures
**Summer high: 90°F (32°C)
Winter low: 28°F (-2°C)**

Tides
**Highest: 30 ft (9 m) near Korean Peninsula
Lowest: 1 ft (0.3 m) near Midway Islands**

Cool creatures: **giant Pacific octopus,
bottlenose whale, clownfish, great
white shark**

CLOWN ANEMONEFISH

ATLANTIC OCEAN

STATS

Surface area
35,338,500 sq mi (91,526,300 sq km)

Portion of Earth's water area
25 percent

Greatest depth
**Puerto Rico Trench
-28,232 ft (-8,605 m)**

Surface temperatures
**Summer high: 90°F (32°C)
Winter low: 28°F (-2°C)**

Tides
**Highest: 52 ft (16 m)
Bay of Fundy, Canada
Lowest: 1.5 ft (0.5 m)
Gulf of Mexico and Mediterranean Sea**

Cool creatures: **blue whale, Atlantic spotted
dolphin, sea turtle**

BOTTLENOSE DOLPHIN

EANS

INDIAN OCEAN

STATS

Surface area
28,839,800 sq mi (74,694,800 sq km)

Portion of Earth's water area
21 percent

Greatest depth
Java Trench
-23,376 ft (-7,125 m)

Surface temperatures
Summer high: 93°F (34°C)
Winter low: 28°F (-2°C)

Tides
Highest: 36 ft (11 m)
Lowest: 2 ft (0.6 m)
Both along Australia's west coast

Cool creatures: **humpback whale, Portuguese man-of-war, dugong (sea cow)**

ARCTIC OCEAN

STATS

Surface area
5,390,000 sq mi (13,960,100 sq km)

Portion of Earth's water area
4 percent

Greatest depth
Molloy Deep
-18,599 ft (-5,669 m)

Surface temperatures
Summer high: 41°F (5°C)
Winter low: 28°F (-2°C)

Tides
Less than 1 ft (0.3 m) variation throughout the ocean

Cool creatures: **beluga whale, orca, harp seal, narwhal**

LEATHERBACK TURTLE

NARWHAL

To see the major oceans and bays in relation to landmasses, look at the map on pages 258 and 259.

Coral Reefs

Just below the surface of the Caribbean Sea's crystal clear water, miles of vivid corals grow in fantastic shapes that shelter tropical fish of every color. Coral reefs account for a quarter of all life in the ocean and are often called the rain forests of the sea. Like big apartment complexes for sea creatures, coral reefs provide a tough limestone skeleton for fish, clams, and other organisms to live in—and plenty of food for them to eat, too.

And how does the coral get its color? It's all about the algae that cling to its limestone polyps. Algae and coral live together in a mutually helpful relationship. The coral provides a home to the algae and helps the algae convert sunlight into food that the corals consume. But as beautiful as coral reefs are, they are also highly sensitive. A jump of even 2°F (1.1°C) in water temperature makes the reef rid itself of the algae, leaving the coral with a sickly, bleached look. Pollution is another threat; it can poison the sensitive corals. Humans pose a threat, too: One clumsy kick from a swimmer can destroy decades of coral growth.

SEA STAR ON A SPONGE

QUEEN ANGELFISH

BY THE NUMBERS

25 percent of all marine creatures are supported by coral reefs.

500 million is how many years ago the world's first coral reefs formed.

4 is the number of countries that border the Mesoamerican Barrier Reef: Mexico, Honduras, Belize, and Guatemala.

THE
GREAT
BARRIER
REEF
IN
AUSTRALIA
IS THE
BIGGEST
LIVING
STRUCTURE
ON EARTH.

MANTA RAY

Try This!
CREATE A
MOTION OCEAN

Shake the jar and watch waves appear!

YOU WILL NEED
- clear jar with lid
- water
- blue food coloring
- glitter
- baby oil
- plastic floating toy

WHAT TO DO
1. Fill the jar halfway with water.
2. Add drops of food coloring until you like the color you see. Shake in a little glitter.
3. Pour in baby oil until the jar is three-quarters full.
4. Place a floating toy on top of the oil, then screw on the lid tightly.
5. Shake the jar gently to set your ocean in motion.

217

QUIZ WHIZ

Quiz yourself to find out if you're a natural when it comes to nature knowledge!

Write your answers on a piece of paper. Then check them below.

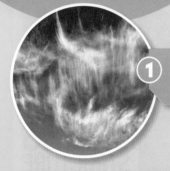

1 **True or false?** Wispy cirrus clouds usually appear where the air is warm.

2 **The Fujita scale measures the speed and intensity of which type of storm?**
a. blizzard
b. tornado
c. hurricane
d. typhoon

3 **The world's first coral reefs formed some _____ years ago.**
a. 5,000
b. 500,000
c. 500 million
d. 5 billion

4 **True or false?** Hurricane John lasted for 31 days in 1994.

 5 **What is the place called where freshwater and salt water meet?**
a. estuary
b. tributary
c. tide pool
d. basin

Not **STUMPED** yet? Check out the *NATIONAL GEOGRAPHIC KIDS QUIZ WHIZ* collection for more crazy **NATURE** questions!

HOMEWORK HELP

Oral Reports Made Easy

TIP: Make sure you practice your presentation a few times. Stand in front of a mirror or have a parent record you so you can see if you need to work on anything, such as eye contact.

Does the thought of public speaking start your stomach churning like a tornado? Would you rather get caught in an avalanche than give a speech?

Giving an oral report does not have to be a natural disaster. The basic format is very similar to that of a written essay. There are two main elements that make up a good oral report—the writing and the presentation. As you write your oral report, remember that your audience will be hearing the information as opposed to reading it. Follow the guidelines below, and there will be clear skies ahead.

Writing Your Material

Follow the steps in the "How to Write a Perfect Essay" section on p. 199, but prepare your report to be spoken rather than written.

Try to keep your sentences short and simple. Long, complex sentences are harder to follow. Limit yourself to just a few key points. You don't want to overwhelm your audience with too much information. To be most effective, hit your key points in the introduction, elaborate on them in the body, and then repeat them once again in your conclusion.

AN ORAL REPORT HAS THREE BASIC PARTS:

- Introduction—This is your chance to engage your audience and really capture their interest in the subject you are presenting. Use a funny personal experience or a dramatic story, or start with an intriguing question.

- Body—This is the longest part of your report. Here you elaborate on the facts and ideas you want to convey. Give information that supports your main idea, and expand on it with specific examples or details. In other words, structure your oral report in the same way you would a written essay, so that your thoughts are presented in a clear and organized manner.

- Conclusion—This is the time to summarize the information and emphasize your most important points to the audience one last time.

Preparing Your Delivery

1 Practice makes perfect. Practice! Practice! Practice! Confidence, enthusiasm, and energy are key to delivering an effective oral report, and they can best be achieved through rehearsal. Ask family and friends to be your practice audience and give you feedback when you're done. Were they able to follow your ideas? Did you seem knowledgeable and confident? Did you speak too slowly or too fast, too softly or too loudly? The more times you practice giving your report, the more you'll master the material. Then you won't have to rely so heavily on your notes or papers, and you will be able to give your report in a relaxed and confident manner.

2 Present with everything you've got. Be as creative as you can. Incorporate videos, sound clips, slide presentations, charts, diagrams, and photos. Visual aids help stimulate your audience's senses and keep them intrigued and engaged. They can also help to reinforce your key points. And remember that when you're giving an oral report, you're a performer. Take charge of the spotlight and be as animated and entertaining as you can. Have fun with it.

3 Keep your nerves under control. Everyone gets a little nervous when speaking in front of a group. That's normal. But the more preparation you've done— meaning plenty of researching, organizing, and rehearsing—the more confident you'll be. Preparation is the key. And if you make a mistake or stumble over your words, just regroup and keep going. Nobody's perfect, and nobody expects you to be.

219

HISTORY
HAPPENS

An amphitheater opened by Emperor Titus in A.D. 80, the Colosseum is among Rome, Italy's most visited monuments today.

EARTH EXPLORER

Meet **Guillermo de Anda!**

The National Geographic emerging explorer dives deep to discover what lies beneath.

Guillermo de Anda's life changed the first time he laid eyes on a submerged human skull. Buried deep inside an underwater cave, this ancient remain intrigued Guillermo—and directed the course of his career.

"That discovery made me want to dedicate my work to underwater archaeology and the study of ancient humans and civilizations," says Guillermo, whose team recently discovered the world's largest underwater cave system in Mexico.

Guillermo's work focuses on the ancient Maya civilization, and his expeditions are centered around cavelike pools called cenotes, which were once used in ancient rituals. In the murky depths of these cenotes, he has found the remains of extinct elephants, sabertoothed cats, and giant sloths—nearly perfectly preserved for as many as 15,000 years.

In particular, Guillermo highlights the Holtun Cenote in Chichén Itzá, Mexico, which contained the

well-preserved remains of human and animal bones as well as jade and ceramics. Because cenotes date back thousands and thousands of years, exploring them may reveal more about the mysterious Maya.

"I am working to get a better understanding of the development of life and civilization over the last 20,000 years," says Guillermo. "Underwater archaeology is amazing, and the potential for research is endless."

GUILLERMO AT A MAYA ARCHAEOLOGICAL SITE IN MEXICO

GUILLERMO IN A CENOTE CALLED "EL PIT"

The world's largest underwater cave is 216 miles (347 km) long.

> One of my biggest career highlights to date is the discovery of the first bears found in Mexico's Yucatán Peninsula. We didn't know they ever existed in this area, and they turned out to be over 12,000 years old.

DIVING IN A CENOTE IN YUCATÁN, MEXICO

Guillermo's team discovered more than 120 artifacts in one cenote, including ceramics and burnt human bones—all dating back some 12,000 years.

CALL TO ACTION!

Before you dive into underwater archaeology, Guillermo suggests you first learn all you can about archaeology in general. "Read books about the Ice Age, about the Maya civilization, and other parts of our past so that you know about a lot of different subjects," he says. As for a specific underwater career, you obviously have to be comfy taking the plunge. Guillermo says learning to scuba dive at an early age is key to avoiding fear when you're swimming through dark spaces. And to keep tabs on Guillermo and his team's progress in Mexico, check out granacuiferomaya.com.

Buried Secrets

Who built this ancient Egyptian monument?

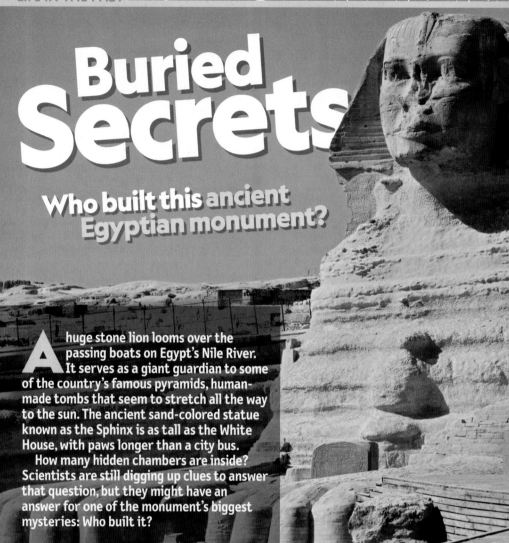

A huge stone lion looms over the passing boats on Egypt's Nile River. It serves as a giant guardian to some of the country's famous pyramids, human-made tombs that seem to stretch all the way to the sun. The ancient sand-colored statue known as the Sphinx is as tall as the White House, with paws longer than a city bus.

How many hidden chambers are inside? Scientists are still digging up clues to answer that question, but they might have an answer for one of the monument's biggest mysteries: Who built it?

SET IN STONE

In ancient Egypt, people worshipped sphinxes as mythical creatures with the power to ward off evil. Some think the Sphinx was built as a protector of the pyramids, which were once used as burial places for Egyptian kings. Nobody's sure when the Sphinx was built, but experts believe it was already ancient when Egyptian queen Cleopatra saw it around 47 B.C. Since then, many other historical figures have visited the monument. But which historical figure *built* the monument?

FACE OFF

Historians' two top suspects are Pharaoh Khufu, who ruled Egypt from 2589 B.C. to 2566 B.C., and his son, Pharaoh Khafre, who reigned from 2558 B.C. to 2532 B.C. Most experts agree that one of these rulers oversaw the construction of the statue and had his own face carved atop the giant lion. But which one was it—Khufu or Khafre?

Some think the Sphinx is the work of Khufu. They say the statue's face matches a sculpture of the king discovered in 1903.

But most experts, including Egyptologist Mark Lehner, think Khufu's son, Khafre, built the Sphinx. As father and son, the pair shared a resemblance.

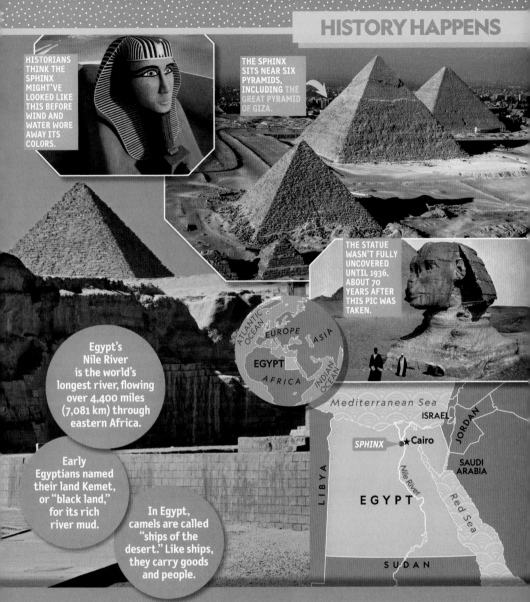

HISTORIANS THINK THE SPHINX MIGHT'VE LOOKED LIKE THIS BEFORE WIND AND WATER WORE AWAY ITS COLORS.

THE SPHINX SITS NEAR SIX PYRAMIDS, INCLUDING THE GREAT PYRAMID OF GIZA.

THE STATUE WASN'T FULLY UNCOVERED UNTIL 1936, ABOUT 70 YEARS AFTER THIS PIC WAS TAKEN.

Egypt's Nile River is the world's longest river, flowing over 4,400 miles (7,081 km) through eastern Africa.

Early Egyptians named their land Kemet, or "black land," for its rich river mud.

In Egypt, camels are called "ships of the desert." Like ships, they carry goods and people.

But Lehner says the most convincing evidence lies in a temple that was built in front of the statue. Lehner believes that the temple and the Sphinx are part of the same master building plan overseen by one person. Ancient workers built the temple on top of part of another structure that's been proven to be the work of Khafre. Lehner believes that this means the Sphinx and its temple must have been constructed after Khafre's first structure was built—Khufu wouldn't have been around to build on top of Khafre's lower structure. "To me, that's strong evidence that the Sphinx couldn't have been Khufu's," Lehner says.

DISAPPEARING ACT

Today the ancient Egyptians' work is crumbling. Centuries of wind and water have ground away at the Sphinx's limestone, and shifting sands have threatened to cover much of it. Archaeologists work tirelessly to repair the structure to keep it from completely disappearing.

By preserving the Sphinx, experts are also protecting clues that might still be hidden in the statue's stone. Someday, these could be the keys that unlock even more of the Sphinx's secrets.

225

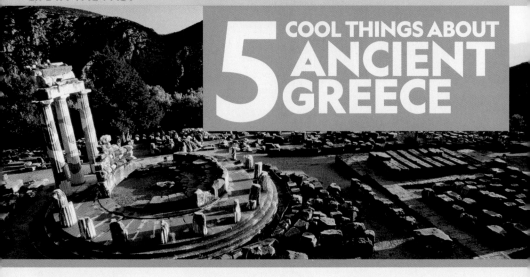

5 COOL THINGS ABOUT ANCIENT GREECE

ALTHOUGH THEY LIVED MORE THAN 2,000 YEARS AGO, the ancient Greeks were clearly ahead of their time. From science to sports, many Greek traditions are alive and well today. Here are some things that make this civilization stand out.

1 START-UP SCHOOL

In 387 B.C., the Greek philosopher Plato founded the Academy in Athens, which was the earliest example of a modern university. Students (including some women, against the traditions of the time) studied astronomy, biology, math, law, politics, and philosophy. Plato's hope was that the Academy would provide a place for all scholars to work toward better government in the Grecian cities. The Academy would become a center of learning for nearly 1,000 years.

2 OUTDOOR STAGE

The Greeks were among the first to perform plays. These performances sprang from festivals honoring their gods in which men would dress up, act out stories, and sing songs. They built large, outdoor theaters in most of their cities—some big enough to hold 15,000 people! The audience was so far away from the stage that the actors would wear elaborate costumes and sad- or happy-face masks so that people could see each character's expressions no matter where they were sitting.

3 CITY-STATES

Experts believe that ancient Greek civilization was likely begun nearly 4,000 years ago by the Mycenaeans of Crete, a Greek island. The ancient Greek Empire spread from Greece through Europe, and in 800 B.C. the Greeks began splitting their land into hundreds of city-states. Although most Greeks shared the same language and religion, each city-state maintained its own laws, customs, and rulers.

4 SUPERSTITIONS

The ancient Greeks were superstitious people. For instance, they originated the idea that breaking a mirror was bad luck. Believing mirrors showed the will of the gods, they thought a broken mirror meant the gods did not want you to see something unpleasant in your future. They also had unique ideas about food—some ancient Greeks would not eat beans because they believed they contained the souls of the dead.

5 ORIGINAL OLYMPICS

The ancient Greeks held many festivals in honor of their gods, including some serious sports competitions. The most famous took place in Olympia, Greece, starting in 776 B.C. Honoring the god Zeus, this two-day event—which inspired the modern-day Olympic Games—included contests in wrestling, boxing, long jump, javelin, discus, and chariot racing. Winners were given a wreath of leaves, free meals, and the best seats in the theater as prizes.

ALEXANDER THE GREAT

A bold military leader, Alexander the Great had a need to lead—and he conquered enough land to create an empire that stretched across 3,000 miles (4,828 km). Get the scoop on the life of this legendary ruler.

Historians think Alexander likely had two different colored eyes—one hazel and one green.

START

ca 356 B.C.

Alexander is born to King Philip II and Queen Olympias, rulers of the ancient Greek kingdom of Macedon. Alexander's tutor is a famous philosopher named Aristotle, who teaches the young prince and his friends about medicine, religion, logic, and art. What, no gym class?

Um—my horse ate my homework?

ca 336 B.C.

Macedon's new king conquers his first city: Thessaly, a neighbor to the south. Alexander and his men sneak up behind Mount Ossa, a nearby mountain range separating the two locations, and surprise the Thessalian guards while they're sleeping. Guess it's true—you snooze, you lose.

ca 338 B.C.

Alexander helps his father command troops at the Battle of Chaeronea (Cair-oh-NEE-ah). He becomes ruler two years later at the age of 20, following King Philip's death.

Historians don't always know the exact dates of events from ancient times. That's why you'll see a "ca" next to the years listed below. It stands for "circa," meaning "around."

ca 331 B.C.

Alexander invades Egypt and takes over the kingdom. The ruler is crowned pharaoh and establishes the famous Egyptian city of Alexandria, naming it after (duh!) himself.

WELCOME TO ALEXANDR

MINE   MINE   MINE

ca 323 B.C.

Alexander gets sick and dies at the age of 32. In just 13 years, he has built a massive empire spreading from Africa to Asia, and introduced Greek culture to much of the world. Now that is pretty great.

GUARDIANS
OF THE TOMB

Back in 1974, some Chinese farmers were digging for water when they got a shock. Staring up from the soil was a face, eyes wide open, with features that looked almost human. But this was not a skeleton: It was one of thousands of life-size soldiers made of baked clay called terra-cotta—and they had been buried for 2,200 years.

BURIED TREASURE

Row upon row of the soldiers—each face as different and as realistic as the next—were hidden in a pit the size of two football fields near Xi'an, which was China's capital city for nearly 2,000 years. Archaeologists eventually found four pits, some containing statues of horse-drawn chariots, cavalry (soldiers on horseback), and high-ranking officers.

BODY GUARDS

Who could have built this huge underground army? Experts assume it was China's first emperor, Qin Shihuangdi (Chin She-hwong-dee). The brilliant but brutal ruler, who created the first unified China, was known for his big ideas and even bigger ego. It's believed that because Qin Shihuangdi had killed so many people during his reign, he may have wanted a large army to protect him from his victims' ghosts once he died. He probably had the clay soldiers created to guard his tomb, which was just one mile (1.6 km) away from where the pits were discovered.

FINAL REWARDS

As it turned out, the emperor's living enemies took revenge—not the dead ones. In 206 B.C., a few years after Qin Shihuangdi's death, invading armies destroyed the pits, burying the warriors and cracking every figure. The pits caved in more as time went on, and the soldiers were lost to the ages.

Experts have since pieced a thousand soldiers back together. But some 6,000 figures are still buried. As work continues, who knows what secrets these soldiers have yet to tell?

STATUES OF ARCHERS, LIKE THE ONE ABOVE, WERE BURIED HOLDING REAL CROSSBOWS.

UNDER
RECONSTRUCTION

Experts have painstakingly rebuilt and restored a thousand terra-cotta warriors found in underground pits near the emperor's tomb. The complex is so vast that excavations may continue for generations.

ANCIENT CRAFTSMEN MADE THOUSANDS OF LIFE-SIZE TERRA-COTTA WARRIORS, EACH WITH A UNIQUE FACE.

ASIA

CHINA

PACIFIC OCEAN

TERRA-COTTA WARRIORS

CHINA

HORSE-DRAWN CHARIOT

A warrior's head poking out of the dirt still has traces of red paint. Originally all of the warriors were painted bright colors.

Workers brush dirt away from the collapsed roof that sheltered the terra-cotta warriors.

A toppled terra-cotta warrior lies in its 2,200-year-old underground tomb.

Secrets of the

SCIENTISTS USE CUTTING-EDGE TECHNOLOGY TO UNCOVER NEW EVIDENCE ABOUT HOW THE SHIP SANK.

Sunday, April 14, 1912: The R.M.S. *Titanic* steams across the North Atlantic Ocean. The 882-foot (269-m)-long passenger ship carries 2,208 people on its maiden voyage from Southampton, England, to New York City, in the United States of America.

Suddenly, a dark shape appears. An iceberg scrapes the ship, and within three hours, the *Titanic* sinks. Almost 1,500 people lose their lives.

Scientists have closely studied the *Titanic's* wreck on the ocean floor since it was discovered in 1985. National Geographic Explorer-in-Residence James Cameron—director of the movies *Titanic* and *Avatar*—assembled a team of experts to examine the shipwreck anew. Using 3D modeling and state-of-the-art technology, the experts reveal new clues about how the *Titanic* sank.

FLOODING

It might have been possible for the ship to sink more slowly, allowing more people to survive. Many of the ship's portholes were found open—most likely because passengers were airing out their rooms and never closed them. This caused the ship to take on water faster.

Something similar also may have happened in one of the grand lobbies, where a large door was found open. "The size of the door is twice the size of the original iceberg damage," Cameron says. "This would have sped up the sinking of the ship."

BREAKING

As the *Titanic* took on water, the front of the ship, called the bow, sank below the surface, causing the back, or stern, to lift into the air. The great stress broke the ship in half. "When the *Titanic* broke in half and the bow pulled away, the bottom likely remained attached to the back of the ship until it, too, was pulled apart," Cameron says.

EXPLORER JAMES CAMERON PILOTS AN UNDERWATER VEHICLE CALLED A SUBMERSIBLE.

SINKING

In its final resting place, the bow looks remarkably intact. But the stern looks like a bomb destroyed it. Why? The bow was filled with water when it sank, so the pressure was the same on the inside as the outside. The stern, however, sank with lots of air inside and imploded from the pressure.

FINAL IMPACT

The sinking ship created a massive trail of water that followed it downward at 20 to 25 miles an hour (32 to 40 km/h). Experts think that this water trail pummeled the *Titanic* after it hit bottom. "Millions of gallons of water came pushing down on it," Cameron says.

With all this new information, is our understanding of the *Titanic* tragedy complete? "I think we have a very good picture of what happened," Cameron says. "But there will always be mysteries."

Titanic

TITANIC
·19· **·12·**
LONDON

SUPERSIZE SHIP
The *Titanic* was almost as long as three football fields. With its smokestacks, the ship was as tall as a 17-story building.

TITANIC

WHAT IF ...
Scientists know a lot about how the *Titanic* sank, but other factors contributed as well.

SAILING SCHEDULE
The *Titanic* set sail more than three weeks behind schedule. If the ship had left on time, an iceberg probably wouldn't have been in its path.

FROM CALM TO CHAOS
The sea was unusually calm on April 14, 1912. Waves would have made the iceberg easier to spot.

MISSED MESSAGES
Two messages were telegraphed from other ships to warn the *Titanic* of icebergs, but they never reached the captain.

We asked oceanographer and National Geographic Explorer-in-Residence Robert Ballard, who led the team that discovered the *Titanic* in 1985, what it felt like to make the discovery of the century.

"My first reaction was one of excitement and celebration. But we were at the **very spot** on the **cold North Atlantic Ocean** where it all happened. So then we had **a quiet moment of remembrance."**

THE GREATEST HEISTS OF ALL TIME!

How criminal masterminds pulled off daring thefts—but still got caught.

TRAIN BANDITS

Where: Buckinghamshire, England
Date: August 8, 1963
The Loot: More than £2.6 million ($7 million) in Scottish banknotes from a Royal Mail Train.
The Master Plan: A team of 15 criminals rigs the train signal so the train stops unexpectedly. When it does, they jump into a car filled with mail sacks carrying the money. The thieves transfer the treasure to their vehicle and speed away to their hideout, a farmhouse 27 miles (43 km) away.
The Outcome: A tip leads investigators to the thieves' hideout, where they find stolen mail sacks and fingerprints on everything. Twelve thieves are taken to jail; three are never found.

THE ARTFUL CROOK

Where: Paris, France
Date: August 21, 1911
The Loot: The priceless "Mona Lisa"
The Master Plan: A man named Vincenzo Perugia poses as a workman at the Louvre art museum in Paris, grabs the famous painting, and walks past an unmanned guard station with it tucked under his smock.
The Outcome: After hiding the painting in a wooden trunk for two years, Perugia takes it to an art dealer in Florence, Italy—the same city where the "Mona Lisa" was painted by Leonardo da Vinci about 400 years earlier. The suspicious dealer calls the police, who arrest Perugia and return the "Mona Lisa" to the Louvre.

A DAZZLING CRIME

Where: Antwerp, Belgium
Date: February 16, 2003
The Loot: More than 75 million euros ($100 million) worth of jewels, gold, and money from a vault under the Antwerp World Diamond Centre.
The Master Plan: Thieves spend two and a half years planning the robbery. Using hair spray, tape, and Styrofoam boxes, the thieves block the heat, light, and motion sensors so they can't detect the men's body temperatures or movements. They figure out the combination to the vault's three-ton (2.7-t) steel door by installing a tiny hidden camera.
The Outcome: Police discover a bag in the woods with two of the robbers' DNA. Four of the thieves go to jail. The stolen gems are never recovered.

CURSE OF THE HOPE DIAMOND

Is the Hope Diamond, one of the world's most valuable jewels, the bearer of bad luck? Legend has it that the stone was stolen from the eye of a sacred statue in India, and Hindu gods cursed the stone to punish the thieves. You decide if the curse is rock solid or just a gem of a tale!

LOSING THEIR HEADS

The French royal family once owned the diamond, but not for too long. After King Louis XVI and his wife, Marie Antoinette, were imprisoned and beheaded during the French Revolution, the government confiscated the stone, which thieves later stole before it was bought by the wealthy Hope family.

LOST HOPE

Lord Francis Hope eventually inherited the diamond, and then his wife left him and he had to sell the pricey stone to help pay off his huge debts. But the gem still bears the Hope family name.

TEMPTING FATE

Millionaire Evalyn McLean bought the diamond in 1911. But luck was not on McLean's side, either. During her lifetime, two of her children died, her husband became mentally ill, and she fell into serious debt.

DOOMED DELIVERY

In 1958 a mailman named James Todd delivered the diamond to its present home—the Smithsonian Institution in Washington, D.C., U.S.A. Within a year Todd's wife died and his house burned down. Was it the curse?

REAL OR FAKE?

"The curse isn't true," says Richard Kurin, author of the book *Hope Diamond: The Legendary History of a Cursed Gem.* It may all just be an eerie coincidence, but one thing's for sure, "The Hope diamond is so valuable because it is a unique stone and because of its famous story," says Kurin.

WHERE DO DIAMONDS COME FROM?

Natural diamonds form about 100 miles (160 km) underground and are the hardest known natural substance. Under extreme heat and pressure, carbon atoms are squeezed together into the hard, clear crystals. Volcanic eruptions carry the diamonds toward Earth's surface, where they are mined for use in industrial tools and sparkly jewelry.

GOING TO WAR

Since the beginning of time, different countries, territories, and cultures have feuded with each other over land, power, and politics. Major military conflicts include the following wars:

1095–1291 THE CRUSADES
Starting late in the 11th century, these wars over religion were fought in the Middle East for nearly 200 years.

1337–1453 HUNDRED YEARS' WAR
France and England battled over rights to land for more than a century before the French eventually drove the English out in 1453.

1754–1763 FRENCH AND INDIAN WAR (part of Europe's Seven Years' War)
A nine-year war between the British and French for control of North America.

1775–1783 AMERICAN REVOLUTION
Thirteen British colonies in America united to reject the rule of the British government and to form the United States of America.

1861–1865 AMERICAN CIVIL WAR
Occurred when the northern states (the Union) went to war with the southern states, which had seceded, or withdrawn, to form the Confederate States of America. Slavery was one of the key issues in the Civil War.

1910–1920 MEXICAN REVOLUTION
The people of Mexico revolted against the rule of dictator President Porfirio Díaz, leading to his eventual defeat and to a democratic government.

1914–1918 WORLD WAR I
The assassination of Austria's Archduke Ferdinand by a Serbian nationalist sparked this wide-spreading war. The U.S. entered after Germany sank the British ship *Lusitania*, killing more than 120 Americans.

1918–1920 RUSSIAN CIVIL WAR
Following the 1917 Russian Revolution, this conflict pitted the Communist Red Army against the foreign-backed White Army. The Red Army won, leading to the establishment of the Union of Soviet Socialist Republics (U.S.S.R.) in 1922.

1936–1939 SPANISH CIVIL WAR
Aid from Italy and Germany helped the Nationalists gain victory over the Communist-supported Republicans. The war resulted in the loss of more than 300,000 lives and increased tension in Europe leading up to World War II.

1939–1945 WORLD WAR II
This massive conflict in Europe, Asia, and North Africa involved many countries that aligned with the two sides: the Allies and the Axis. After the bombing of Pearl Harbor in Hawaii in 1941, the U.S. entered the war on the side of the Allies. More than 50 million people died during the war.

1946–1949 CHINESE CIVIL WAR

Also known as the "War of Liberation," this war pitted the Communist and Nationalist Parties in China against each other. The Communists won.

1950–1953 KOREAN WAR

Kicked off when the Communist forces of North Korea, with backing from the Soviet Union, invaded their democratic neighbor to the south. A coalition of 16 countries from the United Nations stepped in to support South Korea. An armistice ended active fighting in 1953.

1950s–1975 VIETNAM WAR

Fought between the Communist North, supported by allies including China, and the government of South Vietnam, supported by the United States and other anticommunist nations.

1967 SIX-DAY WAR

A battle for land between Israel and the states of Egypt, Jordan, and Syria. The outcome resulted in Israel's gaining control of coveted territory, including the Gaza Strip and the West Bank.

1991–PRESENT SOMALI CIVIL WAR

Began when Somalia's last president, a dictator named Mohamed Siad Barre, was overthrown. The war has led to years of fighting and anarchy.

2001–2014 WAR IN AFGHANISTAN

After attacks in the U.S. by the terrorist group al Qaeda, a coalition that eventually included more than 40 countries invaded Afghanistan to find Osama bin Laden and other al Qaeda members and to dismantle the Taliban. Bin Laden was killed in a U.S. covert operation in 2011. The North Atlantic Treaty Organization (NATO) took control of the coalition's combat mission in 2003. That combat mission officially ended in 2014.

2003–2011 WAR IN IRAQ

A coalition led by the U.S., and including Britain, Australia, and Spain, invaded Iraq over suspicions that Iraq had weapons of mass destruction.

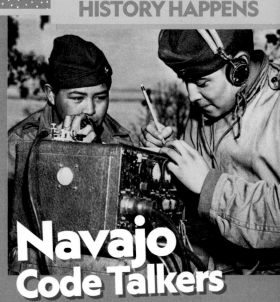

Navajo
Code Talkers

In 1942, the United States was embroiled in World War II over the South Pacific. The Japanese air attacks had crippled the U.S. Pacific Fleet at Pearl Harbor. To outwit Japanese forces, the U.S. needed a secret way to relay sensitive information, like battle plans and enemy positions—without anyone on the outside catching wind of it.

Enter Philip Johnston, a World War I veteran with a plan. Having grown up on a Navajo reservation, he spoke the Navajo language and pitched it to the U.S. Marines as an uncrackable spoken code. After all, the language was unwritten and known to fewer than 30 non-Navajo people. The Marines agreed to recruit other soldiers to test it out. A crew of 29 Navajo speakers were trained as Code Talkers to communicate in a way that would throw off the Japanese.

But the Code Talkers didn't just speak straight Navajo. When they were talking about important military terms, they'd use Navajo words that loosely translated to the term, like "besh-lo," or iron fish, for submarine and "atsá," or eagle, for transport plane. To the enemy's ears, the communication sounded like a bunch of random syllables strung together, but the Code Talkers understood every word.

The Code Talkers were able to deliver thousands of messages to the battlefields and assist in many major turning points during the war, including the U.S. victory at the Battle of Iwo Jima. By the end of World War II, there were more than 400 Code Talkers working to keep opposing forces in the dark.

LEADERS OF THE WORLD

Each of the 195 independent countries in the world has its own leader or leaders. Whatever the leader is called, he or she is called upon to take charge of the direction of the country's growth—politically, economically, and socially.

Some countries have more than one person who has an executive role in the government. That second person is often a prime minister or a chancellor. This varies depending on the type of government in the country.

Over the next several pages, the countries and their leaders are listed in alphabetical order according to the most commonly used version of each country's name. Disputed areas such as Northern Cyprus and Taiwan, and dependencies such as Bermuda, Greenland, and Puerto Rico, which belong to independent nations, are not

included in this listing. The date given for leaders taking office is the date of their first term.

Note the color key at the bottom of the pages, which assigns a color to each country based on the continent on which it is located.

NOTE: These facts are current as of press time.

Color Key by Continent

Afghanistan

President
Ashraf Ghani Ahmadzai
Took office: September 29, 2014

Albania

President
Ilir Meta
Took office: July 24, 2017

Prime Minister
Edi Rama
Took office: September 10, 2013

Algeria

President
Abdelaziz Bouteflika
Took office: April 28, 1999

Prime Minister
Ahmed Ouyahia
Took office: August 16, 2017

To learn more about world leaders, go online:
cia.gov/library/
publications/
world-leaders-1

Andorra

Co-Prince
Emmanuel Macron
Took office: May 14, 2017

Co-Prince
Archbishop Joan-Enric Vives i Sicília
Took office: May 12, 2003

Executive Council President
Antoni Marti Petit
Took office: May 12, 2011

Angola

President
João Manuel Lourenço
Took office: September 26, 2017

Antigua and Barbuda

Governor General
Rodney Williams
Took office: August 14, 2014

Prime Minister
Gaston Browne
Took office: June 13, 2014

Argentina

President
Mauricio Macri
Took office: December 10, 2015

MAURICIO MACRI is the former CHAIRMAN of a PROFESSIONAL SOCCER TEAM.

Armenia

President Armen Sarkissian
Took office: April 9, 2018

Prime Minister
Nikol Pashinyan
Took office: May 8, 2018

Australia

Governor General
Sir Peter Cosgrove
Took office: March 28, 2014

Prime Minister
Scott Morrison
Took office: August 24, 2018

COLOR KEY ● Africa ● Australia, New Zealand, and Oceania

Austria

**President
Alexander Van Der Bellen**
Took office: January 26, 2017

Chancellor Sebastian Kurz
Took office: December 18, 2017

Azerbaijan

President Ilham Aliyev
Took office: October 31, 2003

**Prime Minister
Novruz Mammadov**
Took office: April 21, 2018

Bahamas

**Governor General
Dame Marguerite Pindling**
Took office: July 8, 2014

**Prime Minister
Hubert Minnis**
Took office: May 11, 2017

Bahrain

**King Hamad bin Isa
al-Khalifa**
Began reign: March 6, 1999

**Prime Minister
Khalifa bin Salman al-Khalifa**
Took office: 1971

Bangladesh

President Abdul Hamid
Took office: April 24, 2013

**Prime Minister
Sheikh Hasina**
Took office: January 6, 2009

Barbados

**Governor General
Sandra Mason**
Took office: January 8, 2018

**Prime Minister
Mia Mottley**
Took office: May 25, 2018

Belarus

**President
Aleksandr Lukashenko**
Took office: July 20, 1994

**Prime Minister
Sergey Rumas**
Took office: August 18, 2018

Belgium

King Philippe
Began reign: July 21, 2013

**Prime Minister
Charles Michel**
Took office: October 11, 2014

Belize

**Governor General
Sir Colville Young, Sr.**
Took office: November 17, 1993

**Prime Minister
Dean Oliver Barrow**
Took office: February 8, 2008

Benin

President Patrice Talon
Took office: April 6, 2016

Bhutan

**King Jigme Khesar
Namgyel Wangchuck**
Began reign: December 14, 2006

**Prime Minister
Lotay Tshering**
Took office: November 7, 2018

THE KING OF BHUTAN is officially known as the DRAGON KING.

Bolivia

**President
Juan Evo Morales Ayma**
Took office: January 22, 2006

Bosnia and Herzegovina

**Presidency members:
Milorad Dodik
Sefik Dzaferovic
Zeljko Komsic**
Took office: November 20, 2018

**Chairman of the Council
of Ministers Denis Zvizdic**
Took office: February 11, 2015

Botswana

**President
Mokgweetse Eric Masisi**
Took office: April 1, 2018

MOKGWEETSE ERIC MASISI is a retired high school teacher and actor.

Brazil

**President
Jair Bolsonaro**
Took office: January 1, 2019

Brunei

Sultan Hassanal Bolkiah
Began reign: October 5, 1967

Bulgaria

President Rumen Radev
Took office: January 22, 2016

**Prime Minister
Boyko Borissov**
Took office: May 4, 2017

Burkina Faso

**President Roch Marc
Christian Kabore**
Took office: December 29, 2015

**Interim Prime Minister
Paul Kaba Thieba**
Took office: January 6, 2016

Burundi

President Pierre Nkurunziza
Took office: August 26, 2005

Cabo Verde

**President
Jorge Carlos Fonseca**
Took office: September 9, 2011

**Prime Minister
Ulisses Correia e Silva**
Took office: April 22, 2016

JORGE CARLOS FONSECA has written books of POETRY and ESSAYS.

Cambodia

King Norodom Sihamoni
Began reign: October 29, 2004

Prime Minister Hun Sen
Took office: January 14, 1985

Cameroon

President Paul Biya
Took office: November 6, 1982

Prime Minister Philémon Yang
Took office: June 30, 2009

Canada

**Governor General
Julie Payette**
Took office: October 2, 2017

**Prime Minister
Justin Trudeau**
Took office: November 4, 2015

Central African Republic

President Faustin-Archange Touadera
Took office: March 30, 2016

Prime Minister Simplice Sarandji
Took office: April 2, 2016

Chad

**President
Lt. Gen. Idriss Déby Itno**
Took office: December 4, 1990

Chile

**President
Sebastián Piñera Echenique**
Took office: March 11, 2018

SEBASTIÁN PIÑERA ECHENIQUE owns his own HELICOPTER and has made many public appearances FLYING IT.

Hello from Cambodia

Angkor Wat near Siem Riep, Cambodia

COLOR KEY ● Africa ● Australia, New Zealand, and Oceania

China

President Xi Jinping
Took office: March 14, 2013

Premier Li Keqiang
Took office: March 16, 2013

Colombia

**President
Iván Duque Márquez**
Took office: August 7, 2018

Comoros

**President
Azali Assoumani**
Took office: May 26, 2016

Congo

**President
Denis Sassou-Nguesso**
Took office: October 25, 1997

Costa Rica

**President
Carlos Alvarado Quesada**
Took office: May 8, 2018

CARLOS ALVARADO QUESADA was once the LEAD SINGER in a ROCK BAND.

Côte d'Ivoire (Ivory Coast)

**President
Alassane Ouattara**
Took office: December 4, 2010

**Prime Minister
Amadou Gon Coulibaly**
Took office: January 11, 2017

Croatia

President Kolinda Grabar-Kitarovic
Took office: February 19, 2015

**Prime Minister
Andrej Plenkovic**
Took office: October 19, 2016

Cuba

**President Miguel
Díaz-Canel Bermúdez**
Took office: April 19, 2018

Cyprus

**President
Nikos Anastasiades**
Took office: February 28, 2013

NIKOS ANASTASIADES has a TWIN BROTHER.

Czechia (Czech Republic)

President Milos Zeman
Took office: March 8, 2013

Prime Minister Andrej Babis
Took office: December 13, 2017

Democratic Republic of the Congo

President Joseph Kabila
Took office: January 17, 2001

**Prime Minister
Bruno Tshibala**
Took office: April 7, 2017

Denmark

Queen Margrethe II
Began reign: January 14, 1972

**Prime Minister
Lars Loekke Rasmussen**
Took office: June 28, 2015

Djibouti

**President
Ismail Omar Guelleh**
Took office: May 8, 1999

**Prime Minister
Abdoulkader Kamil
Mohamed**
Took office: April 1, 2013

Dominica

**President
Charles Savarin**
Took office: October 2, 2013

**Prime Minister
Roosevelt Skerrit**
Took office: January 8, 2004

Dominican Republic

**President
Danilo Medina Sánchez**
Took office: August 16, 2012

Ecuador

**President Lenín
Moreno Garces**
Took office: May 24, 2017

LENÍN MORENO GARCES is the first WHEELCHAIR USER to be elected as a HEAD OF STATE IN LATIN AMERICA.

Egypt

**President
Abdelfattah Said Elsisi**
Took office: June 8, 2014

**Prime Minister
Mostafa Madbouly**
Took office: June 7, 2018

El Salvador

President
Salvador Sanchez Ceren
Took office: June 1, 2014

Equatorial Guinea

President Teodoro Obiang Nguema Mbasogo
Took office: August 3, 1979

Prime Minister Francisco Pascual Eyegue Obama Asue
Took office: June 23, 2016

> **TEODORO OBIANG NGUEMA MBASOGO** is Africa's longest serving head of state.

Eritrea

President Isaias Afworki
Took office: June 8, 1993

Estonia

President Kersti Kaljulaid
Took office: October 10, 2016

Prime Minister Juri Ratas
Took office: November 21, 2016

Eswatini

King Mswati III
Began reign: April 25, 1986

Prime Minister Ambrose Mandvulo Dlamini
Took office: October 29, 2018

Ethiopia

President Sahle-Work Zewde
Took office: October 25, 2018

Prime Minister Abiy Ahmed
Took office: April 2, 2018

Fiji

President Jioji Konousi Konrote
Took office: November 12, 2015

Prime Minister Voreqe "Frank" Bainimarama
Took office: September 22, 2014

Finland

President Sauli Ninisto
Took office: March 1, 2012

Prime Minister Juha Sipila
Took office: May 29, 2015

France

President Emmanuel Macron
Took office: May 14, 2017

Prime Minister Edouard Philippe
Took office: May 15, 2017

Gabon

President Ali Ben Bongo Ondimba
Took office: October 16, 2009

Prime Minister Emmanuel Issoze-Ngondet
Took office: September 29, 2016

Gambia

President Adama Barrow
Took office: January 19, 2017

> **ADAMA BARROW** worked as a **DEPARTMENT STORE SECURITY GUARD.**

Georgia

President Giorgi Margvelashvili
Took office: November 17, 2013

Prime Minister Mamuka Bakhtadze
Took office: June 20, 2018

Germany

President Frank-Walter Steinmeier
Took office: March 19, 2017

Chancellor Angela Merkel
Took office: November 22, 2005

Ghana

President Nana Addo Dankwa Akufo-Addo
Took office: January 7, 2017

Greece

President Prokopios Pavlopoulos
Took office: March 13, 2005

Prime Minister Alexis Tsipras
Took office: September 21, 2015

Grenada

Governor General Cecile La Grenade
Took office: May 7, 2013

Prime Minister Keith Mitchell
Took office: February 20, 2013

Guatemala

President Jimmy Ernesto Morales Cabrera
Took office: January 14, 2016

Guinea

President Alpha Condé
Took office: December 21, 2010

Prime Minister Ibrahima Fofana
Took office: May 22, 2018

Guinea-Bissau

President Josse Mario Vaz
Took office: June 17, 2014

Prime Minister Aristides Gomes
Took office: April 16, 2018

240 COLOR KEY ● Africa ● Australia, New Zealand, and Oceania

Guyana

**President
David Granger**
Took office: May 16, 2015

Haiti

**President
Jovenel Moise**
Took office: February 7, 2017

**Prime Minister
Jean Henry Ceant**
Took office: September 16, 2018

**JOVENEL MOISE
has worked as a
BANANA FARMER.**

Honduras

**President
Juan Orlando Hernandez
Alvarado**
Took office: January 27, 2014

Hungary

President Janos Ader
Took office: May 10, 2012

**Prime Minister
Viktor Orban**
Took office: May 29, 2010

Iceland

**President Gudni Thorlacius
Johannesson**
Took office: August 1, 2016

**Acting Prime Minister
Katrin Jakobsdittir**
Took office: November 30, 2017

India

President Ram Nath Kovind
Took office: July 25, 2017

**Prime Minister
Narendra Modi**
Took office: May 26, 2014

Indonesia

President Joko Widodo
Took office: October 20, 2014

**JOKO WIDODO
is a former
FURNITURE MAKER.**

Iran

**Supreme Leader
Ayatollah Ali Hoseini-
Khamenei**
Took office: June 4, 1989

**President
Hasan Fereidun Ruhani**
Took office: August 3, 2013

Iraq

**President
Barham Salih**
Took office: October 1, 2018

**Prime Minister
Abdul Mahdi**
Took office: October 25, 2018

Greetings from
Iceland

Aurora borealis—or northern lights—
above Mount Kirkjufell, Iceland

Ireland

**President
Michael D. Higgins**
Took office: October 29, 2011

**Prime Minister
Leo Varadkar**
Took office: June 14, 2017

Israel

**President
Reuven Rivlin**
Took office: July 27, 2014

**Prime Minister
Binyamin Netanyahu**
Took office: March 31, 2009

REUVEN RIVLIN is a VEGETARIAN.

Italy

President Sergio Mattarella
Took office: February 3, 2015

**Prime Minister
Giuseppe Conte**
Took office: June 1, 2018

Jamaica

**Governor General
Dr. Patrick L. Allen**
Took office: February 26, 2009

**Prime Minister
Andrew Holness**
Took office: March 3, 2016

Japan

Emperor Akihito
Began reign: January 7, 1989

Prime Minister Shinzo Abe
Took office: December 26, 2012

Jordan

King Abdullah II
Began reign: February 7, 1999

**Prime Minister
Omar al-Razzaz**
Took office: June 4, 2018

Kazakhstan

**President
Nursultan A. Nazarbayev**
Took office: December 1, 1991

**Prime Minister
Bakytzhan Sagintayev**
Took office: September 9, 2016

Kenya

**President
Uhuru Kenyatta**
Took office: April 9, 2013

Welcome to Kenya

Zebras in Amboseli, Kenya

COLOR KEY ● Africa ● Australia, New Zealand, and Oceania

Kiribati

**President
Taneti Maamau**
Took office: March 11, 2016

Kosovo

**President
Hashim Thaçi**
Took office: April 7, 2016

**Prime Minister
Ramush Haradinaj**
Took office: September 9, 2017

**HASHIM THAÇI
has 34,000
FOLLOWERS ON
INSTAGRAM.**

Kuwait

**Emir Sabah al-Ahmad
al-Jabir al-Sabah**
Began reign: January 29, 2006

**Prime Minister
Jabir al-Mubarak
al-Hamad al-Sabah**
Took office: November 30, 2011

Kyrgyzstan

**President
Sooronbay Jeenbekov**
Took office: November 24, 2017

**Prime Minister
Mukhammedkalyy
Abylgaziev**
Took office: April 20, 2018

Laos

**President
Bounnyang Vorachit**
Took office: April 20, 2016

**Prime Minister
Thongloun Sisoulit**
Took office: April 20, 2016

Latvia

President Raimonds Vejonis
Took office: July 8, 2015

**Prime Minister
Maris Kucinskis**
Took office: February 11, 2016

Lebanon

President Michel Awn
Took office: October 31, 2016

**Prime Minister
Saad al-Hariri**
Took office: December 18, 2016

Lesotho

King Letsie III
Began reign: February 7, 1996

**Prime Minister
Thomas Motsoahae Thomas
Thabane**
Took office: June 16, 2017

Liberia

President George Weah
Took office: January 22, 2018

**GEORGE WEAH
was named the
WORLD'S SOCCER
PLAYER OF THE
YEAR IN 1995.**

Libya

**Prime Minister
Fayiz al-Saraj**
Took office: April 2016

Liechtenstein

Prince Hans Adam II
Began reign: November 13, 1989

**Prime Minister
Adrian Hasler**
Took office: March 27, 2013

Lithuania

**President
Dalia Grybauskaité**
Took office: July 12, 2009

**Prime Minister
Saulius Skvernelis**
Took office: December 13, 2016

Luxembourg

Grand Duke Henri
Began reign: October 7, 2000

**Prime Minister
Xavier Bettel**
Took office: December 4, 2013

Macedonia

**President
Gjorge Ivanov**
Took office: May 12, 2009

**Prime Minister
Zoran Zaev**
Took office: May 31, 2017

Madagascar

**President
Andry Rajoelina**
Took office: January 2019

**Prime Minister
Christian Ntsay**
Took office: June 6, 2018

Malawi

**President
Arthur Peter Mutharika**
Took office: May 31, 2014

Malaysia

King Muhammad V
Installed: December 13, 2016

**Prime Minister
Mahathir Mohamad**
Took office: May 10, 2018

Maldives

President
Ibrahim Mohamed Solih
Took office: September 23, 2018

Mali

President
Ibrahim Boubacar Keita
Took office: September 4, 2013

Prime Minister
Soumeylou Boubeye Maiga
Took office: December 31, 2017

Malta

President
Marie-Louise Coleiro Preca
Took office: April 4, 2014

Prime Minister
Joseph Muscat
Took office: March 11, 2013

Marshall Islands

President
Hilda C. Heine
Took office: January 28, 2016

Mauritania

President
Mohamed Ould Abdel Aziz
Took office: August 5, 2009

Prime Minister
Mohamed Salem Ould Béchir
Took office: October 29, 2018

Mauritius

Acting President
Paramaslyum (aka Barlen) Pillay Vyapoory
Took office: March 23, 2018

Prime Minister
Pravind Jugnauth
Took office: January 23, 2017

Mexico

President
Enrique Peña Nieto
Took office: December 1, 2012

Micronesia

President
Peter M. Christian
Took office: May 12, 2015

Moldova

President Igor Dodon
Took office: December 23, 2016

Interim Prime Minister
Pavel Filip
Took office: January 20, 2016

Monaco

Prince Albert II
Began reign: April 6, 2005

Minister of State
Serge Telle
Took office: February 1, 2016

Mongolia

President
Khaltmaa Battulga
Took office: July 10, 2017

Prime Minister
Ukhnaa Khurelsukh
Took office: October 4, 2017

UKHNAA KHURELSUKH is a motorbike enthusiast.

Montenegro

President
Milo Djukanovic
Took office: May 20, 2018

Prime Minister
Dusko Markovic
Took office: November 28, 2016

Morocco

King Mohammed VI
Began reign: July 30, 1999

Prime Minister
Saad-Eddine al-Othmani
Took office: March 17, 2017

Mozambique

President
Filipe Jacinto Nyusi
Took office: January 15, 2015

Prime Minister
Carlos Agostinho Do Rosario
Took office: January 17, 2015

Myanmar (Burma)

President
Win Myint
Took office: March 30, 2018

Namibia

President
Hage Geingob
Took office: March 21, 2005

HAGE GEINGOB has a rugby stadium named after him.

Nauru

President
Baron Waqa
Took office: June 11, 2013

Nepal

President
Bidhya Devi Bhandari
Took office: October 29, 2015

Prime Minister Khadga Prasad (KP) Sharma Oli
Took office: February 15, 2018

Netherlands

King Willem-Alexander
Began reign: April 30, 2013

**Prime Minister
Mark Rutte**
Took office: October 14, 2010

New Zealand

**Governor General
Dame Patricia Lee Reddy**
Took office: September 28, 2016

**Prime Minister
Jacinda Ardern**
Took office: October 26, 2017

JACINDA ARDERN had a baby girl eight months after becoming PRIME MINISTER.

Nicaragua

**President
Daniel Ortega Saavedra**
Took office: January 10, 2007

Niger

**President
Issoufou Mahamadou**
Took office: April 7, 2011

**Prime Minister
Brigi Rafini**
Took office: April 7, 2011

Nigeria

**President Maj. Gen. (ret.)
Muhammadu Buhari**
Took office: May 29, 2015

North Korea

**Supreme Leader
Kim Jong-un**
Took office: December 17, 2011

Norway

King Harald V
Began reign: January 17, 1991

**Prime Minister
Erna Solberg**
Took office: October 16, 2013

ERNA SOLBERG plays games on her iPad TO DE-STRESS.

Oman

**Sultan
Qaboos bin Said al-Said**
Began reign: July 23, 1970

Pakistan

**President
Arif Alvi**
Took office: September 9, 2018

**Prime Minister
Imran Khan**
Took office: August 18, 2018

Palau

**President
Tommy Remengesau**
Took office: January 17, 2013

Panama

**President
Juan Carlos Varela**
Took office: July 1, 2014

Papua New Guinea

**Governor General
Grand Chief Sir Bob Dadae**
Took office: February 28, 2017

**Prime Minister
Peter O'Neill**
Took office: August 2, 2011

Paraguay

**President
Mario Abdo Benitez**
Took office: August 15, 2018

Peru

**President
Martin Alberto
Vizcarra Cornejo**
Took office: March 23, 2018

MARTIN ALBERTO VIZCARRA CORNEJO served as Peru's AMBASSADOR to CANADA.

Philippines

**President
Rodrigo Duterte**
Took office: June 30, 2016

Poland

**President
Andrzej Duda**
Took office: August 6, 2015

**Prime Minister
Mateusz Morawiecki**
Took office: December 11, 2017

ANDRZEJ DUDA is an accomplished SKIER.

Portugal

President
Marcelo Rebelo de Sousa
Took office: March 9, 2016

Prime Minister
António Costa
Took office: November 26, 2015

A career as a college instructor earned MARCELO REBELO DE SOUSA the nickname "Professor Marcelo."

Qatar

Amir Tamim bin Hamad Al Thani
Began reign: June 25, 2013

Prime Minister Abdallah bin Nasir bin Khalifa Al Thani
Took office: June 26, 2013

Romania

President Klaus Iohannis
Took office: December 21, 2014

Prime Minister
Viorica Dancila
Took office: January 29, 2018

Russia

President Vladimir Vladimirovich Putin
Took office: May 7, 2012

Premier Dmitriy Anatolyevich Medvedev
Took office: May 8, 2012

Rwanda

President Paul Kagame
Took office: April 22, 2000

Prime Minister
Edouard Ngirente
Took office: August 30, 2017

Samoa

Head of State Tuimaleali'ifano Va'aletoa Sualauvi II
Took office: July 21, 2017

Prime Minister Tuila'epa Lupesoliai Sailele Malielegaoi
Took office: November 23, 1998

San Marino

Co-chiefs of State: Captain Regent Mirco Tomassoni

Captain Regent Luca Santolini
Took office: October 1, 2018

Secretary of State for Foreign and Political Affairs Nicola Renzi
Took office: December 27, 2016

Sao Tome and Principe

President Evaristo Carvalho
Took office: September 3, 2016

Prime Minister Patrice Emery Trovoada
Took office: November 29, 2014

Saudi Arabia

King and Prime Minister Salman bin Abd al-Aziz Al Saud
Began reign: January 23, 2015

Senegal

President Macky Sall
Took office: April 2, 2012

Prime Minister Mohammed Abdallah Boun Dionne
Took office: July 4, 2014

MOHAMMED DIONNE trained as a COMPUTER ENGINEER before entering politics.

Serbia

President
Aleksandar Vucic
Took office: May 31, 2017

Prime Minister Ana Brnabic
Took office: June 29, 2017

Seychelles

President
Danny Faure
Took office: October 16, 2016

Sierra Leone

President
Julius Maada Bio
Took office: April 4, 2018

Singapore

President Halimah Yacob
Took office: September 14, 2017

Prime Minister Lee Hsien Loong
Took office: August 12, 2004

Slovakia

President Andrej Kiska
Took office: June 15, 2014

Prime Minister Peter Pelligrini
Took office: March 22, 2018

ANDREJ KISKA once worked at a GAS STATION in the U.S.A.

Slovenia

President Borut Pahor
Took office: December 22, 2012

Prime Minister Marjan Sarec
Took office: September 13, 2018

COLOR KEY ● Africa ● Australia, New Zealand, and Oceania

Solomon Islands

**Governor General
Frank Kabui**
Took office: July 7, 2009

**Prime Minister
Rick Hou**
Took office: November 16, 2017

Somalia

**President
Mohamed Abdullahi
Mohamed "Farmaajo"**
Took office: February 8, 2017

**Prime Minister
Hassan Ali Khayre**
Took office: March 1, 2017

South Africa

**President Matamela Cyril
Ramaphosa**
Took office: February 15, 2018

South Korea

**President
Moon Jae-in**
Took office: May 10, 2017

**Prime Minister
Lee Nak-yon**
Took office: June 1, 2017

South Sudan

**President
Salva Kiir Mayardit**
Took office: July 9, 2011

Spain

King Felipe VI
Began reign: June 19, 2014

**President of the
Government Pedro Sánchez
Pérez-Castejón**
Took office: June 2, 2018

Sri Lanka

**President
Maithripala Sirisena**
Took office: January 9, 2015

St. Kitts and Nevis

**Governor General
Samuel W. T. Seaton**
Took office: September 2, 2015

**Prime Minister
Timothy Harris**
Took office: February 18, 2015

St. Lucia

**Governor General
Neville Cenac**
Took office: January 12, 2018

**Prime Minister
Allen Chastanet**
Took office: June 7, 2016

Postcard from St. Lucia

Soufrière, Saint Lucia

St. Vincent and the Grenadines

**Governor General
Sir Frederick Nathaniel Ballantyne**
Took office: September 2, 2002

**Prime Minister
Ralph Gonsalves**
Took office: March 29, 2001

Sir Frederick Nathaniel Ballantyne is a trained MEDICAL DOCTOR.

Sudan

President Umar Hassan Ahmad al-Bashir
Took office: October 16, 1993

Suriname

**President
Desiré Delano Bouterse**
Took office: August 12, 2010

Sweden

King Carl XVI Gustaf
Began reign: September 19, 1973

Prime Minister Stefan Löfven leading transitional government
Began: September 25, 2018

KING CARL XVI GUSTAF collects SPORTS CARS.

Switzerland

**President of the Swiss Confederation
Alain Berset**
Took office: January 1, 2018

**Federal Council members:
Doris Leuthard,
Guy Parmelin,
Johann Schneider-Ammann,
Simonetta Sommaruga,
Ueli Maurer,
Ignazio Cassis**
Took office: dates vary

DORIS LEUTHARD speaks fluent French, Italian, German and English.

Syria

**President
Bashar al-Asad**
Took office: July 17, 2000

**Prime Minister
Imad Muhammad Dib Khamis**
Took office: June 22, 2016

Tajikistan

**President
Emomali Rahmon**
Took office: November 19, 1992

**Prime Minister
Qohir Rasulzoda**
Took office: November 23, 2013

EMOMALI RAHMON has nine children— SEVEN daughters and TWO sons.

Tanzania

**President
John Pombe Magufuli**
Took office: November 5, 2015

JOHN POMBE MAGUFULI did push-ups on the campaign trail to prove his FITNESS.

Thailand

King Wachiralongkon Bodinthrathepphay- awarangkun
Began reign: December 1, 2016

**Prime Minister
Prayut Chan-ocha**
Took office: August 25, 2014

Timor-Leste (East Timor)

**President
Francisco Guterres**
Took office: May 20, 2017

**Prime Minister
Taur Matan Ruak**
Took office: June 22, 2018

Togo

**President
Faure Gnassingbé**
Took office: May 4, 2005

**Prime Minister
Komi Klassou**
Took office: June 5, 2015

Tonga

King George Tupou VI
Began reign: March 18, 2012

**Interim Prime Minister
'Akilisi Pohiva**
Took office: December 30, 2014

COLOR KEY ● Africa ● Australia, New Zealand, and Oceania

Trinidad and Tobago

President Paula-Mae Weekes
Took office: March 19, 2018

Prime Minister Keith Rowley
Took office: September 9, 2015

Tunisia

President Beji Caid Essebsi
Took office: December 31, 2014

Prime Minister Youssef Chahed
Took office: August 27, 2016

Turkey

President Recep Tayyip Erdogan
Took office: August 10, 2014

Turkmenistan

President Gurbanguly Berdimuhamedow
Took office: February 14, 2007

Tuvalu

Governor General Iakoba Taeia Italeli
Took office: April 16, 2010

Prime Minister Enele Sopoaga
Took office: August 5, 2013

Uganda

President Yoweri Kaguta Museveni
Took office: January 26, 1986

Ukraine

President Petro Poroshenko
Took office: June 7, 2014

Prime Minister Volodymyr Hroysman
Took office: April 14, 2016

United Arab Emirates

President Khalifa bin Zayid al-Nuhayyan
Took office: November 3, 2004

Prime Minister Muhammad bin Rashid al-Maktum
Took office: January 5, 2006

United Kingdom

Queen Elizabeth II
Began reign: February 6, 1952

Prime Minister Theresa May
Took office: July 13, 2016

A fashion lover, **THERESA MAY** has been spotted wearing **LEOPARD-PRINT SHOES.**

United States

President Donald J. Trump
Took office: January 20, 2017

DONALD J. TRUMP likes **CHERRY VANILLA ICE CREAM.**

Uruguay

President Tabare Vazquez
Took office: March 1, 2015

Uzbekistan

President Shavkat Mirziyoyev
Took office: September 8, 2016

Prime Minister Abdulla Aripov
Took office: December 14, 2016

Vanuatu

President Tallis Obed Moses
Took office: July 6, 2017

Prime Minister Charlot Salwai
Took office: February 11, 2016

Vatican City

Supreme Pontiff Pope Francis
Took office: March 13, 2013

Secretary of State Archbishop Pietro Parolin
Took office: October 15, 2013

Venezuela

President Nicolas Maduro Moros
Took office: April 19, 2013

Vietnam

President Nguyen Phu Trong
Took office: October 21, 2018

Prime Minister Nguyen Xuan Phuc
Took office: April 7, 2016

Yemen

President Abd Rabuh Mansur Hadi
Took office: February 21, 2012

Prime Minister Main Abd al-Malik Said
Took office: October 18, 2018

Zambia

President Edgar Lungu
Took office: January 25, 2015

Zimbabwe

President Emmerson Dambudzo Mnnangagwa
Took office: November 24, 2017

● Asia ● Europe ● North America ● South America

QUIZ WHIZ

Go back in time to seek the answers to this history quiz!

Write your answers on a piece of paper. Then check them below.

1 **True or false?** Ancient Egyptians believed that sphinxes could ward off evil.

2 Including its smokestacks, the R.M.S. *Titanic* was as tall as a _____-story building.
a. 5
b. 30
c. 100
d. 17

3 Bandits in England once stole how much from a Royal Mail Train?
a. $1.7 million
b. $7 million
c. $17 million
d. $170 million

4 **True or false?** Volcanic eruptions help carry diamonds formed underground to Earth's surface.

5 Some ancient Greeks did not eat beans because they believed they contained _____.
a. methane gas
b. the souls of the dead
c. magical powers
d. poison

Not **STUMPED** yet? Check out the *NATIONAL GEOGRAPHIC KIDS QUIZ WHIZ* collection for more crazy **HISTORY** questions!

ANSWERS: 1. True ; 2. d; 3. b; 4. True; 5. b

HOMEWORK HELP

Brilliant Biographies

Malala Yousafzai

A biography is the story of a person's life. It can be a brief summary or a long book. Biographers—those who write biographies—use many different sources to learn about their subjects. You can write your own biography of a famous person you find inspiring.

How to Get Started

Choose a subject you find interesting. If you think Cleopatra is cool, you have a good chance of getting your reader interested, too. If you're bored by ancient Egypt, your reader will be snoring after your first paragraph.

Your subject can be almost anyone: an author, an inventor, a celebrity, a politician, or a member of your family. To find someone to write about, ask yourself these simple questions:

1. Who do I want to know more about?
2. What did this person do that was special?
3. How did this person change the world?

Do Your Research

- Find out as much about your subject as possible. Read books, news articles, and encyclopedia entries. Watch video clips and movies, and search the internet. Conduct interviews, if possible.
- Take notes, writing down important facts and interesting stories about your subject.

Write the Biography

- Come up with a title. Include the person's name.
- Write an introduction. Consider asking a probing question about your subject.
- Include information about the person's childhood. When was this person born? Where did he or she grow up? Who did he or she admire?
- Highlight the person's talents, accomplishments, and personal attributes.
- Describe the specific events that helped to shape this person's life. Did this person ever have a problem and overcome it?
- Write a conclusion. Include your thoughts about why it is important to learn about this person.
- Once you have finished your first draft, revise and then proofread your work.

Here's a **SAMPLE BIOGRAPHY** of Malala Yousafzai, a human rights advocate and the youngest ever recipient of the Nobel Peace Prize. Of course, there is so much more for you to discover and write about on your own!

Malala Yousafzai

Malala Yousafzai was born in Pakistan on July 12, 1997. Malala's father, Ziauddin, a teacher, made it his priority for his daughter to receive a proper education. Malala loved school. She learned to speak three different languages and even wrote a blog about her experiences as a student.

Around the time Malala turned 10, the Taliban—a group of strict Muslims who believe women are to stay at home—took over the region where she lived. The Taliban did not approve of Malala's outspoken love of learning. One day, on her way home from school, Malala was shot in the head by a Taliban gunman. Very badly injured, she was sent to a hospital in England.

Not only did Malala survive the shooting—she thrived. She used her experience as a platform to fight for girls' education worldwide. She began speaking out about educational opportunities for all. Her efforts gained worldwide attention and eventually, she was awarded the Nobel Peace Prize in 2014 at the age of 17. She is the youngest person to earn the prestigious prize.

Each year on July 12, World Malala Day honors her heroic efforts to bring attention to human rights issues.

The all-natural rock rainbows of the Zhangye Danxia National Geological Park in north-central China took millions of years to form.

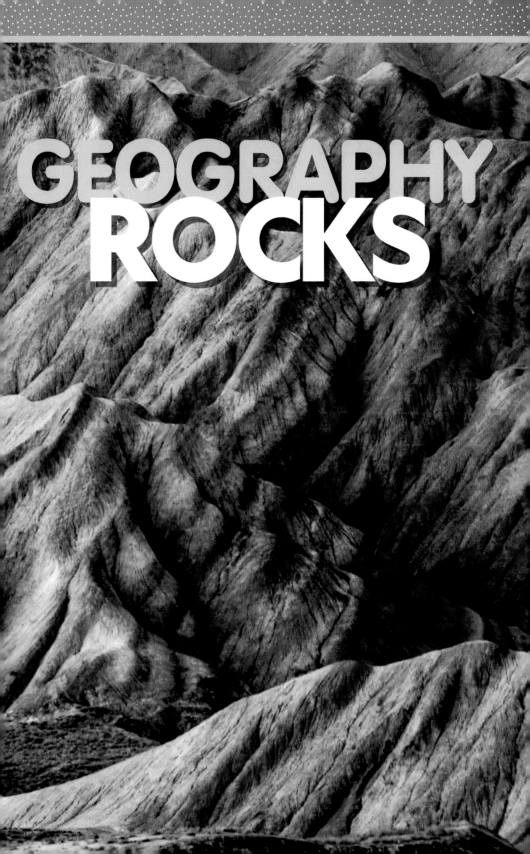

GEOGRAPHY
ROCKS

EARTH EXPLORER
Meet Alex Tait!

How National Geographic's Geographer put his passion on the map.

When an iceberg the size of Delaware recently sheared off the Antarctic Peninsula, Alex Tait was watching—and waiting. As the Geographer at National Geographic, Alex keeps the maps up to date. So as the giant iceberg, one of the world's largest, broke away and essentially changed the shape of the continent, Alex took note.

Updating National Geographic's maps of Antarctica to reflect the fractured ice shelf is just one of many jobs Alex tackles in his position. He also monitors other shifts in the world, like boundary changes; creates custom maps; updates existing maps; and makes sure that there's consistency among all of the many maps published in National Geographic's books and magazines, and on its website.

"Maps tell us stories and give us an easier way to understand and care about our world," says Alex.

Alex fell in love with geography as a kid while poring over paper maps as he planned hiking trips with his dad. While technology has changed the way many of us view maps today, Alex believes that the beauty of geography remains the same, whether maps are on a screen or folded out in front of you.

And as technology continues to advance, so will our access to see places from around the globe, says Alex. Want to see the top of Mount Everest? You may one day soon be able to get live images of the famous summit and other far-flung places around the planet.

"Geographic data is getting so comprehensive and maps are getting more and more realistic," says Alex. "And with virtual reality (VR) and augmented reality (AR), you will be able to use a map to go anywhere you want—from the tops of mountains to the bottom of the ocean. Maps literally change the way we view the world."

A person who makes and studies maps is called a cartographer.

A MAP OF MOUNT WASHINGTON IN NEW HAMPSHIRE, U.S.A., THAT ALEX WORKED ON

"Maps are tools to show changes happening on our planet. We recently made a map showing the impact of human activity on the planet, like fishing, shipping, and climate change.

The earliest maps were drawn on clay tablets some 3,500 years ago.

CALL TO ACTION!

Want to get into geography? It all starts with learning to understand and read maps—and even making some of your own. Whether you use a paper and pencil to draw out the boundaries of your backyard or create a map on your computer, Alex says that making and studying maps will help you get a stronger grip on geography. "I still make my own maps sometimes," says Alex. "Understanding maps is like learning a language. The more you do it and the more you practice, the better you'll be at interpreting it all." (Get started on your own maps by visiting mapmaker.nationalgeographic.org today!)

THE POLITICAL WORLD

Earth's land area is made up of seven continents, but people have divided much of the land into smaller political units called countries. Australia is a continent made up of a single country, and Antarctica is used for scientific research. But the other five continents include almost 200 independent countries. The political map shown here depicts boundaries—imaginary lines created by treaties—that separate countries. Some boundaries, such as the one between the United States and Canada, are very stable and have been recognized for many years.

ARCTIC

Queen Elizabeth Is.

Chukchi Sea

Beaufort Sea

Baffin Bay

Greenland (Denmark)

Greenland Sea

RUSSIA

Alaska (U.S.)

Bering Sea

Gulf of Alaska

60°

Great Bear Lake

Great Slave Lake

CANADA

Hudson Bay

Labrador Sea

ARCTIC CIRCLE

ICELAND

UNITED KINGDOM

IRELAND (ÉIRE)

FRANCE

PORT. SPAIN

Lake Winnipeg

Great Lakes

Great Salt Lake

UNITED STATES

30°

See Europe map for more detail.

MOROCCO

TROPIC OF CANCER

Hawai'i (U.S.)

MEXICO

Gulf of Mexico

BAHAMAS

Western Sahara (Morocco)

CUBA

HAITI

DOMINICAN REP.

Puerto Rico (U.S.)

ST. KITTS & NEVIS

ANTIGUA & BARBUDA

Guadeloupe (France)

DOMINICA

Martinique (France)

CABO VERDE

MAURITANIA

MALI

BELIZE

JAMAICA

GUATEMALA

HONDURAS

EL SALVADOR

NICARAGUA

Caribbean Sea

ST. LUCIA

GRENADA

BARBADOS

ST. VINCENT & THE GRENADINES

TRINIDAD AND TOBAGO

SENEGAL

GAMBIA

GUINEA-BISSAU

GUINEA

BURKINA FASO

GHANA

COSTA RICA

PANAMA

VENEZUELA

GUYANA

French Guiana (France)

SIERRA LEONE

LIBERIA

PACIFIC

COLOMBIA

SURINAME

CÔTE D'IVOIRE (IVORY COAST)

EQUATOR

150°

120°

90°

30°

0°

KIRIBATI

OCEAN

Galápagos Islands (Ecuador)

ECUADOR

EQ. GUINEA

Marquesas Islands (France)

PERU

BRAZIL

SAO TOME AND PRINCIPE

SAMOA

American Samoa (U.S.)

French Polynesia (France)

BOLIVIA

ATLANTIC

TONGA

PARAGUAY

TROPIC OF CAPRICORN

OCEAN

30°

URUGUAY

CHILE

ARGENTINA

0   miles   2000

0   kilometers   3000

Winkel Tripel Projection

Chatham Is. (N.Z.)

Falkland Islands (U.K.)

Tierra del Fuego

Strait of Magellan

Drake Passage

Meridian of Greenwich (London)

ANTARCTIC

60°

Weddell Sea

Ross Sea

A N T

Other boundaries, such as the one between Sudan and South Sudan in northeast Africa, are relatively new and still disputed. Countries come in all shapes and sizes. Russia and Canada are giants; others, such as El Salvador and Qatar, are small. Some countries are long and skinny—look at Chile in South America! Still other countries—such as Indonesia and Japan in Asia—are made up of groups of islands. The political map is a clue to the diversity that makes Earth so fascinating.

OCEAN

Svalbard (Norway)

Barents Sea
Novaya Zemlya
Kara Sea
North Land
New Siberian Islands
Laptev Sea
East Siberian Sea

NORWAY
SWEDEN
FINLAND
DEN.
GERMANY
LATV.
EST.
LITH.
BELARUS
POLAND
UKRAINE
MOLD.
ROMANIA
BULGARIA
GEORGIA
ALBANIA
GREECE
ITALY
TURKEY
ARM. AZER.
TUNISIA
CYPRUS
SYRIA
LEBANON
ISRAEL
JORDAN
IRAQ
ALGERIA
LIBYA
EGYPT

R U S S I A

Sea of Okhotsk
Bering Sea
60°

Lake Baikal

KAZAKHSTAN
MONGOLIA
UZBEK.
KYRGYZSTAN
TURKMEN.
TAJIKISTAN
AFGHAN.
C H I N A
NORTH KOREA
SOUTH KOREA
JAPAN

Caspian Sea
Mediterranean Sea
Red Sea

IRAN
PAKISTAN
NEPAL
BHUTAN
KUWAIT
BAHRAIN
QATAR
SAUDI ARABIA
U.A.E.
OMAN
YEMEN
DJIBOUTI

BANGLADESH
INDIA
MYANMAR (BURMA)
THAILAND
LAOS
VIETNAM
CAMBODIA

30°

TAIWAN
The People's Republic of China claims Taiwan as its 23rd province. Taiwan's government (Republic of China) maintains that there are two political entities.

Taiwan

South China Sea
Philippine Sea
Northern Mariana Islands (U.S.)
Guam (U.S.)
PHILIPPINES
PALAU

PACIFIC
OCEAN
MARSHALL ISLANDS

FEDERATED STATES OF MICRONESIA
KIRIBATI
NAURU

NIGER
CHAD
SUDAN
ERITREA
SOUTH SUDAN
ETHIOPIA
SOMALIA
BENIN
NIGERIA
CAMEROON
TOGO
C.A.R.
GABON
CONGO
DEM. REP. OF THE CONGO
Cabinda (Angola)
RWANDA
BURUNDI
UGANDA
KENYA
TANZANIA
SEYCHELLES

Arabian Sea
Bay of Bengal
SRI LANKA
MALDIVES

BRUNEI
MALAYSIA
SINGAPORE
I N D O N E S I A
New Guinea
PAPUA NEW GUINEA
TIMOR-LESTE (EAST TIMOR)
SOLOMON ISLANDS
TUVALU

EQUATOR 0°
150°

I N D I A N

ANGOLA
ZAMBIA
ZIMBABWE
NAMIBIA
BOTSWANA
SOUTH AFRICA
ESWATINI (SWAZILAND)
LESOTHO
MALAWI
MOZAMBIQUE
MADAGASCAR
COMOROS
MAURITIUS
Réunion (France)

O C E A N

Coral Sea
VANUATU
FIJI
New Caledonia (France)

Kerguelen Islands (France)

A U S T R A L I A

Great Australian Bight
Tasman Sea
Tasmania
North Island
NEW ZEALAND
South Island

30°

60°
90°
60°

CIRCLE

Ross Sea

A R C T I C A

THE PHYSICAL WORLD

Earth is dominated by large landmasses called continents—seven in all—and by an interconnected global ocean that is divided into four parts by the continents. More than 70 percent of Earth's surface is covered by oceans, and the rest is made up of land areas.

Different landforms give variety to the surface of the continents. The Rocky Mountains divide North America, the Andes mark the western edge of South America, and the Himalaya tower above South Asia. The Plateau of Tibet forms the rugged core of Asia, while

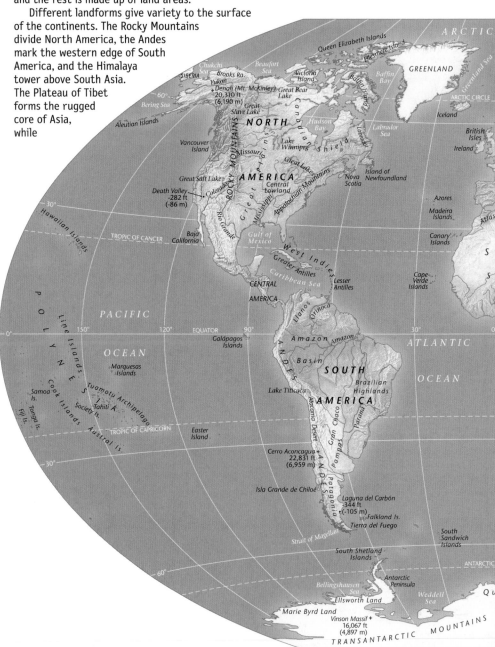

the Northern European Plain extends from the North Sea to the Ural Mountains. Much of Africa is a plateau, and dry plains cover large areas of Australia. Mountains rise more than 16,000 feet (4,877 m) above Antarctica's massive ice sheets. Mountains and trenches make the ocean floors as varied as any continent. A mountain chain called the Mid-Atlantic Ridge runs the length of the Atlantic Ocean. In the western Pacific, trenches drop deep into the ocean floor.

OCEAN

Svalbard
Norwegian Sea
Barents Sea
Novaya Zemlya
North Land
New Siberian Islands
Kara Sea
Laptev Sea
East Siberian Sea
Scandinavia
Yenisey
West Siberian Plain
Central Siberian Plateau
SIBERIA
Lena
Angara
Bering Sea
Kamchatka Peninsula
Aleutian Is.
North Sea
Northern European Plain
Ural Mountains
Ob
Irtysh
Volga
Ob
Lena
Sea of Okhotsk
Kuril Islands
EUROPE
Alps
The Steppes
El'brus 18,510 ft (5,642 m)
Altay Mountains
Lake Baikal
Amur
GOBI
Hokkaido
JAPAN
Nampo Shoto
Danube
Caucasus Mts.
Black Sea
Caspian Sea
Tian Shan
ASIA
Kunlun Mountains
Sea of Japan East Sea
Honshu
Mediterranean Sea
Mts.
Zagros Mts.
Dead Sea -1,388 ft (-423 m)
Plateau of Tibet
HIMALAYA
Brahmaputra
Yellow
Yangtze
North China Plain
Korea
East China Sea
Ryukyu Is.
30°
SAHARA
Libyan Desert
Nile
ARABIAN PENINSULA
Indus
Ganges
Mt. Everest 29,035 ft (8,850 m)
Salween
Taiwan
PACIFIC
SAHEL
Niger
Lake Chad
Lake Assal -509 ft (-151 m)
Gulf of Aden
Somali Peninsula
Arabian Sea
INDIA
Bay of Bengal
Mekong
Hainan
Luzon
Philippine Sea
Mariana Islands
OCEAN
AFRICA
Ethiopian Highlands
Sri Lanka
Andaman Islands
Indochina Peninsula
South China Sea
Philippine Islands
MICRONESIA
Marshall Islands
Congo Basin
Lake Victoria
Great Rift Valley
Kilimanjaro 19,340 ft (5,895 m)
Seychelles
Maldive Islands
Nicobar Is.
Malay Peninsula
INDONESIA
Borneo
Celebes
Moluccas
60°
EQUATOR
150°
Gilbert Islands
Lake Tanganyika
Comoros Is.
90°
Sumatra
Greater Sunda Islands
Java
New Guinea
MELANESIA
Bismarck Archipelago
Zambezi
Madagascar
Mascarene Is.
INDIAN
Timor
Arafura Sea
Mt. Wilhelm 14,793 ft (4,509 m)
Solomon Islands
Kalahari Desert
OCEAN
Coral Sea
Vanuatu
Fiji Islands
Great Sandy Desert
AUSTRALIA
Lake Eyre -49 ft (-15 m)
Great Victoria Desert
Great Central Lowlands
Great Dividing Range
New Caledonia
0   miles   2000
0   kilometers   3000
Winkel Tripel Projection
Kerguelen Islands
Tasman Sea
Darling
30°
Tasmania
North Island
ZEALAND
South Island
NEW
Auckland Islands
60°
CIRCLE
een Maud Land
ANTARCTICA
Transantarctic Mountains
Byrd Glacier -9,416 ft (-2,870 m)
Victoria Land

KINDS OF MAPS

Maps are special tools that geographers use to tell a story about Earth. Maps can be used to show just about anything related to places. Some maps show physical features, such as mountains or vegetation. Maps can also show climates or natural hazards and other things we cannot easily see. Other maps illustrate different features on Earth—political boundaries, urban centers, and economic systems.

AN IMPERFECT TOOL

Maps are not perfect. A globe is a scale model of Earth with accurate relative sizes and locations. Because maps are flat, they involve distortions of size, shape, and direction. Also, cartographers—people who create maps—make choices about what information to include. Because of this, it is important to study many different types of maps to learn the complete story of Earth. Three commonly found kinds of maps are shown on this page.

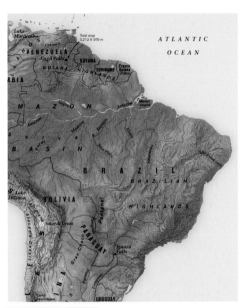

PHYSICAL MAPS. Earth's natural features—landforms, water bodies, and vegetation—are shown on physical maps. The map above uses color and shading to illustrate mountains, lakes, rivers, and deserts of central South America. Country names and borders are added for reference, but they are not natural features.

POLITICAL MAPS. These maps represent characteristics of the landscape created by humans, such as boundaries, cities, and place-names. Natural features are added only for reference. On the map above, capital cities are represented with a star inside a circle, while other cities are shown with black dots.

THEMATIC MAPS. Patterns related to a particular topic or theme, such as population distribution, appear on these maps. The map above displays the region's climate zones, which range from tropical wet (bright green) to tropical wet and dry (light green) to semiarid (dark yellow) to arid or desert (light yellow).

MAKING MAPS

Long ago, cartographers worked with pen and ink, carefully handcrafting maps based on explorers' observations and diaries. Today, mapmaking is a high-tech business. Cartographers use Earth data stored in "layers" in a Geographic Information System (GIS) and special computer programs to create maps that can be easily updated as new information becomes available.

National Geographic staff cartographers Mike McNey and Rosemary Wardley review a map of Africa for the *National Geographic Kids World Atlas.*

Satellites in orbit around Earth act as eyes in the sky, recording data about the planet's land and ocean areas. The data is converted to numbers that are transmitted back to computers that are specially programmed to interpret the data. They record it in a form that cartographers can use to create maps.

MAP PROJECTIONS

To create a map, cartographers transfer an image of the round Earth to a flat surface, a process called projection. All projections involve distortion. For example, an interrupted projection (bottom map) shows accurate shapes and relative sizes of land areas, but oceans have gaps. Other types of projections are cylindrical, conic, or azimuthal—each with certain advantages, but all with some distortion.

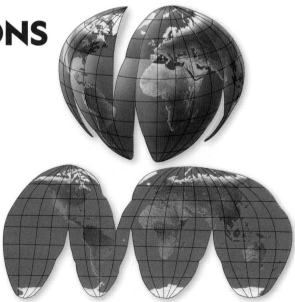

261

GEOGRAPHIC FEATURES

From roaring rivers to parched deserts, from underwater canyons to jagged mountains, Earth is covered with beautiful and diverse environments. Here are examples of the most common types of geographic features found around the world.

WATERFALL

Waterfalls form when a river reaches an abrupt change in elevation. At left, the Iguazú waterfall system—on the border of Brazil and Argentina—is made up of 275 falls.

VALLEY

Valleys, cut by running water or moving ice, may be broad and flat or narrow and steep, such as the Indus River Valley in Ladakh, India (above).

RIVER

As a river moves through flatlands, it twists and turns. Above, the Rio Los Amigos winds through a rain forest in Peru.

MOUNTAIN

Mountains are Earth's tallest landforms, and Mount Everest (above) rises highest of all, at 29,035 feet (8,850 m) above sea level.

GLACIER

Glaciers—"rivers" of ice—such as Alaska's Hubbard Glacier (above) move slowly from mountains to the sea. Global warming is shrinking them.

CANYON

Steep-sided valleys called canyons are created mainly by running water. Buckskin Gulch in Utah (above) is the deepest "slot" canyon in the American Southwest.

DESERT

Deserts are land features created by climate, specifically by a lack of water. Here, a camel caravan crosses the Sahara in North Africa.

Bet You Didn't Know!

7 awesome facts about Earth

1 There are **volcanoes inside glaciers in Iceland.**

5 The **oldest water on Earth**— some 1 to 2.5 billion years old— **was found 1.5 miles** (2.4 km) down a mine in **Canada.**

2 Antarctica is the only **continent** with no rain forests.

3 There are more **geysers** in U.S.A.'s **Yellowstone National Park** than anywhere else on **Earth.**

6 The **ocean below** the **North Pole** is more than **13,000** feet (3,960 m) deep.

7 Two lakes continue to exist in the **Sahara,** fed by water from underground.

4 More than **100** million years ago, **India** was an island.

Old Faithful geyser, in Yellowstone National Park, Wyoming, U.S.A.

AFRICA

In 1979 and 2012, snow fell in parts of the Sahara in North Africa.

A zebra's night vision is thought to be as good as an owl's.

Zebra

The massive continent of Africa, where humankind began millions of years ago, is second only to Asia in size. Stretching nearly as far from west to east as it does from north to south, Africa is home to both the longest river in the world (the Nile) and the largest hot desert on Earth (the Sahara).

The Great Sphinx at Giza in Egypt

SPEEDY SPECIES

Some of the world's fastest animals live in Africa, such as cheetahs, pronghorn antelopes, wildebeests, and lions. Each of these species can reach speeds topping 50 miles an hour (80 km/h).

ADVANCED ANCESTORS

Our earliest ancestors lived in Africa—and experts say these humans were rather evolved. Artifacts recently discovered in Kenya from some 320,000 years ago show that the *Homo sapiens*—our early ancestor—made tools with sharp blades from volcanic rock and created their own bright red dye from clay, which they may have used as body paint. Scientists think this early civilization also traded for goods with other groups in distant lands, a surprisingly sophisticated system for people who lived so long ago.

Protecting the Environment

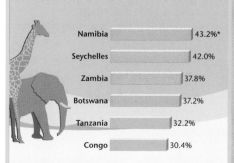

Country	Percent
Namibia	43.2%*
Seychelles	42.0%
Zambia	37.8%
Botswana	37.2%
Tanzania	32.2%
Congo	30.4%

*Figures represent percent of total land area set aside as protected area

MAJOR MINES

Bling it on! Africa is home to many gold and diamond mines, including the deepest mine in the world. The Mponeng mine in South Africa is deeper than 13,000 feet (3,960 m) and features tunnels that are many miles long. It takes over an hour to get to the bottom, where temps top 140°F (60°C). As for diamonds? Botswana's Jwaneng mine produces up to 15 million carats of bling every year—making it the world's most valuable diamond mine.

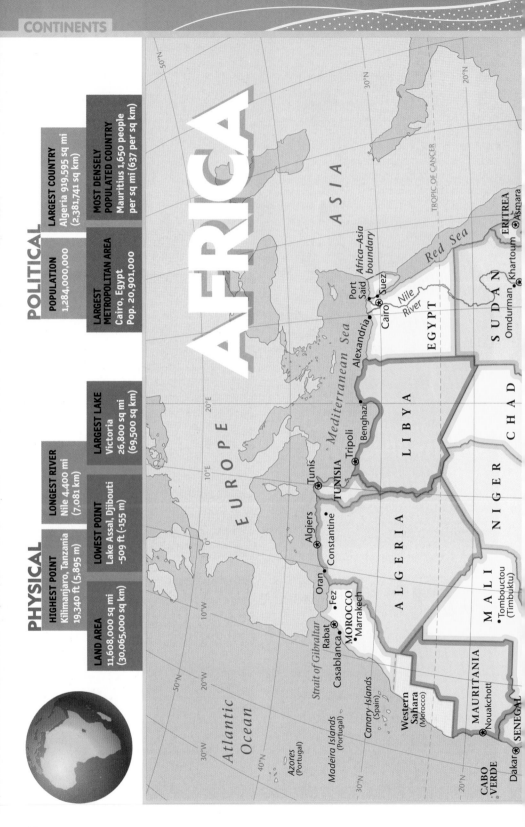

AFRICA

PHYSICAL

LAND AREA	HIGHEST POINT	LOWEST POINT	LONGEST RIVER	LARGEST LAKE
11,608,000 sq mi (30,065,000 sq km)	Kilimanjaro, Tanzania 19,340 ft (5,895 m)	Lake Assal, Djibouti -509 ft (-155 m)	Nile 4,400 mi (7,081 km)	Victoria 26,800 sq mi (69,500 sq km)

POLITICAL

POPULATION	LARGEST METROPOLITAN AREA	LARGEST COUNTRY	MOST DENSELY POPULATED COUNTRY
1,284,000,000	Cairo, Egypt Pop. 20,901,000	Algeria 919,595 sq mi (2,381,741 sq km)	Mauritius 1,650 people per sq mi (637 per sq km)

Map labels:

ASIA

EUROPE

Atlantic Ocean

Mediterranean Sea

Red Sea

TROPIC OF CANCER

Africa-Asia boundary

Port Said · Suez
Cairo
Alexandria
Nile River

EGYPT

SUDAN
Omdurman · Khartoum
ERITREA · Asmara

LIBYA
Benghazi ·
Tripoli ·

TUNISIA
Tunis ·

CHAD

NIGER

ALGERIA
Algiers ·
Constantine ·
Oran ·

Fez ·
MOROCCO
Rabat
Casablanca ·
Marrakech ·

MALI
Tombouctou (Timbuktu) ·

Strait of Gibraltar

Canary Islands (Spain)

Western Sahara (Morocco)

MAURITANIA
Nouakchott ·

SENEGAL
Dakar ·

CABO VERDE

Madeira Islands (Portugal)

Azores (Portugal)

50°N, 40°N, 30°N, 20°N, 10°N

30°W, 20°W, 10°W, 0°, 10°E, 20°E, 30°E, 50°E

Map Key

⊗ National capital
• Other city
▲ Highest point
▼ Lowest point

800 Miles

800 Kilometers

Azimuthal Equal-Area Projection

Indian Ocean

MAURITIUS
Port Louis
Réunion (France)

SEYCHELLES
Victoria

MADAGASCAR
Antananarivo

COMOROS
Moroni

Mozambique Channel

SOMALILAND
SOMALIA
Mogadishu
Djibouti
DJIBOUTI

Gulf of Aden

Lake Assal
(-155 m) -509 ft ▼

Addis Ababa
ETHIOPIA

Juba
SOUTH SUDAN

DARFUR

UGANDA
Kampala

KENYA
Nairobi
Mombasa
Kilimanjaro
19,340 ft ▲
(5,895 m)

Lake Victoria

RWANDA
Kigali
BURUNDI
Bujumbura

TANZANIA
Dodoma
Dar es Salaam

MALAWI
Lilongwe

MOZAMBIQUE

CENTRAL AFRICAN REPUBLIC
Bangui

DEMOCRATIC REPUBLIC OF THE CONGO
Kisangani
Kananga
Mbuji-Mayi
Kinshasa

ZAMBIA
Lubumbashi
Kolwezi
Kitwe
Lusaka

ZIMBABWE
Harare

BOTSWANA
Gaborone

ESWATINI (SWAZILAND)
Mbabane
Lobamba

LESOTHO
Maseru

Pretoria
(Tshwane)
Johannesburg
Bloemfontein
SOUTH AFRICA
Durban
Port Elizabeth
Cape Town

Maputo

NAMIBIA
Windhoek

ANGOLA
Luanda

CONGO
Brazzaville
Pointe-Noire
Cabinda
(Angola)

GABON
Libreville

CAMEROON
Yaoundé
Douala

EQUATORIAL GUINEA
Malabo

SAO TOME & PRINCIPE
São Tomé

N'Djamena

NIGERIA
Kano
Abuja
Ogbomosho
Lagos
Porto-Novo
BENIN
Cotonou
TOGO
Lomé
GHANA
Accra

BURKINA FASO
Ouagadougou
Niamey

Bamako
MALI

GAMBIA
Banjul
GUINEA-BISSAU
Bissau
GUINEA
Conakry
SIERRA LEONE
Freetown
LIBERIA
Monrovia
CÔTE D'IVOIRE
(IVORY COAST)
Yamoussoukro
Abidjan

Atlantic Ocean

St. Helena (U.K.)

Ascension (U.K.)

TROPIC OF CAPRICORN

EQUATOR

267

ANTARCTICA

Gentoo penguin

There are mountains buried under ice in Antarctica.

An adult gentoo penguin makes as many as 450 dives a day looking for food.

This frozen continent may be a cool place to visit, but unless you're a penguin, you probably wouldn't want to hang out in Antarctica for long. The fact that it's the coldest, windiest, and driest continent helps explain why humans never colonized this ice-covered land surrounding the South Pole.

Weddell seal

GOING THE DISTANCE

Each year, a few hundred runners from around the world compete in the Antarctica Marathon and Half-Marathon, a hilly and twisty race along the continent's icy peninsula.

A DAY TO CELEBRATE

DECEMBER 1

Signed in 1959, the Antarctic Treaty, which governs Antarctica, says that the continent should be used only for peaceful purposes. The treaty, which has now been signed by 53 countries, also established Antarctica as a scientific reserve and a place for scientific exploration. Any activities that may disrupt the natural environment are prohibited. Each year on December 1, World Antarctica Day marks the signing of the treaty and celebrates this unique and fascinating place on Earth.

FREAKY FALLS

Five-story-tall Blood Falls in Antarctica oozes red water from an ancient lake trapped under Taylor Glacier. First discovered in 1911, the falls' creepy color baffled experts, who originally thought it came from red algae. But recent studies show that the lake deep beneath the glacier is super-salty and full of iron, which turns the water red. Another fascinating fact about the falls? Scientists say it takes approximately 1.5 million years for the ancient lake water to travel through tiny cracks and channels in Taylor Glacier before it sees the light of day.

Earth's Largest Deserts

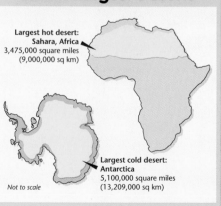

Largest hot desert:
Sahara, Africa
3,475,000 square miles
(9,000,000 sq km)

Largest cold desert:
Antarctica
5,100,000 square miles
(13,209,000 sq km)

Not to scale

PHYSICAL

LAND AREA
5,100,000 sq mi
(13,209,000 sq km)

HIGHEST POINT
Vinson Massif
16,067 ft (4,897 m)

LOWEST POINT
Byrd Glacier
-9,416 ft (-2,870 m)

COLDEST PLACE
Ridge A, annual
average temperature
-94°F (-70°C)

**AVERAGE
PRECIPITATION ON
THE POLAR PLATEAU**
Less than 2 in (5 cm)

POLITICAL

POPULATION
There are no
indigenous inhabitants,
but there are both
permanent and
summer-only staffed
research stations.

**NUMBER OF
INDEPENDENT
COUNTRIES** 0

**NUMBER OF
COUNTRIES
CLAIMING LAND** 7

**NUMBER OF
COUNTRIES
OPERATING YEAR-
ROUND RESEARCH
STATIONS** 20

**NUMBER OF YEAR-
ROUND RESEARCH
STATIONS** 40

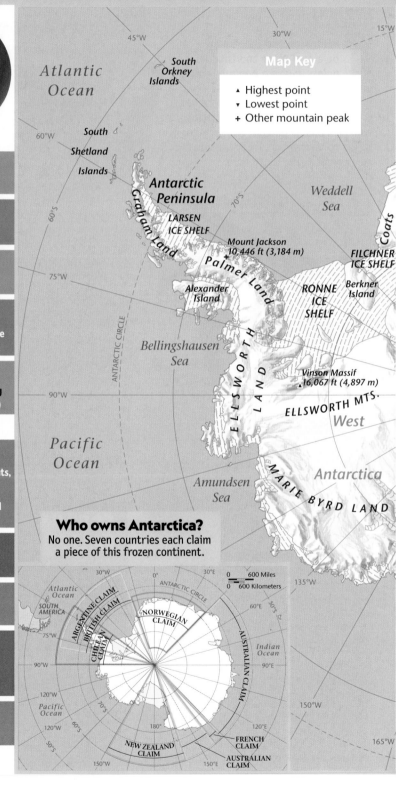

Map Key

▲ Highest point
▼ Lowest point
+ Other mountain peak

Atlantic Ocean

South Orkney Islands

South Shetland Islands

Antarctic Peninsula

Graham Land

LARSEN ICE SHELF

Weddell Sea

Coats

Mount Jackson
10,446 ft (3,184 m)

FILCHNER ICE SHELF

Palmer Land

Alexander Island

RONNE ICE SHELF

Berkner Island

Bellingshausen Sea

ELLSWORTH LAND

Vinson Massif
▲16,067 ft (4,897 m)

ELLSWORTH MTS.

West

Pacific Ocean

Amundsen Sea

MARIE BYRD LAND

Antarctica

ANTARCTIC CIRCLE

Who owns Antarctica?
No one. Seven countries each claim
a piece of this frozen continent.

Atlantic Ocean

SOUTH AMERICA

ARGENTINE CLAIM
BRITISH CLAIM
CHILEAN CLAIM

NORWEGIAN CLAIM

AUSTRALIAN CLAIM

Indian Ocean

Pacific Ocean

NEW ZEALAND CLAIM

FRENCH CLAIM

AUSTRALIAN CLAIM

ANTARCTIC CIRCLE

0   600 Miles
0   600 Kilometers

ANTARCTICA

FIMBUL
ICE SHELF

0°

RIISER-LARSEN
ICE SHELF

Q U E E N   M A U D   L A N D

ENDERBY
LAND

60°E

Land

Valkyrie
Dome

*Indian
Ocean*

Lambert
Glacier

MacKenzie Bay

75°E

AMERY ICE SHELF

AMERICAN

HIGHLAND

WEST
ICE SHELF

T
R
A
N
S
A
N
T
A
R
C
T
I
C

Ridge A +

East

90°E

POLAR PLATEAU

South Pole

Antarctica

SHACKLETON
ICE SHELF

M
O
U
N
T
A
I
N
S

80°S

ROSS
ICE
SHELF

105°E

Byrd Glacier
-9,416 ft (-2,870 m)

Roosevelt
Island

Taylor
Glacier

W
I
L
K
E
S

L
A
N
D

Ross Island

Mount Erebus
12,448 ft
(3,794 m)

*Ross
Sea*

V
I
C
T
O
R
I
A

L
A
N
D

70°S

120°E

180°

Talos
Dome

60°S

| 0 | | 600 Miles |
| 0 | | 600 Kilometers |

Azimuthal Equidistant Projection

150°E

135°E

*Indian
Ocean*

ASIA

Children with a water buffalo
in Sa Pa, Vietnam

A water buffalo's wide hooves keep it from sinking in mud.

About 73 percent of Japan is covered with mountains.

Kuala Lumpur, Malaysia

Made up of 46 countries, Asia is the world's largest continent. Just how big is it? From western Turkey to the eastern tip of Russia, Asia spans nearly half the globe! Home to more than four billion citizens—that's three out of five people on the planet—Asia's population is bigger than that of all the other continents combined.

ON THE MOVE

About a third of the population of Mongolia moves seasonally. They live in portable huts called *ger* while traveling up to 70 miles (112 km) on foot to find food sources for their livestock.

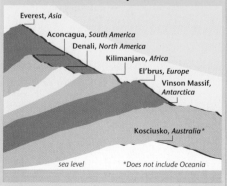

ON THE BORDER

Asia is the only continent that shares borders with two other continents: Africa and Europe. Here a marker identifies the border between Europe and Asia in western Russia.

Tallest Peaks by Continent

Everest, *Asia*

Aconcagua, *South America*

Denali, *North America*

Kilimanjaro, *Africa*

El'brus, *Europe*

Vinson Massif, *Antarctica*

Kosciusko, *Australia**

sea level   *Does not include Oceania

GOING BATTY

From the hefty golden-crowned flying fox to the itty-bitty bumblebee bat, Asia is home to at least 435 of the world's more than 1,300 species of bats. Indonesia has the world's largest number of species, with more than 175 different types of bats. And in Malaysia? Bats outnumber all other mammals in the country, including humans! The winged mammals help keep the ecosystem healthy, especially in Southeast Asia's forests where the bats play a key role in spreading the seeds of trees and other plants.

PHYSICAL

LAND AREA
17,208,000 sq mi
(44,570,000 sq km)

HIGHEST POINT
Mount Everest,
China–Nepal
29,035 ft (8,850 m)

LOWEST POINT
Dead Sea,
Israel–Jordan
-1,388 ft (-423 m)

LONGEST RIVER
Yangtze, China
3,880 mi (6,244 km)

**LARGEST LAKE
ENTIRELY IN ASIA**
Lake Baikal, Russia
12,200 sq mi
(31,500 sq km)

POLITICAL

POPULATION
4,536,000,000

**LARGEST
METROPOLITAN AREA**
Tokyo, Japan
Pop. 37,393,000

**LARGEST COUNTRY
ENTIRELY IN ASIA**
China
3,705,406 sq mi
(9,596,960 sq km)

**MOST DENSELY
POPULATED COUNTRY**
Singapore
22,745 people
per sq mi
(8,788 per sq km)

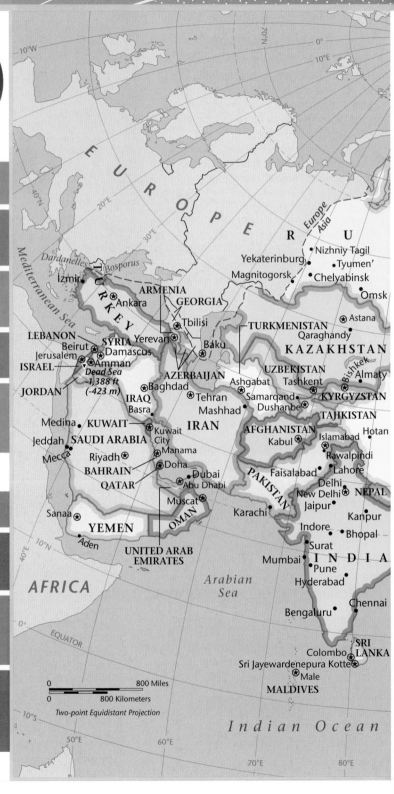

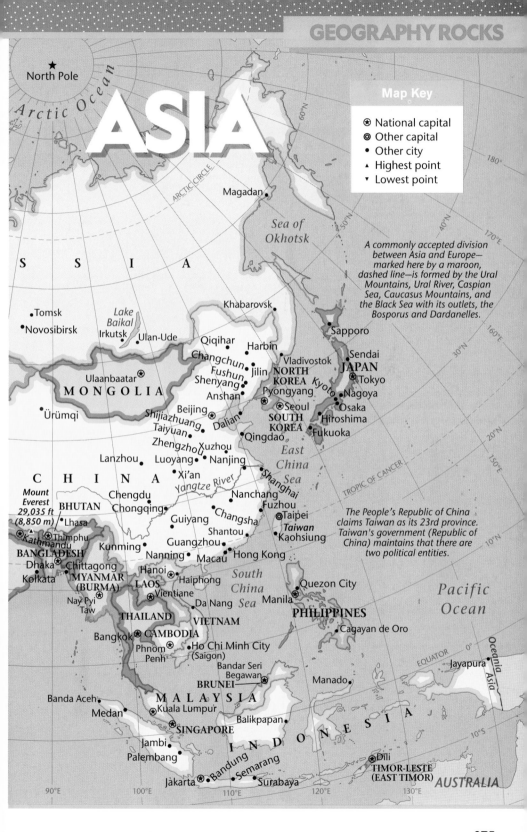

★ North Pole

Arctic Ocean

ASIA

Map Key

⊛ National capital
◎ Other capital
• Other city
▲ Highest point
▼ Lowest point

Arctic Circle

Magadan

Sea of Okhotsk

A commonly accepted division between Asia and Europe— marked here by a maroon, dashed line—is formed by the Ural Mountains, Ural River, Caspian Sea, Caucasus Mountains, and the Black Sea with its outlets, the Bosporus and Dardanelles.

S S I A

•Tomsk
Lake Baikal
•Novosibirsk   Irkutsk •Ulan-Ude

Khabarovsk

Sapporo

Qiqihar   Harbin
Changchun   •Jilin   Vladivostok
Fushun   NORTH
Shenyang   KOREA
Anshan   Pyongyang

Ulaanbaatar ⊛

MONGOLIA

Beijing⊛
Dalian•

JAPAN
•Sendai
Tokyo⊛
Kyoto Nagoya
Osaka
Hiroshima
Fukuoka

•Ürümqi

Shijiazhuang•
Taiyuan•
Zhengzhou•
Xuzhou
Seoul⊛
SOUTH
KOREA
Qingdao•

East China Sea

Lanzhou• Luoyang• •Nanjing

C H I N A

Mount Everest
29,035 ft
(8,850 m)

Xi'an•
Yangtze River
Chengdu
Chongqing•
Nanchang•
Shanghai•
Fuzhou•

BHUTAN
•Lhasa
Thimphu

Guiyang•
Changsha•
Shantou•

Taipei◎
Taiwan
Kaohsiung•

TROPIC OF CANCER

The People's Republic of China claims Taiwan as its 23rd province. Taiwan's government (Republic of China) maintains that there are two political entities.

•Kathmandu
BANGLADESH
Dhaka• •Chittagong
Kolkata

Kunming•
Guangzhou•
Nanning• •Macau Hong Kong

Hanoi•
MYANMAR
(BURMA) LAOS •Haiphong
Nay Pyi Taw⊛ ◎Vientiane •Da Nang

South China Sea

•Quezon City

Manila⊛

PHILIPPINES

•Cagayan de Oro

Pacific Ocean

THAILAND VIETNAM
Bangkok⊛ •CAMBODIA
Phnom ⊛ •Ho Chi Minh City
Penh   (Saigon)

Bandar Seri
Begawan•
BRUNEI

•Manado

EQUATOR

•Jayapura

Oceania
Asia

Banda Aceh•
Medan• ⊛Kuala Lumpur

M A L A Y S I A

Balikpapan•

⊛SINGAPORE

Jambi•
Palembang•

I N D O N E S I A

•Dili
TIMOR-LESTE
(EAST TIMOR)

AUSTRALIA

Jakarta⊛ •Bandung •Semarang •Surabaya

90°E 100°E 110°E 120°E 130°E

AUSTRALIA,
NEW ZEALAND, AND OCEANIA

More than one-third of New Zealand's population lives in the city of Auckland.

Australia's capitol building was designed in the shape of a boomerang.

Auckland Harbour in Auckland, New Zealand

G'day, mate! This vast region, covering almost 3.3 million square miles (8.5 million sq km), includes Australia—the world's smallest and flattest continent—and New Zealand, as well as a fleet of mostly tiny islands scattered across the Pacific Ocean. Also known as "down under," most of the countries in this region are in the Southern Hemisphere, and below the Equator.

Aboriginal children of Australia in ceremonial dress

ROCK STARS

Most of Australia is a rural desert, also known as the outback. Here you can also find a giant rock formation called Uluru, or Ayers Rock, which appears to change color during the day.

FOR THE DOGS

Dingos are wild dogs found almost exclusively in Australia. But these canines aren't actually native to down under—they likely arrived 1,000–5,000 years ago by boat from Asia. Today, these social dogs travel in packs throughout the forests, plains, mountains, and deserts of northern, northwestern, and central Australia. As the largest land predator in Australia, they prey on small to medium animals, such as lizards, rodents, and rabbits.

Sizing Up the Great Barrier Reef

Just how big is the Great Barrier Reef Marine Park? It's approximately as large as:

Great Barrier Reef Marine Park

Germany

Vietnam

Australia

or the Republic of Congo

*Based on an area of 133,000 square miles (344,400 sq km)

GROW ON

About 80 percent of the plants in New Zealand are not found anywhere else in the world. And some of them doubled as dinosaur snacks! Plants like the kauri—a coniferous tree—have ancestors that date back to the Jurassic period. And New Zealand's magnificent lowland forests have been nicknamed "dinosaur forests" because of the prehistoric plants that grow there.

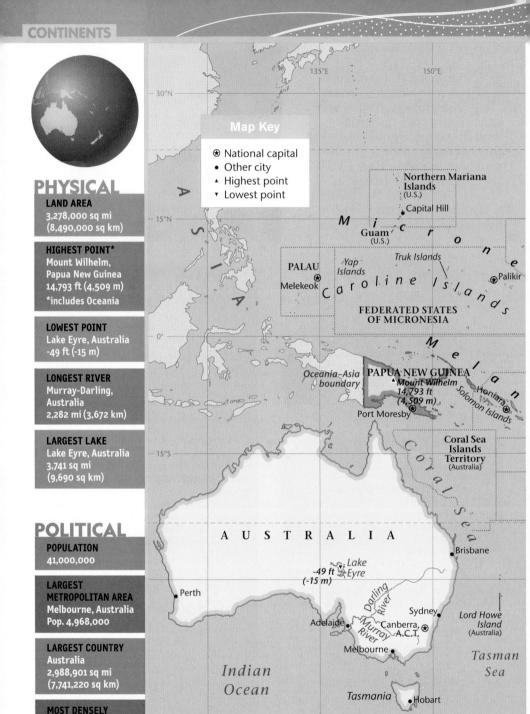

PHYSICAL

LAND AREA
3,278,000 sq mi
(8,490,000 sq km)

HIGHEST POINT*
Mount Wilhelm,
Papua New Guinea
14,793 ft (4,509 m)
*includes Oceania

LOWEST POINT
Lake Eyre, Australia
-49 ft (-15 m)

LONGEST RIVER
Murray-Darling,
Australia
2,282 mi (3,672 km)

LARGEST LAKE
Lake Eyre, Australia
3,741 sq mi
(9,690 sq km)

POLITICAL

POPULATION
41,000,000

**LARGEST
METROPOLITAN AREA**
Melbourne, Australia
Pop. 4,968,000

LARGEST COUNTRY
Australia
2,988,901 sq mi
(7,741,220 sq km)

**MOST DENSELY
POPULATED COUNTRY**
Nauru
1,250 people per sq mi
(476 per sq km)

Map Key

⊛ National capital
• Other city
▲ Highest point
▼ Lowest point

30°N

135°E   150°E

A S I A

15°N

Northern Mariana
Islands
(U.S.)
• Capital Hill

M i c r o n e

Guam
(U.S.)

PALAU
Melekeok ⊛

Yap
Islands

Truk Islands

Caroline Islands

Palikir

FEDERATED STATES
OF MICRONESIA

0°

M e l a n

Oceania–Asia
boundary

PAPUA NEW GUINEA
▲ Mount Wilhelm
14,793 ft
(4,509 m)

Honiara
Solomon Islands

e s i a

Port Moresby

15°S

Coral Sea
Islands
Territory
(Australia)

C o r a l   S e a

A U S T R A L I A

Brisbane

▼ Lake
Eyre
-49 ft
(-15 m)

Darling
River

Perth

Sydney

Lord Howe
Island
(Australia)

Adelaide
Murray
River

Canberra, ⊛
A.C.T.

Indian
Ocean

Melbourne

Tasman
Sea

Tasmania

Hobart

45°S

0   800 Miles
0   800 Kilometers

Mercator Projection

120°E   135°E   150°E

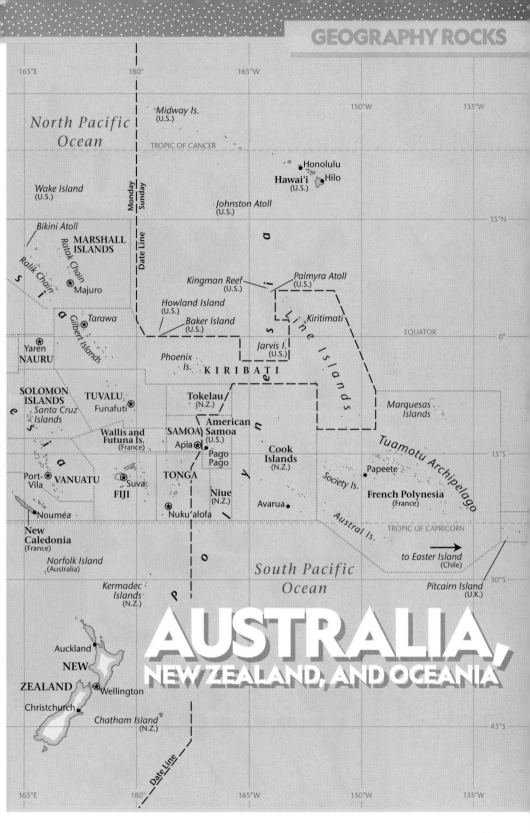

North Pacific Ocean

165°E 180° 165°W 150°W 135°W

Midway Is. (U.S.)

TROPIC OF CANCER

Honolulu
Hawai'i (U.S.) Hilo

Wake Island (U.S.)

Monday | Sunday

Johnston Atoll (U.S.)

15°N

Bikini Atoll

MARSHALL ISLANDS

Date Line

Ralik Chain
Ratak Chain

Majuro

Kingman Reef (U.S.)
Palmyra Atoll (U.S.)

Howland Island (U.S.)

Tarawa

Gilbert Islands

Baker Island (U.S.)

Kiritimati

EQUATOR 0°

Yaren
NAURU

Jarvis I. (U.S.)

Line Islands

Phoenix Is.

KIRIBATI

SOLOMON ISLANDS

TUVALU
Funafuti

Tokelau (N.Z.)

Santa Cruz Islands

Wallis and Futuna Is. (France)

SAMOA
Apia

American Samoa (U.S.)
Pago Pago

Marquesas Islands

15°S

Port- Vila **VANUATU**

Suva
FIJI

TONGA

Cook Islands (N.Z.)

Papeete

Tuamotu Archipelago

Nouméa

Nuku'alofa

Niue (N.Z.)

Avarua

Society Is.

French Polynesia (France)

Austral Is.

New Caledonia (France)

Norfolk Island (Australia)

TROPIC OF CAPRICORN

to Easter Island (Chile)

30°S

Kermadec Islands (N.Z.)

South Pacific Ocean

Pitcairn Island (U.K.)

Date Line

AUSTRALIA, NEW ZEALAND, AND OCEANIA

Auckland

NEW ZEALAND

Wellington

Christchurch

Chatham Island (N.Z.)

45°S

165°E 180° 165°W 150°W 135°W

279

EUROPE

A pastry chef in Paris is known for his foie gras macarons—or goose liver cookies.

It's considered rude to write in red ink in Portugal.

Macarons in a pastry shop

A cluster of islands and peninsulas jutting west from Asia, Europe is bordered by the Atlantic and Arctic Oceans and more than a dozen seas. Here you'll find a variety of scenery, from mountains to countryside to coastlines. Europe is also known for its rich culture and fascinating history, which make it one of the most visited continents on Earth.

Traditional dance performed in Greece

SPOT IT

Dalmatians get their name from Dalmatia, a region of Croatia along the Adriatic Sea. The spotted canines have served as border guard dogs during conflicts in the region.

BERRY GOOD

Most of the world's raspberries are grown in Europe. Russia, Serbia, and Poland rank among the world's leading producers. The fertile soil and temperate climate in those countries create ideal growing conditions. Raspberries are native to Europe, and there are records of them being cultivated in Greece and Turkey more than 2,000 years ago. Now that's some sweet history!

Europe's Longest Rivers

Volga	2,290 miles (3,685 km)
Danube	1,770 miles (2,848 km)
Dnieper	1,420 miles (2,285 km)
Rhine	765 miles (1,230 km)
Elbe	724 miles (1,165 km)

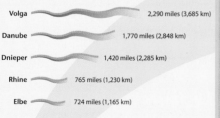

SEEING THE LIGHT

The midnight sun is a natural phenomenon that occurs every summer near the Arctic Circle when the sun can still be seen at midnight. Several places in northern Europe—including parts of Iceland, Norway, Finland, Sweden, Denmark, and Russia—experience the phenomena. Svalbard, Norway, experiences the longest period of the midnight sun in that country, with the sun staying visible in the night sky between April 20 and August 22.

PHYSICAL

LAND AREA
3,841,000 sq mi
(9,947,000 sq km)

HIGHEST POINT
El'brus, Russia
18,510 ft (5,642 m)

LOWEST POINT
Caspian Sea
-92 ft (-28 m)

LONGEST RIVER
Volga, Russia
2,290 mi
(3,685 km)

**LARGEST LAKE
ENTIRELY IN EUROPE**
Ladoga, Russia
6,900 sq mi
(17,872 sq km)

POLITICAL

POPULATION
746,000,000

**LARGEST
METROPOLITAN AREA**
Moscow, Russia
Pop. 12,538,000

**LARGEST COUNTRY
ENTIRELY IN EUROPE**
Ukraine
233,030 sq mi
(603,550 sq km)

**MOST DENSELY
POPULATED COUNTRY**
Monaco
50,000 people per sq
mi (20,000 per sq km)

Map Key

⊛ National capital
• Other city
▫ Small country
▲ Highest point
▾ Lowest point

Jan Mayen
(Norway)

Reykjavík
ICELAND

ARCTIC CIRCLE

*Norwegian
Sea*

Faroe Islands
(Denmark)

Shetland
Islands

Orkney Islands

Oslo

Göteborg

SCOTLAND
Glasgow
N. IRELAND
Edinburgh
Belfast

*North
Sea*

DENMARK
Copenhagen

**IRELAND
(ÉIRE)**
Dublin

UNITED KINGDOM
Liverpool • Manchester
WALES Birmingham
Cardiff ENGLAND
London ⊛

Kiel

*Atlantic
Ocean*

The **NETH.** Hamburg
Hague ⊛ Amsterdam Berlin ⊛

Brussels ⊛
BELGIUM

GERMANY
Frankfurt
⌐LUX. Prague

⊛ Paris

• Nantes

*Bay of
Biscay*

FRANCE Zürich
Bern ⊛
Lyon • SWITZ.

Munich
LIECH.

AUSTRIA
Ljubljana
SLOV.

Bordeaux •

Milan
Turin Venice

Oporto
Bilbao•
Valladolid

• Toulouse

MONACO Nice
Marseille

Genoa
SAN
MARINO

PORTUGAL

ANDORRA
•Zaragoza

Corsica
(France)

ITALY
VATICAN
CITY ⊛
Rome

Lisbon ⊛ Madrid ⊛

SPAIN
Valencia•

Barcelona

Sardinia
(Italy)

Naples•

Seville• Murcia•
Málaga•

Balearic Is.
(Spain)

Mediterra

Gibraltar (U.K.)

Messina
Palermo• Catania•
Sicily

0   400 Miles
0   400 Kilometers
Azimuthal Equidistant Projection

Valletta ⊛
○ **MALTA**

AFRICA

EUROPE

Barents Sea

Murmansk

Archangel

RUSSIA

ASIA

SWEDEN

NORWAY

FINLAND

Lake Ladoga

Helsinki

Tallinn
Stockholm
ESTONIA

St. Petersburg

Tver'

Yaroslavl'
Volga River Kazan'

Ufa

Nizhniy Novgorod

Samara Orenburg

Baltic Sea

Riga
LATVIA

Moscow
Ryazan'

LITHUANIA
Kaliningrad
(Russia)
Kaunas Vilnius

Vitsyebsk
Minsk

Smolensk

Penza

Saratov

Gdańsk

Bryansk

KAZAKHSTAN

POLAND
Warsaw

BELARUS
Homyel'

Kursk

Bydgoszcz
Łódź
Wrocław

Kraków

Kiev

Kharkiv

Volgograd

Astrakhan'

CZECHIA
(CZECH REP.)

L'viv
UKRAINE
Vinnytsya

Poltava
Donets'k

Rostov

Vienna
SLOVAKIA
Bratislava
Budapest

Dnipropetrovs'k

-92 ft
(-28 m)

Caspian Sea

HUNGARY

MOLDOVA
Chişinău

El'brus
(5,642 m) 18,510 ft

Groznyy

Zagreb

ROMANIA

Odesa
CRIMEA
Simferopol'

Sochi

GEORGIA

CROATIA
BOSNIA &
HERZEGOVINA
SERBIA
Belgrade
Bucharest

Sevastopol'

AZERBAIJAN

Baku

Sarajevo

MONTENEGRO
KOSOVO
Pristina
BULGARIA
Varna

Black Sea

Podgorica
Skopje
Sofia
Tirana
MACED.

Bosporus

ALBANIA
Thessaloniki

Istanbul

T U R K E Y

Dardanelles

GREECE

Athens

A commonly accepted division
between Asia and Europe—
marked here by a maroon,
dashed line—is formed by the
Ural Mountains, Ural River, Caspian
Sea, Caucasus Mountains, and
the Black Sea with its outlets, the
Bosporus and Dardanelles.

NORTHERN CYPRUS
Nicosia
CYPRUS

Sea

Crete

NORTH AMERICA

There are more than 100,000 coffee farms in Mexico.

Polar bears have no natural predators.

Polar bear with cub, Manitoba, Canada

F rom the Great Plains of the United States and Canada to the rain forests of Panama, North America stretches 5,500 miles (8,850 km) from north to south. The third largest continent, North America can be divided into five regions: the mountainous west (including parts of Mexico and Central America's western coast), the Great Plains, the Canadian Shield, the varied eastern region (including Central America's lowlands and coastal plains), and the Caribbean.

Onlookers celebrate the opening of the Panama Canal expansion in 2016.

VIKINGS LIVED HERE

Some 1,000 years ago, a troop of Norse explorers traveled by boat from Norway to the banks of Newfoundland, Canada. There, they found plenty of salmon, wild grapes, and timber—and set up camp. Today, the only known Viking settlement in North America can be found at L'Anse aux Meadows in the northernmost tip of Newfoundland. Archaeological evidence shows that these adventurous seafarers may have spent time in northeastern New Brunswick as well.

HIGH ENERGY

The United States is one of the top producers of geothermal energy— energy from the natural heat of the ground. Among the states, California leads the geothermal charge, with some 5 percent of the state's total power generated from underground heat. In New York City, St. Patrick's Cathedral (above) recently installed a geothermal plant for heating and cooling that stretches as deep as 2,200 feet (670 m) below the building.

TAKING FLIGHT

Millions of monarchs migrate up to 3,000 miles (4,828 km) to Mexico every year from the United States and Canada. They're the only butterflies to make such a massive journey.

World's Longest Coastlines

Canada	151,023 miles (243,048 km)
Indonesia	33,998 miles (54,716 km)
Russia	23,397 miles (37,653 km)
Philippines	22,549 miles (36,289 km)
Japan	18,486 miles (29,751 km)

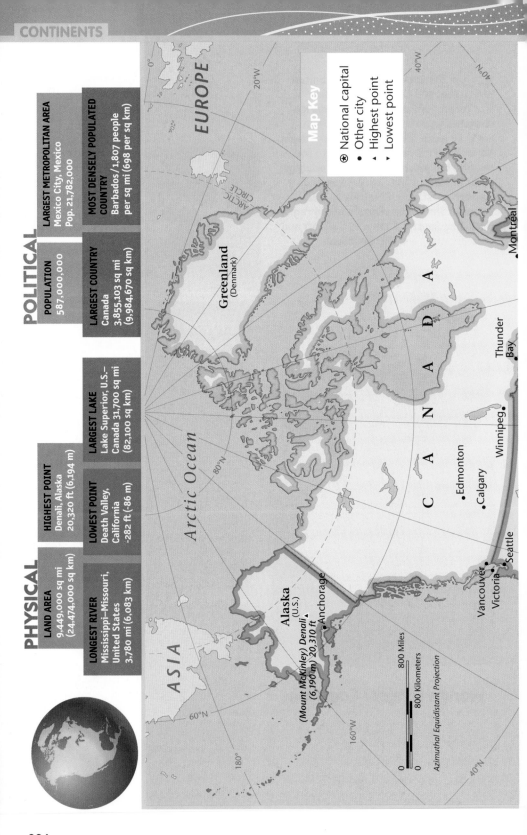

PHYSICAL

LAND AREA
9,449,000 sq mi
(24,474,000 sq km)

LONGEST RIVER
Mississippi–Missouri,
United States
3,780 mi (6,083 km)

HIGHEST POINT
Denali, Alaska
20,320 ft (6,194 m)

LOWEST POINT
Death Valley,
California
-282 ft (-86 m)

LARGEST LAKE
Lake Superior, U.S.–
Canada 31,700 sq mi
(82,100 sq km)

POLITICAL

POPULATION
587,000,000

LARGEST COUNTRY
Canada
3,855,103 sq mi
(9,984,670 sq km)

LARGEST METROPOLITAN AREA
Mexico City, Mexico
Pop. 21,782,000

MOST DENSELY POPULATED COUNTRY
Barbados/1,807 people
per sq mi (698 per sq km)

Map Key
✪ National capital
• Other city
▲ Highest point
▼ Lowest point

EUROPE

ASIA

Arctic Ocean

Greenland
(Denmark)

ARCTIC CIRCLE

C A N A D A

Alaska
(U.S.)
(Mount McKinley) Denali 20,310 ft
(6,190 m) Denali ▲
• Anchorage

Edmonton •
Calgary •

Winnipeg •

Thunder
Bay

Montreal

Vancouver •
Victoria •
Seattle •

800 Miles
800 Kilometers
Azimuthal Equidistant Projection

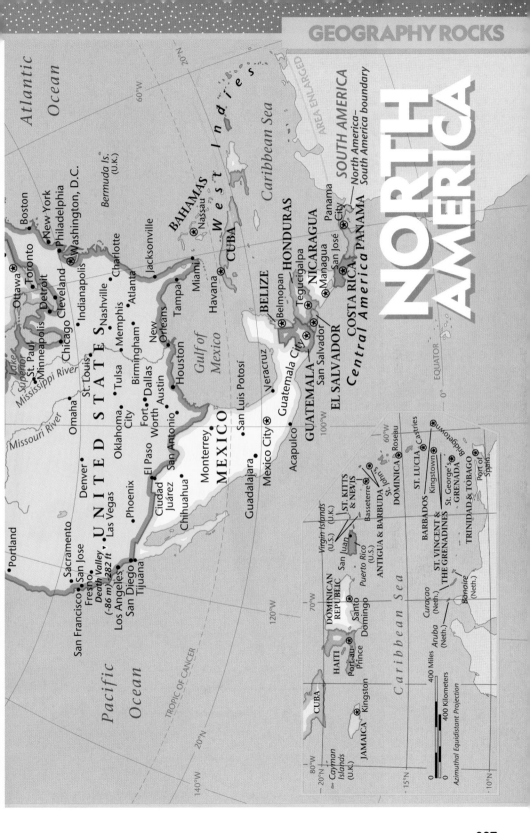

NORTH AMERICA

AREA ENLARGED

SOUTH AMERICA
North America–
South America boundary

PANAMA
Central America
COSTA RICA
San José
Panama
City

NICARAGUA
Managua

HONDURAS
Tegucigalpa

NASSAU
BAHAMAS

West Indies

Caribbean Sea

CUBA

BELIZE
Belmopan

Havana

GUATEMALA
Guatemala City
San Salvador
EL SALVADOR
San Salvador

Veracruz

Gulf of
Mexico

MEXICO

Acapulco

Mexico City

San Luis Potosí

Guadalajara

Monterrey

Chihuahua

Ciudad
Juárez

El Paso

San Antonio

Austin
Fort
Worth

Dallas

Houston

New
Orleans

Birmingham

Memphis

Tulsa

Oklahoma
City

UNITED STATES

Nashville

Indianapolis

Atlanta

Charlotte

Jacksonville

Tampa

Miami

Fort
Worth

Denver

Las Vegas

Death Valley
(-86 m) -282 ft ▼

Phoenix

Tijuana
San Diego
Los Angeles

Fresno
San Jose
San Francisco

Sacramento

Portland

Pacific
Ocean

TROPIC OF CANCER

20°N

140°W

120°W

Omaha

St. Louis

Missouri River

Mississippi River

Lake
Superior

St. Paul
Minneapolis

Chicago

Detroit

Cleveland

Ottawa

Toronto

Boston
New York
Philadelphia
Washington, D.C.

Bermuda Is.
(U.K.)

Atlantic
Ocean

20°N

60°W

EQUATOR

0°

100°W

80°W

70°W

60°W

Caribbean Sea

Virgin Islands
(U.S.) (U.K.)

San Juan

Puerto Rico
(U.S.)

ANTIGUA & BARBUDA

ST. KITTS
& NEVIS
Basseterre

St. John's

DOMINICA
Roseau

ST. LUCIA
Castries

BARBADOS
Bridgetown

ST. VINCENT &
THE GRENADINES
Kingstown
St. George's
GRENADA

TRINIDAD & TOBAGO
Port of
Spain

Bonaire
(Neth.)

Curaçao
(Neth.)

Aruba
(Neth.)

DOMINICAN
REPUBLIC
Santo
Domingo

HAITI
Port-au-
Prince

CUBA

JAMAICA
Kingston

Cayman
Islands
(U.K.)

15°N

20°N

10°N

400 Miles
0
400 Kilometers
0
Azimuthal Equidistant Projection

SOUTH AMERICA

Brazil has participated in the FIFA World Cup 21 times—more than any other team.

Ancient tombs in Peru contain kernels of popcorn, some of which still pop.

A boy plays soccer in Manaus, Brazil.

South America is bordered by three major bodies of water—the Caribbean Sea, Atlantic Ocean, and Pacific Ocean. The world's fourth largest continent extends over a range of climates from tropical in the north to subarctic in the south. South America produces a rich diversity of natural resources, including nuts, fruits, sugar, grains, coffee, and chocolate.

Santiago Cathedral in Santiago, Chile

BIG BIRD

The Andean condor, which lives exclusively in the mountains and valleys of the Andes, is the largest raptor in the world and the largest flying bird in South America.

OCEANS ALL AROUND

South America is surrounded by both the Pacific and Atlantic Oceans. Experts think that the two oceans used to be one massive body of water until North and South America joined together at the Isthmus of Panama some three million years ago. That move, scientists think, divided the original ocean into two. Today, Colombia and Chile are the only two countries in South America with a coastline on each ocean.

ICE LAND

Patagonia in southern Chile is home to one of the largest ice fields in the world. The Southern Patagonia Icefield, which stretches across the Andes Mountains and occupies parts of Argentina and Chile, feeds some 50 major glaciers that flow into the Pacific Ocean or freshwater lakes. The ice field takes up an area almost as large as the Bahamas and is so big, it can be seen from space on a clear day.

South America's Deepest Canyon

Peru's Cotahuasi Canyon is more than 11,500 feet (3,500 m) deep!

Almost twice as deep as the Grand Canyon — 6,000 feet (1,830 m) —

Burj Khalifa 2,717 feet (828 m)

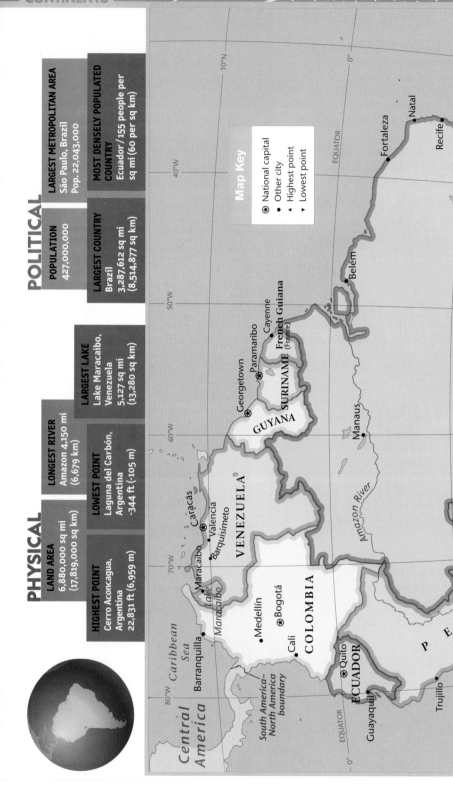

PHYSICAL

LAND AREA
6,880,000 sq mi
(17,819,000 sq km)

HIGHEST POINT
Cerro Aconcagua,
Argentina
22,831 ft (6,959 m)

LOWEST POINT
Laguna del Carbón,
Argentina
-344 ft (-105 m)

LONGEST RIVER
Amazon 4,150 mi
(6,679 km)

LARGEST LAKE
Lake Maracaibo,
Venezuela
5,127 sq mi
(13,280 sq km)

POLITICAL

POPULATION
427,000,000

LARGEST COUNTRY
Brazil
3,287,612 sq mi
(8,514,877 sq km)

LARGEST METROPOLITAN AREA
São Paulo, Brazil
Pop. 22,043,000

**MOST DENSELY POPULATED
COUNTRY**
Ecuador / 155 people per
sq mi (60 per sq km)

Map Key

⊛ National capital
• Other city
▲ Highest point
▼ Lowest point

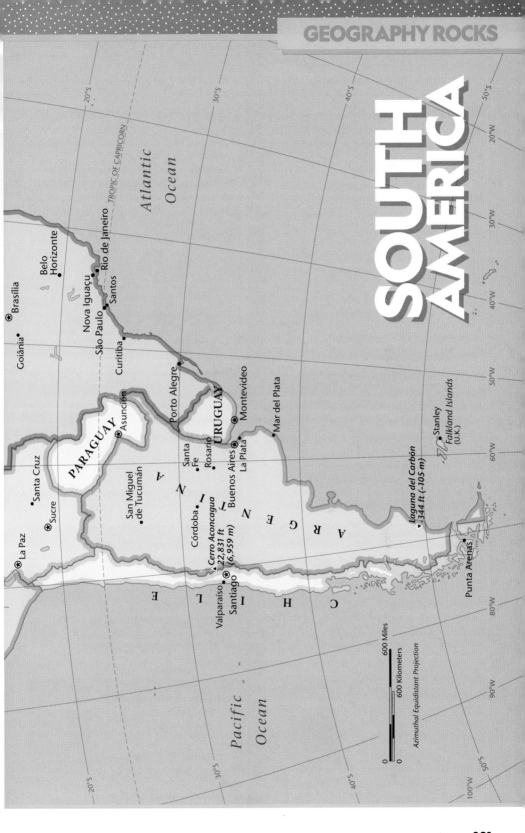

SOUTH AMERICA

Atlantic Ocean

TROPIC OF CAPRICORN

20°S
30°S
40°S
50°S

20°W
30°W
40°W
50°W
60°W
70°W
80°W

Belo Horizonte
Rio de Janeiro
Nova Iguaçu
Santos
São Paulo
Curitiba
Brasília
Goiânia
Porto Alegre
Asunción
PARAGUAY
Santa Cruz
Sucre
La Paz
San Miguel de Tucumán
Córdoba
Cerro Aconcagua
22,831 ft
(6,959 m)
Valparaíso
Santiago
C H I L E
A R G E N T I N A
Santa Fe
Rosario
URUGUAY
Montevideo
Buenos Aires
La Plata
Mar del Plata
Laguna del Carbón
-344 ft (-105 m)
Punta Arenas
Stanley
Falkland Islands
(U.K.)

Pacific Ocean

100°W
90°W
80°W

20°S
30°S
40°S
50°S

600 Miles
600 Kilometers
Azimuthal Equidistant Projection
0

COUNTRIES OF THE WORLD

The following pages present a general overview of all 195 independent countries recognized by the National Geographic Society, including the newest nation, South Sudan, which gained independence in 2011.

The flags of each independent country symbolize diverse cultures and histories. The statistical data cover highlights of geography and demography and provide a brief overview of each country. They present general characteristics and are not intended to be comprehensive. For example, not every language spoken in a specific country can be listed. Thus, languages shown are the most representative of that area. This is also true of the religions mentioned.

A country is defined as a political body with its own independent government, geographical space, and, in most cases, laws, military, and taxes.

Disputed areas such as Northern Cyprus and Taiwan, and dependencies of independent nations, such as Bermuda and Puerto Rico, are not included in this listing.

Note the color key at the bottom of the pages and the locator map below, which assign a color to each country based on the continent on which it is located. Some capital city populations include that city's metro area. All information is accurate as of press time.

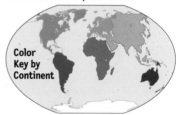

Color Key by Continent

Afghanistan

Area: 251,773 sq mi (652,090 sq km)
Population: 36,500,000
Capital: Kabul, pop. 4,012,000
Currency: afghani
Religions: Sunni Muslim, Shiite Muslim
Languages: Afghan Persian (Dari), Pashto, Turkic languages (primarily Uzbek and Turkmen), Baluchi, 30 minor languages (including Pashai)

Albania

Area: 11,100 sq mi (28,748 sq km)
Population: 2,900,000
Capital: Tirana, pop. 476,000
Currency: lek
Religions: Muslim, Albanian Orthodox, Roman Catholic
Languages: Albanian, Greek, Vlach, Romani, Slavic dialects

Algeria

Area: 919,595 sq mi (2,381,741 sq km)
Population: 42,700,000
Capital: Algiers, pop. 2,694,000
Currency: Algerian dinar
Religion: Sunni Muslim
Languages: Arabic, French, Berber dialects

Andorra

Area: 181 sq mi (469 sq km)
Population: 80,000
Capital: Andorra la Vella, pop. 23,000
Currency: euro
Religion: Roman Catholic
Languages: Catalan, French, Castilian, Portuguese

Angola

Area: 481,354 sq mi (1,246,700 sq km)
Population: 30,400,000
Capital: Luanda, pop. 7,774,000
Currency: kwanza
Religions: indigenous beliefs, Roman Catholic, Protestant
Languages: Portuguese, Bantu, other African languages

Antigua and Barbuda

Area: 171 sq mi (442 sq km)
Population: 100,000
Capital: St. John's, pop. 21,000
Currency: East Caribbean dollar
Religions: Anglican, Seventh-day Adventist, Pentecostal, Moravian, Roman Catholic, Methodist, Baptist, Church of God, other Christian
Languages: English, local dialects

Argentina

Area: 1,073,518 sq mi
(2,780,400 sq km)
Population: 44,500,000
Capital: Buenos Aires,
pop. 14,967,000
Currency: Argentine peso
Religion: Roman Catholic
Languages: Spanish, English, Italian, German, French

Armenia

Area: 11,484 sq mi
(29,743 sq km)
Population: 3,000,000
Capital: Yerevan,
pop. 1,080,000
Currency: dram
Religions: Armenian Apostolic, other Christian
Language: Armenian

3 cool things about ARMENIA

1. As the first country in the world to adopt Christianity as a state religion, Armenia earns its nickname, "Land of Churches," for its many places of worship. Some still-standing churches date back thousands of years.

2. A 5,500-year-old leather shoe—considered the oldest—was found in an Armenian cave. It looked like a moccasin and was stuffed with grasses.

3. The town of Yerevan is also known as the "Pink City" because many of its buildings and homes are made from a blush-colored volcanic rock.

Australia

Area: 2,988,901 sq mi
(7,741,220 sq km)
Population: 24,100,000
Capital: Canberra, A.C.T.,
pop. 448,000
Currency: Australian dollar
Religions: Roman Catholic, Anglican
Language: English

Austria

Area: 32,378 sq mi (83,858 sq km)
Population: 8,800,000
Capital: Vienna, pop. 1,901,000
Currency: euro
Religions: Roman Catholic, Protestant, Muslim
Language: German

Azerbaijan

Area: 33,436 sq mi
(86,600 sq km)
Population: 9,900,000
Capital: Baku, pop. 2,286,000
Currency: Azerbaijani manat
Religion: Muslim
Language: Azerbaijani (Azeri)

Bahamas

Area: 5,382 sq mi
(13,939 sq km)
Population: 400,000
Capital: Nassau, pop. 280,000
Currency: Bahamian dollar
Religions: Baptist, Anglican, Roman Catholic, Pentecostal, Church of God
Languages: English, Creole

Bahrain

Area: 277 sq mi (717 sq km)
Population: 1,500,000
Capital: Manama, pop. 565,000
Currency: Bahraini dinar
Religions: Shiite Muslim, Sunni Muslim, Christian
Languages: Arabic, English, Farsi, Urdu

Bangladesh

Area: 55,598 sq mi
(143,998 sq km)
Population: 166,400,000
Capital: Dhaka, pop. 19,578,000
Currency: taka
Religions: Muslim, Hindu
Languages: Bangla (Bengali), English

 ● Asia ● Europe ● North America ● South America

Barbados

Area: 166 sq mi (430 sq km)
Population: 300,000
Capital: Bridgetown, pop. 89,000
Currency: Barbadian dollar
Religions: Anglican, Pentecostal, Methodist, other Protestant, Roman Catholic
Language: English

Belarus

Area: 80,153 sq mi (207,595 sq km)
Population: 9,500,000
Capital: Minsk, pop. 2,005,000
Currency: Belarusian ruble
Religions: Eastern Orthodox, other (includes Roman Catholic, Protestant, Jewish, Muslim)
Languages: Belarusian, Russian

Belgium

Area: 11,787 sq mi (30,528 sq km)
Population: 11,400,000
Capital: Brussels, pop. 2,050,000
Currency: euro
Religions: Roman Catholic, other (includes Protestant)
Languages: Dutch, French

Belize

Area: 8,867 sq mi (22,965 sq km)
Population: 400,000
Capital: Belmopan, pop. 23,000
Currency: Belizean dollar
Religions: Roman Catholic, Protestant (includes Pentecostal, Seventh-day Adventist, Mennonite, Methodist)
Languages: Spanish, Creole, Mayan dialects, English, Garifuna (Carib), German

Benin

Area: 43,484 sq mi (112,622 sq km)
Population: 11,500,000
Capitals: Porto-Novo, pop. 285,000; Cotonou, pop. 685,000
Currency: Communauté Financière Africaine franc
Religions: Christian, Muslim, Vodoun
Languages: French, Fon, Yoruba, tribal languages

Bhutan

Area: 17,954 sq mi (46,500 sq km)
Population: 800,000
Capital: Thimphu, pop. 203,000
Currencies: ngultrum; Indian rupee
Religions: Lamaistic Buddhist, Indian- and Nepalese-influenced Hindu
Languages: Dzongkha, Tibetan dialects, Nepalese dialects

Bolivia

Area: 424,164 sq mi (1,098,581 sq km)
Population: 11,300,000
Capitals: La Paz, pop. 1,814,000; Sucre, pop. 278,000
Currency: boliviano
Religions: Roman Catholic, Protestant (includes Evangelical Methodist)
Languages: Spanish, Quechua, Aymara

Bosnia and Herzegovina

Area: 19,741 sq mi (51,129 sq km)
Population: 3,500,000
Capital: Sarajevo, pop. 343,000
Currency: konvertibilna marka (convertible mark)
Religions: Muslim, Orthodox, Roman Catholic
Languages: Bosnian, Croatian, Serbian

Botswana

Area: 224,607 sq mi (581,730 sq km)
Population: 2,200,000
Capital: Gaborone, pop. 269,000
Currency: pula
Religions: Christian, Badimo
Languages: Setswana, Kalanga

Brazil

Area: 3,287,612 sq mi (8,514,877 sq km)
Population: 209,400,000
Capital: Brasília, pop. 4,470,000
Currency: real
Religions: Roman Catholic, Protestant
Language: Portuguese

COLOR KEY ● Africa ● Australia, New Zealand, and Oceania

Brunei

Area: 2,226 sq mi (5,765 sq km)
Population: 400,000
Capital: Bandar Seri Begawan, pop. 41,000
Currency: Bruneian dollar
Religions: Muslim, Buddhist, Christian, other (includes indigenous beliefs)
Languages: Malay, English, Chinese

Burkina Faso

Area: 105,869 sq mi (274,200 sq km)
Population: 20,300,000
Capital: Ouagadougou, pop. 2,531,000
Currency: Communauté Financière Africaine franc
Religions: Muslim, indigenous beliefs, Christian
Languages: French, native African languages

Bulgaria

Area: 42,855 sq mi (110,994 sq km)
Population: 7,000,000
Capital: Sofia, pop. 1,272,000
Currency: lev
Religions: Bulgarian Orthodox, Muslim
Languages: Bulgarian, Turkish, Roma

Burundi

Area: 10,747 sq mi (27,834 sq km)
Population: 11,800,000
Capital: Bujumbura, pop. 899,000
Currency: Burundi franc
Religions: Roman Catholic, indigenous beliefs, Muslim, Protestant
Languages: Kirundi, French, Swahili

SNAPSHOT
Bulgaria

Traditional clothing is worn during the Festival of the National Costume in Zheravna, Bulgaria.

● Asia ● Europe ● North America ● South America

Cabo Verde

Area: 1,558 sq mi (4,036 sq km)
Population: 600,000
Capital: Praia, pop. 168,000
Currency: Cape Verdean escudo
Religions: Roman Catholic (infused with indigenous beliefs), Protestant (mostly Church of the Nazarene)
Languages: Portuguese, Crioulo

Cameroon

Area: 183,569 sq mi (475,442 sq km)
Population: 25,600,000
Capital: Yaoundé, pop. 3,656,000
Currency: Communauté Financière Africaine franc
Religions: indigenous beliefs, Christian, Muslim
Languages: 24 major African language groups, English, French

Cambodia

Area: 69,898 sq mi (181,035 sq km)
Population: 16,000,000
Capital: Phnom Penh, pop. 1,952,000
Currency: riel
Religion: Theravada Buddhist
Language: Khmer

Canada

Area: 3,855,103 sq mi (9,984,670 sq km)
Population: 37,200,000
Capital: Ottawa, pop. 1,363,000
Currency: Canadian dollar
Religions: Roman Catholic, Protestant (includes United Church, Anglican), other Christian
Languages: English, French

SNAPSHOT
Colombia

A long-tailed sylph hummingbird feeds on a tropical flower in Colombia.

COLOR KEY ● Africa ● Australia, New Zealand, and Oceania

Central African Republic

Area: 240,535 sq mi
(622,984 sq km)
Population: 4,700,000
Capital: Bangui, pop. 851,000
Currency: Communauté Financière Africaine franc
Religions: indigenous beliefs, Protestant, Roman Catholic, Muslim
Languages: French, Sangho, tribal languages

Chad

Area: 495,755 sq mi
(1,284,000 sq km)
Population: 15,400,000
Capital: N'Djamena, pop. 1,323,000
Currency: Communauté Financière Africaine franc
Religions: Muslim, Catholic, Protestant, animist
Languages: French, Arabic, Sara, more than 120 languages and dialects

Chile

Area: 291,930 sq mi
(756,096 sq km)
Population: 18,600,000
Capital: Santiago, pop. 6,680,000
Currency: Chilean peso
Religions: Roman Catholic, Evangelical
Language: Spanish

China

Area: 3,705,406 sq mi
(9,596,960 sq km)
Population: 1,393,800,000
Capital: Beijing, pop. 19,618,000
Currency: renminbi (yuan)
Religions: Taoist, Buddhist, Christian
Languages: Standard Chinese or Mandarin, Yue, Wu, Minbei, Minnan, Xiang, Gan, Hakka dialects

Colombia

Area: 440,831 sq mi
(1,141,748 sq km)
Population: 49,800,000
Capital: Bogotá, pop. 10,574,000
Currency: Colombian peso
Religion: Roman Catholic
Language: Spanish

Comoros

Area: 863 sq mi (2,235 sq km)
Population: 800,000
Capital: Moroni, pop. 62,000
Currency: Comoran franc
Religion: Sunni Muslim
Languages: Arabic, French, Shikomoro

Congo

Area: 132,047 sq mi (342,000 sq km)
Population: 5,400,000
Capital: Brazzaville, pop. 2,230,000
Currency: Communauté Financière Africaine franc
Religions: Christian, animist
Languages: French, Lingala, Monokutuba, local languages

Costa Rica

Area: 19,730 sq mi
(51,100 sq km)
Population: 5,000,000
Capital: San José, pop. 1,358,000
Currency: Costa Rican colón
Religions: Roman Catholic, Evangelical
Languages: Spanish, English

Côte d'Ivoire (Ivory Coast)

Area: 124,503 sq mi
(322,462 sq km)
Population: 24,900,000
Capitals: Abidjan, pop. 4,921,000; Yamoussoukro, pop. 231,000
Currency: Communauté Financière Africaine franc
Religions: Muslim, indigenous beliefs, Christian
Languages: French, Dioula, other native dialects

Croatia

Area: 21,831 sq mi
(56,542 sq km)
Population: 4,100,000
Capital: Zagreb, pop. 686,000
Currency: kuna
Religions: Roman Catholic, Orthodox
Language: Croatian

Cuba

Area: 42,803 sq mi
(110,860 sq km)
Population: 11,100,000
Capital: Havana, pop. 2,136,000
Currency: Cuban peso
Religions: Roman Catholic, Protestant, Jehovah's Witnesses, Jewish, Santería
Language: Spanish

3 cool things about CUBA

1. The world's smallest bird, the bee hummingbird, inhabits Cuba's Isla de la Juventud. The tiny birds, which grow to be about the size of the insect they're named for, build nests the size of quarters and lay pea-size eggs.

2. The national sport of Cuba is baseball, which was brought to the country in the 1860s. Today, the country has one of the top national teams in the world and many major league players come from Cuba.

3. Cuba is nicknamed *El Cocodrilo* (Spanish for crocodile), after the shape of the island. It's also home to some 3,000 Cuban crocodiles, a critically endangered species that can grow to be almost as long as a full-size car.

Cyprus

Area: 3,572 sq mi (9,251 sq km)
Population: 1,200,000
Capital: Nicosia, pop. 269,000
Currencies: euro; new Turkish lira in Northern Cyprus
Religions: Greek Orthodox, Muslim, Maronite, Armenian Apostolic
Languages: Greek, Turkish, English

Czechia (Czech Republic)

Area: 30,450 sq mi (78,866 sq km)
Population: 10,600,000
Capital: Prague, pop. 1,292,000
Currency: koruny
Religion: Roman Catholic
Language: Czech

Democratic Republic of the Congo

Area: 905,365 sq mi
(2,344,885 sq km)
Population: 84,300,000
Capital: Kinshasa, pop. 13,171,000
Currency: Congolese franc
Religions: Roman Catholic, Protestant, Kimbanguist, Muslim, syncretic sects, indigenous beliefs
Languages: French, Lingala, Kingwana, Kikongo, Tshiluba

Denmark

Area: 16,640 sq mi (43,098 sq km)
Population: 5,800,000
Capital: Copenhagen, pop. 1,321,000
Currency: Danish krone
Religions: Evangelical Lutheran, other Protestant, Roman Catholic
Languages: Danish, Faroese, Greenlandic, German, English as second language

Djibouti

Area: 8,958 sq mi
(23,200 sq km)
Population: 1,000,000
Capital: Djibouti, pop. 562,000
Currency: Djiboutian franc
Religions: Muslim, Christian
Languages: French, Arabic, Somali, Afar

Dominica

Area: 290 sq mi (751 sq km)
Population: 70,000
Capital: Roseau, pop. 15,000
Currency: East Caribbean dollar
Religions: Roman Catholic, Seventh-day Adventist, Pentecostal, Baptist, Methodist, other Christian
Languages: English, French patois

Dominican Republic

Area: 18,704 sq mi
(48,442 sq km)
Population: 10,800,000
Capital: Santo Domingo, pop. 3,172,000
Currency: Dominican peso
Religion: Roman Catholic
Language: Spanish

COLOR KEY ● Africa ● Australia, New Zealand, and Oceania

Ecuador

Area: 109,483 sq mi (283,560 sq km)
Population: 17,000,000
Capital: Quito, pop. 1,822,000
Currency: U.S. dollar
Religion: Roman Catholic
Languages: Spanish, Quechua, other Amerindian languages

Egypt

Area: 386,874 sq mi (1,002,000 sq km)
Population: 97,000,000
Capital: Cairo, pop. 20,901,000
Currency: Egyptian pound
Religions: Muslim (mostly Sunni), Coptic Christian
Languages: Arabic, English, French

El Salvador

Area: 8,124 sq mi (21,041 sq km)
Population: 6,500,000
Capital: San Salvador, pop. 1,107,000
Currency: U.S. dollar
Religions: Roman Catholic, Protestant
Languages: Spanish, Nahua

Equatorial Guinea

Area: 10,831 sq mi (28,051 sq km)
Population: 1,300,000
Capital: Malabo, pop. 297,000
Currency: Communauté Financière Africaine franc
Religions: Christian (predominantly Roman Catholic), pagan practices
Languages: Spanish, French, Fang, Bubi

Eritrea

Area: 45,406 sq mi (117,600 sq km)
Population: 6,000,000
Capital: Asmara, pop. 896,000
Currency: nakfa
Religions: Muslim, Coptic Christian, Roman Catholic
Languages: Afar, Arabic, Tigre, Kunama, Tigrinya, other Cushitic languages

Estonia

Area: 17,462 sq mi (45,227 sq km)
Population: 1,300,000
Capital: Tallinn, pop. 437,000
Currency: euro
Religions: Evangelical Lutheran, Orthodox
Languages: Estonian, Russian

Eswatini

Area: 6,704 sq mi (17,363 sq km)
Population: 1,400,000
Capitals: Mbabane, pop. 68,000; Lobamba, pop. 11,000
Currency: lilangeni
Religions: Zionist, Roman Catholic, Muslim
Languages: English, siSwati

Ethiopia

Area: 426,373 sq mi (1,104,300 sq km)
Population: 107,500,000
Capital: Addis Ababa, pop. 4,400,000
Currency: birr
Religions: Christian, Muslim, traditional
Languages: Amharic, Oromigna, Tigrinya, Guaragigna

Fiji

Area: 7,095 sq mi (18,376 sq km)
Population: 900,000
Capital: Suva, pop. 178,000
Currency: Fijian dollar
Religions: Christian (Methodist, Roman Catholic, Assembly of God), Hindu (Sanatan), Muslim (Sunni)
Languages: English, Fijian, Hindustani

Finland

Area: 130,558 sq mi (338,145 sq km)
Population: 5,500,000
Capital: Helsinki, pop. 1,279,000
Currency: euro
Religion: Lutheran Church of Finland
Languages: Finnish, Swedish

France

Area: 210,026 sq mi
(543,965 sq km)
Population: 65,100,000
Capital: Paris, pop. 10,901,000
Currency: euro
Religions: Roman Catholic, Muslim
Language: French

Gambia

Area: 4,361 sq mi (11,295 sq km)
Population: 2,200,000
Capital: Banjul, pop. 437,000
Currency: dalasi
Religions: Muslim, Christian
Languages: English, Mandinka, Wolof, Fula,
other indigenous vernaculars

Gabon

Area: 103,347 sq mi (267,667 sq km)
Population: 2,100,000
Capital: Libreville, pop. 813,000
Currency: Communauté Financière
Africaine franc
Religions: Christian, animist
Languages: French, Fang, Myene, Nzebi, Bapounou/
Eschira, Bandjabi

Georgia

Area: 26,911 sq mi (69,700 sq km)
Population: 3,900,000
Capital: Tbilisi, pop. 1,077,000
Currency: lari
Religions: Orthodox Christian, Muslim,
Armenian-Gregorian
Languages: Georgian, Russian, Armenian, Azeri, Abkhaz

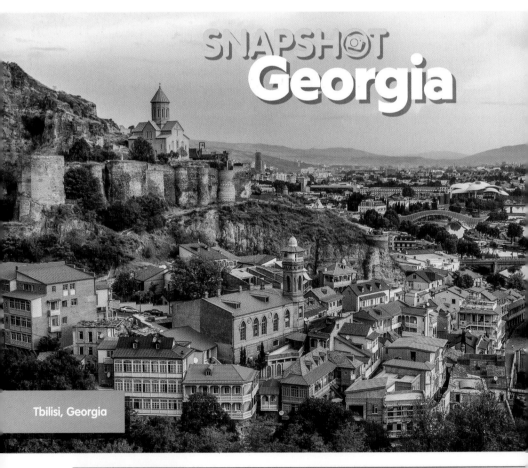

SNAPSHOT
Georgia

Tbilisi, Georgia

COLOR KEY ● Africa ● Australia, New Zealand, and Oceania

Germany

Area: 137,847 sq mi
(357,022 sq km)
Population: 82,800,000
Capital: Berlin, pop. 3,552,000
Currency: euro
Religions: Protestant, Roman Catholic, Muslim
Language: German

Ghana

Area: 92,100 sq mi (238,537 sq km)
Population: 29,500,000
Capital: Accra, pop. 2,439,000
Currency: Ghana cedi
Religions: Christian (Pentecostal/Charismatic, Protestant, Roman Catholic, other), Muslim, traditional beliefs
Languages: Asante, Ewe, Fante, Boron (Brong), Dagomba, Dangme, Dagarte (Dagaba), Akyem, Ga, English

Greece

Area: 50,949 sq mi (131,957 sq km)
Population: 10,600,000
Capital: Athens, pop. 3,156,000
Currency: euro
Religion: Greek Orthodox
Languages: Greek, English, French

Grenada

Area: 133 sq mi (344 sq km)
Population: 100,000
Capital: St. George's, pop. 39,000
Currency: East Caribbean dollar
Religions: Roman Catholic, Anglican, other Protestant
Languages: English, French patois

Guatemala

Area: 42,042 sq mi (108,889 sq km)
Population: 17,200,000
Capital: Guatemala City, pop. 2,851,000
Currency: quetzal
Religions: Roman Catholic, Protestant, indigenous Maya beliefs
Languages: Spanish, 23 official Amerindian languages

Guinea

Area: 94,926 sq mi (245,857 sq km)
Population: 11,900,000
Capital: Conakry, pop. 1,843,000
Currency: Guinean franc
Religions: Muslim, Christian, indigenous beliefs
Languages: French, ethnic languages

Guinea-Bissau

Area: 13,948 sq mi
(36,125 sq km)
Population: 1,900,000
Capital: Bissau, pop. 558,000
Currency: Communauté Financière Africaine franc
Religions: indigenous beliefs, Muslim, Christian
Languages: Portuguese, Crioulo, African languages

Guyana

Area: 83,000 sq mi
(214,969 sq km)
Population: 800,000
Capital: Georgetown, pop. 110,000
Currency: Guyanese dollar
Religions: Christian, Hindu, Muslim
Languages: English, Amerindian dialects, Creole, Hindustani, Urdu

Haiti

Area: 10,714 sq mi (27,750 sq km)
Population: 10,800,000
Capital: Port-au-Prince, pop. 2,637,000
Currency: gourde
Religions: Roman Catholic, Protestant (Baptist, Pentecostal, other)
Languages: French, Creole

Honduras

Area: 43,433 sq mi
(112,492 sq km)
Population: 9,000,000
Capital: Tegucigalpa, pop. 1,363,000
Currency: lempira
Religions: Roman Catholic, Protestant
Languages: Spanish, Amerindian dialects

Hungary

Area: 35,919 sq mi (93,030 sq km)
Population: 9,800,000
Capital: Budapest, pop. 1,759,000
Currency: forint
Religions: Roman Catholic, Calvinist, Lutheran
Language: Hungarian

Iceland

Area: 39,769 sq mi
(103,000 sq km)
Population: 400,000
Capital: Reykjavík, pop. 216,000
Currency: Icelandic krona
Religion: Lutheran Church of Iceland
Languages: Icelandic, English, Nordic
languages, German

India

Area: 1,269,221 sq mi (3,287,270 sq km)
Population: 1,371,300,000
Capital: New Delhi, pop. 28,514,000
(part of Delhi metropolitan area)
Currency: Indian rupee
Religions: Hindu, Muslim
Languages: Hindi, 21 other official languages,
Hindustani (popular Hindi/Urdu variant in the north)

Indonesia

Area: 742,308 sq mi
(1,922,570 sq km)
Population: 265,200,000
Capital: Jakarta, pop. 10,517,000
Currency: Indonesian rupiah
Religions: Muslim, Protestant, Roman Catholic
Languages: Bahasa Indonesia (modified form of Malay),
English, Dutch, Javanese, local dialects

Iran

Area: 636,296 sq mi
(1,648,000 sq km)
Population: 81,600,000
Capital: Tehran, pop. 8,896,000
Currency: Iranian rial
Religions: Shiite Muslim, Sunni Muslim
Languages: Persian, Turkic, Kurdish, Luri,
Baluchi, Arabic

Iraq

Area: 168,754 sq mi
(437,072 sq km)
Population: 40,200,000
Capital: Baghdad, pop. 6,812,000
Currency: Iraqi dinar
Religions: Shiite Muslim, Sunni Muslim
Languages: Arabic, Kurdish, Assyrian, Armenian

Ireland (Éire)

Area: 27,133 sq mi
(70,273 sq km)
Population: 4,900,000
Capital: Dublin, pop. 1,201,000
Currency: euro
Religions: Roman Catholic, Church of Ireland
Languages: Irish (Gaelic), English

Israel

Area: 8,550 sq mi (22,145 sq km)
Population: 8,500,000
Capital: Jerusalem, pop. 907,000
Currency: new Israeli sheqel
Religions: Jewish, Muslim
Languages: Hebrew, Arabic, English

Italy

Area: 116,345 sq mi
(301,333 sq km)
Population: 60,600,000
Capital: Rome, pop. 4,210,000
Currency: euro
Religions: Roman Catholic, Protestant, Jewish, Muslim
Languages: Italian, German, French, Slovene

Jamaica

Area: 4,244 sq mi
(10,991 sq km)
Population: 2,900,000
Capital: Kingston, pop. 589,000
Currency: Jamaican dollar
Religions: Protestant (Church of God, Seventh-day
Adventist, Pentecostal, Baptist, Anglican, other)
Languages: English, English patois

Japan

Area: 145,902 sq mi (377,887 sq km)
Population: 126,500,000
Capital: Tokyo, pop. 37,393,000
Currency: yen
Religions: Shinto, Buddhist
Language: Japanese

Kazakhstan

Area: 1,049,155 sq mi (2,717,300 sq km)
Population: 18,400,000
Capital: Astana, pop. 1,068,000
Currency: tenge
Religions: Muslim, Russian Orthodox
Languages: Kazakh (Qazaq), Russian

Jordan

Area: 34,495 sq mi (89,342 sq km)
Population: 10,200,000
Capital: Amman, pop. 2,065,000
Currency: Jordanian dinar
Religions: Sunni Muslim, Christian
Languages: Arabic, English

Kenya

Area: 224,081 sq mi (580,367 sq km)
Population: 51,000,000
Capital: Nairobi, pop. 4,386,000
Currency: Kenyan shilling
Religions: Protestant, Roman Catholic, Muslim, indigenous beliefs
Languages: English, Kiswahili, many indigenous languages

SNAPSHOT
Jamaica

Children dance in Kingston, Jamaica, wearing yellow, green, and black—Jamaica's national colors.

● Asia ● Europe ● North America ● South America

Kiribati

Area: 313 sq mi (811 sq km)
Population: 100,000
Capital: Tarawa, pop. 64,000
Currency: Australian dollar
Religions: Roman Catholic, Protestant (Congregational)
Languages: I-Kiribati, English

Kuwait

Area: 6,880 sq mi (17,818 sq km)
Population: 4,200,000
Capital: Kuwait City, pop. 2,989,000
Currency: Kuwaiti dinar
Religions: Sunni Muslim, Shiite Muslim
Languages: Arabic, English

Kosovo

Area: 4,203 sq mi (10,887 sq km)
Population: 1,800,000
Capital: Pristina, pop. 205,000
Currency: euro
Religions: Muslim, Serbian Orthodox, Roman Catholic
Languages: Albanian, Serbian, Bosnian, Turkish, Roma

Kyrgyzstan

Area: 77,182 sq mi (199,900 sq km)
Population: 6,100,000
Capital: Bishkek, pop. 996,000
Currency: som
Religions: Muslim, Russian Orthodox
Languages: Kyrgyz, Uzbek, Russian

SNAPSHOT
Luxembourg

Pretzel from Grevenmacher, Luxembourg

COLOR KEY ● Africa ● Australia, New Zealand, and Oceania

Laos

Area: 91,429 sq mi
(236,800 sq km)
Population: 7,000,000
Capital: Vientiane, pop. 665,000
Currency: kip
Religions: Buddhist, animist
Languages: Lao, French, English, various ethnic languages

Libya

Area: 679,362 sq mi
(1,759,540 sq km)
Population: 6,500,000
Capital: Tripoli, pop. 1,158,000
Currency: Libyan dinar
Religion: Sunni Muslim
Languages: Arabic, Italian, English

Latvia

Area: 24,938 sq mi
(64,589 sq km)
Population: 1,900,000
Capital: Riga, pop. 637,000
Currency: Latvian lat
Religions: Lutheran, Roman Catholic, Russian Orthodox
Languages: Latvian, Russian, Lithuanian

Liechtenstein

Area: 62 sq mi (160 sq km)
Population: 40,000
Capital: Vaduz, pop. 5,000
Currency: Swiss franc
Religions: Roman Catholic, Protestant
Languages: German, Alemannic dialect

Lebanon

Area: 4,036 sq mi (10,452 sq km)
Population: 6,100,000
Capital: Beirut, pop. 2,385,000
Currency: Lebanese pound
Religions: Muslim, Christian
Languages: Arabic, French, English, Armenian

Lithuania

Area: 25,212 sq mi
(65,300 sq km)
Population: 2,800,000
Capital: Vilnius, pop. 536,000
Currency: litas
Religions: Roman Catholic, Russian Orthodox
Languages: Lithuanian, Russian, Polish

Lesotho

Area: 11,720 sq mi (30,355 sq km)
Population: 2,300,000
Capital: Maseru, pop. 202,000
Currencies: loti; South African rand
Religions: Christian, indigenous beliefs
Languages: Sesotho, English, Zulu, Xhosa

Luxembourg

Area: 998 sq mi (2,586 sq km)
Population: 600,000
Capital: Luxembourg,
pop. 120,000
Currency: euro
Religions: Roman Catholic, Protestant, Jewish, Muslim
Languages: Luxembourgish, German, French

Liberia

Area: 43,000 sq mi
(111,370 sq km)
Population: 4,900,000
Capital: Monrovia,
pop. 1,418,000
Currency: Liberian dollar
Religions: Christian, indigenous beliefs, Muslim
Languages: English, some 20 ethnic languages

Macedonia

Area: 9,928 sq mi
(25,713 sq km)
Population: 2,100,000
Capital: Skopje, pop. 584,000
Currency: Macedonian denar
Religions: Macedonian Orthodox, Muslim
Languages: Macedonian, Albanian, Turkish

Madagascar

Area: 226,658 sq mi (587,041 sq km)
Population: 26,300,000
Capital: Antananarivo, pop. 3,058,000
Currency: Madagascar ariary
Religions: indigenous beliefs, Christian, Muslim
Languages: English, French, Malagasy

Malawi

Area: 45,747 sq mi (118,484 sq km)
Population: 19,100,000
Capital: Lilongwe, pop. 1,030,000
Currency: Malawian kwacha
Religions: Christian, Muslim
Languages: Chichewa, Chinyanja, Chiyao, Chitumbuka

Malaysia

Area: 127,355 sq mi (329,847 sq km)
Population: 32,500,000
Capital: Kuala Lumpur, pop. 7,564,000
Currency: ringgit
Religions: Muslim, Buddhist, Christian, Hindu
Languages: Bahasa Malaysia, English, Chinese, Tamil, Telugu, Malayalam, Panjabi, Thai, indigenous languages

Maldives

Area: 115 sq mi (298 sq km)
Population: 400,000
Capital: Male, pop. 177,000
Currency: rufiyaa
Religion: Sunni Muslim
Languages: Maldivian Dhivehi, English

Mali

Area: 478,841 sq mi (1,240,192 sq km)
Population: 19,400,000
Capital: Bamako, pop. 2,447,000
Currency: Communauté Financière Africaine franc
Religions: Muslim, indigenous beliefs
Languages: Bambara, French, numerous African languages

Malta

Area: 122 sq mi (316 sq km)
Population: 500,000
Capital: Valletta, pop. 213,000
Currency: euro
Religion: Roman Catholic
Languages: Maltese, English

Marshall Islands

Area: 70 sq mi (181 sq km)
Population: 60,000
Capital: Majuro, pop. 31,000
Currency: U.S. dollar
Religions: Protestant, Assembly of God, Roman Catholic
Language: Marshallese

Mauritania

Area: 397,955 sq mi (1,030,700 sq km)
Population: 4,500,000
Capital: Nouakchott, pop. 1,205,000
Currency: ouguiya
Religion: Muslim
Languages: Arabic, Pulaar, Soninke, French, Hassaniya, Wolof

3 cool things about MAURITANIA

1. Nouakchott was designated as Mauritania's capital when the country gained independence in 1960, making it one of the world's newest capitals. Once a tiny fishing village, Nouakchott is now the country's largest city.

2. "The Eye of Africa"—a 30-mile (50-km)-wide bull's-eye rock formation in the Sahara in Mauritania can be seen from space. The natural phenomenon was likely formed by geological shifts and exposed over time by wind and water erosion.

3. The rusty remains of some 300 ships once bobbed along in Mauritania's Bay of Nouadhibou. It was one of the world's biggest ship cemeteries, and boats from all over the world were abandoned there during the 1980s.

COLOR KEY ● Africa ● Australia, New Zealand, and Oceania

Mauritius

Area: 788 sq mi (2,040 sq km)
Population: 1,300,000
Capital: Port Louis, pop. 149,000
Currency: Mauritian rupee
Religions: Hindu, Roman Catholic, Muslim, other Christian
Languages: Creole, Bhojpuri, French

Mexico

Area: 758,449 sq mi (1,964,375 sq km)
Population: 130,800,000
Capital: Mexico City, pop. 21,782,000
Currency: Mexican peso
Religions: Roman Catholic, Protestant
Languages: Spanish, Mayan, other indigenous languages

Micronesia

Area: 271 sq mi (702 sq km)
Population: 100,000
Capital: Palikir, pop. 7,000
Currency: U.S. dollar
Religions: Roman Catholic, Protestant
Languages: English, Trukese, Pohnpeian, Yapese, other indigenous languages

Moldova

Area: 13,050 sq mi (33,800 sq km)
Population: 3,500,000
Capital: Chișinău, pop. 510,000
Currency: Moldovan leu
Religion: Eastern Orthodox
Languages: Moldovan, Russian, Gagauz

Monaco

Area: 0.8 sq mi (2 sq km)
Population: 40,000
Capital: Monaco, pop. 39,000
Currency: euro
Religion: Roman Catholic
Languages: French, English, Italian, Monegasque

Mongolia

Area: 603,909 sq mi (1,564,116 sq km)
Population: 3,200,000
Capital: Ulaanbaatar, pop. 1,520,000
Currency: togrog/tugrik
Religions: Buddhist Lamaist, Shamanist, Christian
Languages: Khalkha Mongol, Turkic, Russian

Montenegro

Area: 5,333 sq mi (13,812 sq km)
Population: 600,000
Capital: Podgorica, pop. 177,000
Currency: euro
Religions: Orthodox, Muslim, Roman Catholic
Languages: Serbian (Ijekavian dialect), Bosnian, Albanian, Croatian

MONTENEGRO— WHICH MEANS "BLACK MOUNTAIN"—is home to many DARK MOUNTAIN FORESTS.

Morocco

Area: 172,414 sq mi (446,550 sq km)
Population: 35,200,000
Capital: Rabat, pop. 1,847,000
Currency: Moroccan dirham
Religion: Muslim
Languages: Arabic, Berber dialects, French

Mozambique

Area: 308,642 sq mi (799,380 sq km)
Population: 30,500,000
Capital: Maputo, pop. 1,102,000
Currency: metical
Religions: Roman Catholic, Muslim, Zionist Christian
Languages: Emakhuwa, Xichangana, Portuguese, Elomwe, Cisena, Echuwabo, other local languages

 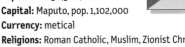

Myanmar (Burma)

Area: 261,218 sq mi
(676,552 sq km)
Population: 53,900,000
Capital: Nay Pyi Taw,
pop. 500,000
Currency: kyat
Religions: Buddhist, Christian, Muslim
Languages: Burmese, minority ethnic languages

Nauru

Area: 8 sq mi (21 sq km)
Population: 11,000
Capital: Yaren, pop. 11,000
Currency: Australian dollar
Religions: Protestant, Roman Catholic
Languages: Nauruan, English

Namibia

Area: 318,261 sq mi
(824,292 sq km)
Population: 2,500,000
Capital: Windhoek, pop. 404,000
Currencies: Namibian dollar;
South African rand
Religions: Lutheran, other Christian, indigenous beliefs
Languages: Afrikaans, German, English

Nepal

Area: 56,827 sq mi
(147,181 sq km)
Population: 29,700,000
Capital: Kathmandu, pop. 1,330,000
Currency: Nepalese rupee
Religions: Hindu, Buddhist, Muslim, Kirant
Languages: Nepali, Maithali, Bhojpuri, Tharu, Tamang, Newar, Magar

SNAPSHOT
Nepal

A street vendor sells flowers
and vegetables in Patan, Nepal.

COLOR KEY ● Africa ● Australia, New Zealand, and Oceania

Netherlands

Area: 16,034 sq mi
(41,528 sq km)
Population: 17,200,000
Capital: Amsterdam, pop. 1,132,000;
The Hague, pop. 685,000
Currency: euro
Religions: Roman Catholic, Dutch Reformed,
Calvinist, Muslim
Languages: Dutch, Frisian

New Zealand

Area: 104,454 sq mi
(270,534 sq km)
Population: 4,900,000
Capital: Wellington, pop. 411,000
Currency: New Zealand dollar
Religions: Anglican, Roman Catholic, Presbyterian,
other Christian
Languages: English, Maori

Nicaragua

Area: 50,193 sq mi
(130,000 sq km)
Population: 6,300,000
Capital: Managua, pop. 1,048,000
Currency: gold cordoba
Religions: Roman Catholic, Evangelical
Language: Spanish

Niger

Area: 489,191 sq mi (1,267,000 sq km)
Population: 22,200,000
Capital: Niamey, pop. 1,214,000
Currency: Communauté
Financière Africaine franc
Religions: Muslim, other (includes indigenous
beliefs and Christian)
Languages: French, Hausa, Djerma

Nigeria

Area: 356,669 sq mi
(923,768 sq km)
Population: 195,900,000
Capital: Abuja, pop. 2,919,000
Currency: naira
Religions: Muslim, Christian, indigenous beliefs
Languages: English, Hausa, Yoruba, Igbo (Ibo), Fulani

North Korea

Area: 46,540 sq mi
(120,538 sq km)
Population: 25,600,000
Capital: Pyongyang,
pop. 3,038,000
Currency: North Korean won
Religions: Buddhist, Confucianist, some Christian
and syncretic Chondogyo
Language: Korean

Norway

Area: 125,004 sq mi
(323,758 sq km)
Population: 5,300,000
Capital: Oslo, pop. 1,012,000
Currency: Norwegian krone
Religion: Church of Norway (Lutheran)
Languages: Bokmal Norwegian, Nynorsk
Norwegian, Sami

Oman

Area: 119,500 sq mi
(309,500 sq km)
Population: 4,700,000
Capital: Muscat, pop. 1,447,000
Currency: Omani rial
Religions: Ibadhi Muslim, Sunni Muslim,
Shiite Muslim, Hindu
Languages: Arabic, English, Baluchi, Urdu, Indian dialects

Pakistan

Area: 307,374 sq mi
(796,095 sq km)
Population: 200,600,000
Capital: Islamabad, pop. 1,061,000
Currency: Pakistani rupee
Religions: Sunni Muslim, Shiite Muslim
Languages: Punjabi, Sindhi, Siraiki, Pashto, Urdu,
Baluchi, Hindko, English

Palau

Area: 189 sq mi (489 sq km)
Population: 20,000
Capital: Melekeok, pop. 11,000
Currency: U.S. dollar
Religions: Roman Catholic, Protestant, Modekngei,
Seventh-day Adventist
Languages: Palauan, Filipino, English, Chinese

Panama

Area: 29,157 sq mi (75,517 sq km)
Population: 4,200,000
Capital: Panama City, pop. 1,783,000
Currencies: balboa; U.S. dollar
Religions: Roman Catholic, Protestant
Languages: Spanish, English

Papua New Guinea

Area: 178,703 sq mi (462,840 sq km)
Population: 8,500,000
Capital: Port Moresby, pop. 367,000
Currency: kina
Religions: indigenous beliefs, Roman Catholic, Lutheran, other Protestant
Languages: Melanesian Pidgin, 820 indigenous languages

Paraguay

Area: 157,048 sq mi (406,752 sq km)
Population: 6,900,000
Capital: Asunción, pop. 3,222,000
Currency: guarani
Religions: Roman Catholic, Protestant
Languages: Spanish, Guarani

Peru

Area: 496,224 sq mi (1,285,216 sq km)
Population: 32,200,000
Capital: Lima, pop. 10,391,000
Currency: nuevo sol
Religion: Roman Catholic
Languages: Spanish, Quechua, Aymara, minor Amazonian languages

Philippines

Area: 115,831 sq mi (300,000 sq km)
Population: 107,000,000
Capital: Manila, pop. 13,482,000
Currency: Philippine peso
Religions: Roman Catholic, Muslim, other Christian
Languages: Filipino (based on Tagalog), English

Poland

Area: 120,728 sq mi (312,685 sq km)
Population: 38,400,000
Capital: Warsaw, pop. 1,768,000
Currency: zloty
Religion: Roman Catholic
Language: Polish

Portugal

Area: 35,655 sq mi (92,345 sq km)
Population: 10,300,000
Capital: Lisbon, pop. 2,927,000
Currency: euro
Religion: Roman Catholic
Languages: Portuguese, Mirandese

Qatar

Area: 4,448 sq mi (11,521 sq km)
Population: 2,700,000
Capital: Doha, pop. 633,000
Currency: Qatari rial
Religions: Muslim, Christian
Languages: Arabic; English commonly a second language

Romania

Area: 92,043 sq mi (238,391 sq km)
Population: 19,500,000
Capital: Bucharest, pop. 1,821,000
Currency: new leu
Religions: Eastern Orthodox, Protestant, Roman Catholic
Languages: Romanian, Hungarian

Russia

Area: 6,592,850 sq mi (17,075,400 sq km)
Population: 147,300,000
Capital: Moscow, pop. 12,538,000
Currency: ruble
Religions: Russian Orthodox, Muslim
Languages: Russian, many minority languages
Note: Russia is in both Europe and Asia, but its capital is in Europe, so it is classified here as a European country.

COLOR KEY ● Africa ● Australia, New Zealand, and Oceania

Rwanda

Area: 10,169 sq mi
(26,338 sq km)
Population: 12,600,000
Capital: Kigali, pop. 1,058,000
Currency: Rwandan franc
Religions: Roman Catholic, Protestant,
Adventist, Muslim
Languages: Kinyarwanda, French, English, Kiswahili

San Marino

Area: 24 sq mi (61 sq km)
Population: 30,000
Capital: San Marino, pop. 4,000
Currency: euro
Religion: Roman Catholic
Language: Italian

Samoa

Area: 1,093 sq mi (2,831 sq km)
Population: 200,000
Capital: Apia, pop. 36,000
Currency: tala
Religions: Congregationalist, Roman Catholic,
Methodist, Church of Jesus Christ of Latter-day
Saints, Assembly of God, Seventh-day Adventist
Languages: Samoan (Polynesian), English

Sao Tome and Principe

Area: 386 sq mi (1,001 sq km)
Population: 200,000
Capital: São Tomé,
pop. 80,000
Currency: dobra
Religions: Roman Catholic, Evangelical
Language: Portuguese

SNAPSHOT
Papua New Guinea

Children ride in a homemade canoe in
Kavieng, New Ireland, Papua New Guinea.

Saudi Arabia

Area: 756,985 sq mi
(1,960,582 sq km)
Population: 33,400,000
Capital: Riyadh, pop. 6,907,000
Currency: Saudi riyal
Religion: Muslim
Language: Arabic

Senegal

Area: 75,955 sq mi
(196,722 sq km)
Population: 16,300,000
Capital: Dakar, pop. 2,978,000
Currency: Communauté
Financière Africaine franc
Religions: Muslim, Christian (mostly Roman Catholic)
Languages: French, Wolof, Pulaar, Jola, Mandinka

Serbia

Area: 29,913 sq mi (77,474 sq km)
Population: 7,000,000
Capital: Belgrade, pop. 1,389,000
Currency: Serbian dinar
Religions: Serbian Orthodox, Roman Catholic, Muslim
Languages: Serbian, Hungarian

Seychelles

Area: 176 sq mi (455 sq km)
Population: 100,000
Capital: Victoria, pop. 28,000
Currency: Seychelles rupee
Religions: Roman Catholic, Anglican, other Christian
Languages: Creole, English

Sierra Leone

Area: 27,699 sq mi (71,740 sq km)
Population: 7,700,000
Capital: Freetown, pop. 1,136,000
Currency: leone
Religions: Muslim, indigenous beliefs, Christian
Languages: English, Mende, Temne, Krio

Singapore

Area: 255 sq mi (660 sq km)
Population: 5,800,000
Capital: Singapore, pop. 5,792,000
Currency: Singapore dollar
Religions: Buddhist, Muslim, Taoist, Roman Catholic, Hindu, other Christian
Languages: Mandarin, English, Malay, Hokkien, Cantonese, Teochew, Tamil

Slovakia

Area: 18,932 sq mi
(49,035 sq km)
Population: 5,400,000
Capital: Bratislava, pop. 430,000
Currency: euro
Religions: Roman Catholic, Protestant, Greek Catholic
Languages: Slovak, Hungarian

Slovenia

Area: 7,827 sq mi
(20,273 sq km)
Population: 2,100,000
Capital: Ljubljana,
pop. 286,000
Currency: euro
Religions: Roman Catholic, Muslim, Orthodox
Languages: Slovene, Croatian, Serbian

3 cool things about SLOVENIA

1. Some 54 percent of Slovenia's land is forest. Kočevje, a town that is made up of about 90 percent forest, is also known as Slovenia's Bear Forest, as it's home to much of the country's 500-strong brown bear population.

2. There are about 10,000 caves in Slovenia, including Postojna Cave, which has 15 miles (24 km) of passages, galleries, and chambers that started forming some three million years ago.

3. A 1,181-foot (360-m)-tall chimney soars above the city of Trbovlje, Slovenia. The tallest chimney in Europe, it's part of the old Trbovlje Power Station and is a destination for climbers, who scale the more than 50-year-old tower.

Solomon Islands

Area: 10,954 sq mi
(28,370 sq km)
Population: 700,000
Capital: Honiara, pop. 82,000
Currency: Solomon Islands dollar
Religions: Church of Melanesia, Roman Catholic,
South Seas Evangelical, other Christian
Languages: Melanesian pidgin, 120 indigenous languages

Somalia

Area: 246,201 sq mi
(637,657 sq km)
Population: 15,200,000
Capital: Mogadishu, pop. 2,082,000
Currency: Somali shilling
Religion: Sunni Muslim
Languages: Somali, Arabic, Italian, English

South Africa

Area: 470,693 sq mi (1,219,090 sq km)
Population: 57,700,000
Capitals: Pretoria (Tshwane),
pop. 2,378,000; Bloemfontein,
pop. 546,000; Cape Town, pop. 4,430,000
Currency: rand
Religions: Zion Christian, Pentecostal, Catholic,
Methodist, Dutch Reformed, Anglican, other Christian
Languages: IsiZulu, IsiXhosa, Afrikaans, Sepedi, English

South Korea

Area: 38,321 sq mi
(99,250 sq km)
Population: 51,800,000
Capital: Seoul, pop. 9,963,000
Currency: South Korean won
Religions: Christian, Buddhist
Languages: Korean, English

South Sudan

Area: 248,777 sq mi
(644,329 sq km)
Population: 13,000,000
Capital: Juba, pop. 369,000
Currency: South Sudan pound
Religions: animist, Christian
Languages: English, Arabic, regional languages
(Dinke, Nuer, Bari, Zande, Shilluk)

Spain

Area: 195,363 sq mi (505,988 sq km)
Population: 46,700,000
Capital: Madrid, pop. 6,497,000
Currency: euro
Religion: Roman Catholic
Languages: Castilian Spanish, Catalan,
Galician, Basque

Sri Lanka

Area: 25,299 sq mi
(65,525 sq km)
Population: 21,700,000
Capitals: Colombo, pop. 600,000;
Sri Jayewardenepura Kotte, pop. 103,000
Currency: Sri Lankan rupee
Religions: Buddhist, Muslim, Hindu, Christian
Languages: Sinhala, Tamil

St. Kitts and Nevis

Area: 104 sq mi (269 sq km)
Population: 50,000
Capital: Basseterre, pop. 14,000
Currency: East Caribbean dollar
Religions: Anglican, other Protestant,
Roman Catholic
Language: English

St. Lucia

Area: 238 sq mi (616 sq km)
Population: 200,000
Capital: Castries, pop. 22,000
Currency: East Caribbean
dollar
Religions: Roman Catholic, Seventh-day Adventist,
Pentecostal
Languages: English, French patois

St. Vincent and the Grenadines

Area: 150 sq mi (389 sq km)
Population: 100,000
Capital: Kingstown, pop. 27,000
Currency: East Caribbean dollar
Religions: Anglican, Methodist, Roman Catholic
Languages: English, French patois

Sudan

Area: 718,722 sq mi
(1,861,484 sq km)
Population: 41,700,000
Capital: Khartoum, pop. 5,534,000
Currency: Sudanese pound
Religions: Sunni Muslim, indigenous beliefs, Christian
Languages: Arabic, Nubian, Ta Bedawie, many diverse
dialects of Nilotic, Nilo-Hamitic, Sudanic languages

Suriname

Area: 63,037 sq mi (163,265 sq km)
Population: 600,000
Capital: Paramaribo, pop. 239,000
Currency: Suriname dollar
Religions: Hindu, Protestant (predominantly
Moravian), Roman Catholic, Muslim, indigenous beliefs
Languages: Dutch, English, Sranang Tongo,
Hindustani, Javanese

Sweden

Area: 173,732 sq mi
(449,964 sq km)
Population: 10,200,000
Capital: Stockholm, pop. 1,583,000
Currency: Swedish krona
Religion: Lutheran
Languages: Swedish, Sami, Finnish

Switzerland

Area: 15,940 sq mi
(41,284 sq km)
Population: 8,500,000
Capital: Bern, pop. 422,000
Currency: Swiss franc
Religions: Roman Catholic, Protestant, Muslim
Languages: German, French, Italian, Romansh

Syria

Area: 71,498 sq mi (185,180 sq km)
Population: 18,300,000
Capital: Damascus, pop. 2,320,000
Currency: Syrian pound
Religions: Sunni, other Muslim (includes Alawite,
Druze), Christian
Languages: Arabic, Kurdish, Armenian, Aramaic,
Circassian

Tajikistan

Area: 55,251 sq mi
(143,100 sq km)
Population: 9,100,000
Capital: Dushanbe,
pop. 873,000
Currency: somoni
Religions: Sunni Muslim, Shiite Muslim
Languages: Tajik, Russian

There's a flag
pole as high as a
50-story building
in DUSHANBE,
TAJIKISTAN.

Tanzania

Area: 364,900 sq mi (945,087 sq km)
Population: 59,100,000
Capitals: Dar es Salaam, pop.
6,048,000; Dodoma, pop. 262,000
Currency: Tanzanian shilling
Religions: Muslim, indigenous beliefs, Christian
Languages: Kiswahili, Kiunguja, English, Arabic,
local languages

Thailand

Area: 198,115 sq mi
(513,115 sq km)
Population: 66,200,000
Capital: Bangkok, pop. 10,156,000
Currency: baht
Religions: Buddhist, Muslim
Languages: Thai, English, ethnic dialects

Timor-Leste (East Timor)

Area: 5,640 sq mi
(14,609 sq km)
Population: 1,200,000
Capital: Dili, pop. 281,000
Currency: U.S. dollar
Religion: Roman Catholic
Languages: Tetum, Portuguese, Indonesian, English,
indigenous languages

COLOR KEY ● Africa ● Australia, New Zealand, and Oceania

Togo

Area: 21,925 sq mi (56,785 sq km)
Population: 8,000,000
Capital: Lomé, pop. 1,746,000
Currency: Communauté Financière Africaine franc
Religions: indigenous beliefs, Christian, Muslim
Languages: French, Ewe, Mina, Kabye, Dagomb

Tonga

Area: 289 sq mi (748 sq km)
Population: 100,000
Capital: Nuku'alofa, pop. 23,000
Currency: pa'anga
Religion: Christian
Languages: Tongan, English

Trinidad and Tobago

Area: 1,980 sq mi (5,128 sq km)
Population: 1,400,000
Capital: Port of Spain, pop. 544,000
Currency: Trinidad and Tobago dollar
Religions: Roman Catholic, Hindu, Anglican, Baptist
Languages: English, Caribbean Hindustani, French, Spanish, Chinese

LEATHERBACK SEA TURTLES nest on the beaches of TRINIDAD and TOBAGO.

Tunisia

Area: 63,170 sq mi (163,610 sq km)
Population: 11,600,000
Capital: Tunis, pop. 2,291,000
Currency: Tunisian dinar
Religion: Muslim
Languages: Arabic, French

Turkey

Area: 300,948 sq mi (779,452 sq km)
Population: 81,300,000
Capital: Ankara, pop. 4,919,000
Currency: new Turkish lira
Religion: Muslim (mostly Sunni)
Languages: Turkish, Kurdish, Dimli (Zaza), Azeri, Kabardian, Gagauz

Turkmenistan

Area: 188,456 sq mi (488,100 sq km)
Population: 5,900,000
Capital: Ashgabat, pop. 810,000
Currency: Turkmen manat
Religions: Muslim, Eastern Orthodox
Languages: Turkmen, Russian, Uzbek

Tuvalu

Area: 10 sq mi (26 sq km)
Population: 10,000
Capital: Funafuti, pop. 7,000
Currencies: Australian dollar; Tuvaluan dollar
Religion: Church of Tuvalu (Congregationalist)
Languages: Tuvaluan, English, Samoan, Kiribati

Tuvalu's land area has grown by about 3 PERCENT since the EARLY 1970s.

Uganda

Area: 93,104 sq mi (241,139 sq km)
Population: 44,100,000
Capital: Kampala, pop. 2,986,000
Currency: Ugandan shilling
Religions: Protestant, Roman Catholic, Muslim
Languages: English, Ganda, other local languages, Kiswahili, Arabic

Ukraine

Area: 233,030 sq mi
(603,550 sq km)
Population: 42,300,000
Capital: Kiev, pop. 2,957,000
Currency: hryvnia
Religions: Ukrainian Orthodox, Orthodox, Ukrainian Greek Catholic
Languages: Ukrainian, Russian

United Kingdom

Area: 93,788 sq mi
(242,910 sq km)
Population: 66,400,000
Capital: London, pop. 9,046,000
Currency: British pound
Religions: Anglican, Roman Catholic, Presbyterian, Methodist
Languages: English, Welsh, Scottish form of Gaelic

United Arab Emirates

Area: 30,000 sq mi
(77,700 sq km)
Population: 9,500,000
Capital: Abu Dhabi, pop. 1,420,000
Currency: Emirati dirham
Religion: Muslim
Languages: Arabic, Persian, English, Hindi, Urdu

United States

Area: 3,794,083 sq mi
(9,826,630 sq km)
Population: 328,000,000
Capital: Washington, D.C., pop. 5,207,000
Currency: U.S. dollar
Religions: Protestant, Roman Catholic
Languages: English, Spanish

SNAPSHOT
Zambia

Victoria Falls on the border of Zambia and Zimbabwe

COLOR KEY ● Africa ● Australia, New Zealand, and Oceania

Uruguay

Area: 68,037 sq mi
(176,215 sq km)
Population: 3,500,000
Capital: Montevideo, pop. 1,737,000
Currency: Uruguayan peso
Religion: Roman Catholic
Language: Spanish

> ## There are about FOUR TIMES MORE COWS in Uruguay than people.

Venezuela

Area: 352,144 sq mi
(912,050 sq km)
Population: 31,800,000
Capital: Caracas, pop. 2,935,000
Currency: bolivar
Religion: Roman Catholic
Languages: Spanish, numerous indigenous dialects

Vietnam

Area: 127,844 sq mi
(331,114 sq km)
Population: 94,700,000
Capital: Hanoi, pop. 4,283,000
Currency: dong
Religions: Buddhist, Roman Catholic
Languages: Vietnamese, English, French, Chinese, Khmer

Uzbekistan

Area: 172,742 sq mi
(447,400 sq km)
Population: 32,900,000
Capital: Tashkent,
pop. 2,464,000
Currency: Uzbekistani sum
Religions: Muslim (mostly Sunni), Eastern Orthodox
Languages: Uzbek, Russian, Tajik

Yemen

Area: 207,286 sq mi
(536,869 sq km)
Population: 28,900,000
Capital: Sanaa, pop. 2,779,000
Currency: Yemeni rial
Religions: Muslim, including Shaf'i (Sunni) and Zaydi (Shiite)
Language: Arabic

Vanuatu

Area: 4,707 sq mi (12,190 sq km)
Population: 300,000
Capital: Port Vila, pop. 53,000
Currency: vatu
Religions: Presbyterian, Anglican, Roman Catholic, other Christian, indigenous beliefs
Languages: more than 100 local languages, pidgin (known as Bislama or Bichelama)

Zambia

Area: 290,586 sq mi
(752,614 sq km)
Population: 17,700,000
Capital: Lusaka, pop. 2,524,000
Currency: Zambian kwacha
Religions: Christian, Muslim, Hindu
Languages: English, Bemba, Kaonda, Lozi, Lunda, Luvale, Nyanja, Tonga, about 70 other indigenous languages

Vatican City

Area: 0.2 sq mi (0.4 sq km)
Population: 800
Capital: Vatican City, pop. 800
Currency: euro
Religion: Roman Catholic
Languages: Italian, Latin, French

Zimbabwe

Area: 150,872 sq mi
(390,757 sq km)
Population: 14,000,000
Capital: Harare, pop. 1,515,000
Currency: Zimbabwean dollar
Religions: Syncretic (part Christian, part indigenous beliefs), Christian, indigenous beliefs
Languages: English, Shona, Sindebele, tribal dialects

EXTREME RECORDS

THE TALLEST, FASTEST, COOLEST, HOTTEST STUFF ON EARTH

Mauna Loa is so massive that it actually sank the ocean floor 26,200 feet (7,986 m) in the shape of an inverted cone.

TALLEST
MOUNTAIN ON EARTH

MAUNA LOA VOLCANO

Think the tallest mountain on Earth is Mount Everest? Surprise! It's Mauna Loa, an active volcano in Hawaii. Before you demand a re-measure, here's the scoop: At 56,000 feet (17,069 m) from its peak to its base, Mauna Loa is almost twice as tall as Mount Everest's 29,035 feet (8,850 m). So why doesn't it look like it? Because only a quarter of Mauna Loa is above water! Its base is depressed 26,200 feet (7,986 m) below the ocean floor.

FASTEST TRAIN

JAPAN'S MAGLEV PROTOTYPE

Japan currently holds the title for fastest passenger train. A prototype maglev (short for magnetic levitation) train, which uses electrically charged magnets to lift the train and move it along the rails, reached speeds of 374 miles an hour (603 km/h) in a test run. The plan is to use the train for service between the cities of Tokyo and Nagoya by 2027. The 174-mile (280-km) journey would be whittled down to 40 minutes, less than half the time it takes now!

COOLEST BALANCING ACT

DRINA RIVER HOUSE

Talk about remote. You'll need a canoe and a whole lot of patience to get to this cabin, carefully balanced on a rocky outcrop of the Drina River in the eastern European country of Serbia. The far-out abode has been around for more than 40 years, carefully built from materials that were floated over or brought by boat. You can really live on the edge in this cozy cabin!

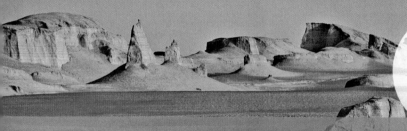

It's so hot and dry in parts of the Lut Desert that not even bacteria can survive there.

HOTTEST PLACE ON EARTH

LUT DESERT

The Lut Desert in southeast Iran is so hot that scientists once thought it was impossible for animals or plants to live there. Satellite measurements in 2005 found an air temperature of 159.3°F (70.7°C) —the highest ever recorded. (Dalol, Ethiopia, has the highest recorded ground temperatures.) The desert is full of sand dunes and open spaces with dark, pebbled ground perfect for soaking up the sun's heat. For humans that can be deadly, but reptiles, spiders, and Blanford's foxes all make this scorching spot their home.

awes8me
SUPERSIZE SCULPTURES

ROCK STAR ②
In Romania, the hills have ... a bushy beard? This stone sculpture—carved into a rock wall near the Danube River—represents Decebal, a mighty ruler from ancient times. Some 130 feet (40 m) high, it's the tallest rock sculpture in all of Europe.

BIG BUDDHAS ①
These colossal statues are found in Myanmar, a country in Southeast Asia. The standing sculpture (seen on the right) stretches 423 feet (129 m) tall, making it one of the biggest Buddhas on Earth.

READY, SET, SWIM ③
A 46-foot (14-m)-long swimmer strokes along the grassy banks of the Thames River in London, England. The temporary statue—made of Styrofoam hand-painted to look like real flesh—was set up in the British capital to promote a TV show.

HORSING AROUND ④
A pair of steel horse heads greet visitors in Falkirk, Scotland. You can enter the sculptures—known as "Kelpies," the name of the working horses that once pulled barges in the area—to admire the artwork from the inside out.

THUMBS-UP ⑤
The artist who created this four-story thumb seen in the La Défense district of Paris, France, cast it from an impression of his own thumb and fingerprint. Now where's the rest of his hand?

REALLY HIGH HEEL ⑥
Cinderella would never be able to leave this supersize shoe behind! A Portuguese artist used stainless-steel pots and lids to create a colossal version of the famed fairy-tale slipper.

TOP BRASS ⑦
Perched high on a hill, this 160-foot (49-m)-tall bronze monument of a man, woman, and child overlooks the Atlantic Ocean in Dakar, Senegal. The tallest statue in Africa, it celebrates the country's independence from French rule.

HEAD ABOVE THE REST
What a big head you have! This 10-story-tall bust of 20th-century Chinese leader Mao Zedong looms large over Changsha, China. More than 8,000 pieces of granite were used to create the mammoth statue. ⑧

CHOOSE

THIS:

HOP IN THE OCEAN WITH SHARKS THE SIZE OF WHALES.

OR

CHOOSE

THAT:

DRIFT IN THE SHALLOWS WITH "SEA COWS."

Seriously? A shark the size of a whale? Getting the underwater photo of a lifetime. Sea cows sound cute. They also sound boring.

MUSE BEFORE YOU CHOOSE

THIS OR THAT?

A WACKY CHOICES TO REVEAL THE HIDDEN YOU

CHECK OUT THE BOOK!

TURN TO FIND OUT

IF YOU CHOSE **THIS:**

Strap on your dive mask and splash around with **WHALE SHARKS,** the world's largest fish. Although they grow to a size rivaling that of a humpback whale, whale sharks are peaceful beasts. They have a mouth that could swallow you whole and thousands of tiny teeth, but they'd rather sift pinhead-size plankton through their gills than gobble up curious swimmers. Their skin—the thickest of any animal—is covered in constellations of yellow spots that are unique to each animal. These elusive sharks roam in tropical seas around the world, but they're easiest to find off Mexico's Holbox Island, where they gather to feed each summer.

IF YOU CHOSE **THAT:**

MANATEES are better known as sea cows for their constant aquatic grazing, but a more suitable nickname might be "sea teddy bear." Lacking natural predators, these half-ton (450-kg) distant relatives of elephants aren't skittish around humans and will even approach swimmers for a tummy rub. See for yourself in Crystal River, Florida, U.S.A., the only place in the world where you're guaranteed to see manatees swim by. These docile endangered giants migrate to the river each winter to keep warm in the spring-fed waters. (Despite their blubbery appearance, manatees lack insulating fat.) Unfortunately, their incautious nature puts them in danger from boat impacts and entanglement in fishing nets.

A Whale of a Time ...
Landlubbers prone to seasickness can skip the boat trip off Holbox Island and swim with whale sharks in Atlanta at the Georgia Aquarium, one of the world's largest aquariums.

COUNTING UP THE NUMBERS FOR
THE COLOSSEUM

Rome's Colosseum was built to impress.
It was the largest amphitheater in the Roman world—and its
numbers still measure up. Let the games begin!

It took less than
10 years to build the
620-by-513-foot (189-by-156-m)
Colosseum, which was
ellipse-shaped to give
everyone the best
view possible.

The arena was
surrounded by an
18-foot (5-m)-
high wall to protect
spectators from
being attacked by
wild beasts.

Sailors
raised and lowered
240 wooden masts
connected to long strips
of fabriclike sails on a
ship to provide
shade over the
amphitheater.

When the
Colosseum
opened in
A.D. 80, there were
100 days
of games to
celebrate.

The
Colosseum
could hold
50,000
spectators.

Beneath
the Colosseum,
animals and
gladiators stayed in
32 cages waiting
to be hoisted up into
the performance
area.

Weird but true!

Check out these outrageous facts.

Buttered **bread** topped with **sprinkles** is a popular **breakfast** in the **Netherlands.**

I'd better call Mom to tell her I'll be late for dinner.

THERE IS CELL PHONE RECEPTION AT THE SUMMIT OF MOUNT EVEREST.

PATO, THE NATIONAL SPORT OF **ARGENTINA,** IS A MIX OF **POLO AND BASKETBALL.**

Belgium once released **postage stamps** that smelled **like chocolate.**

Mexico City has sunk more than **32 feet** (10 m) in the past **100 years.**

A HIGHWAY RUNS THROUGH THE MIDDLE OF AN OFFICE BUILDING IN OSAKA, JAPAN.

IN AUSTRALIA, **"BLUEY"** IS A NICKNAME FOR **REDHEADS.**

Located in **Reutlingen, Germany,** the narrowest street in the world is only **one foot** (30 cm) **wide.**

The entire land area of the **United States** could fit in the **Sahara.**

A TRAFFIC JAM IN CHINA LASTED FOR **MORE THAN** A WEEK.

ADDING UP THE NUMBERS FOR THE WORLD-FAMOUS
SYDNEY OPERA HOUSE

Located in Sydney, Australia, the Sydney Opera House hosts some 40 shows every week, from opera and theater to rock concerts and dance. It's also jam-packed with numbers.

THE CONCERT HALL ORGAN HAS **10,154** PIPES.

15,500 LIGHTBULBS ARE REPLACED EVERY YEAR.

1,000 ROOMS **2,679** SEATS IN THE CONCERT HALL

It took **14** years and **10,000** construction workers to build the Opera House; it was expected to only take **4** years.

COST TO BUILD: **$102,000,000** AUSTRALIAN DOLLARS (That's $72,000,000 in U.S. dollars today.)

HIGHEST ROOF SHELL (OR SAIL) **220** FEET (67 m) ABOVE SEA LEVEL, AS TALL AS A 22-STORY BUILDING

MORE THAN **100,000,000** ROOF TILES

WORLD'S WILDEST THEME PARKS

Kids all over the world flock to theme parks for thrills and chills. Check out the awesome attractions at these amazing theme parks around the globe.

OCEAN PARK
HONG KONG, CHINA

WHY IT'S COOL Almost completely surrounded by the South China Sea, Ocean Park mixes wildlife with wild rides. For instance, visitors can watch an exciting live show at Ocean Theatre, or they can wade in a pool to pet dolphins.

SIGNATURE RIDE High-rise cable cars carry people 673 feet (205 m) to the top of the hilly park.

PLUS Animals at Ocean Park aren't all wet: Bamboo-munching giant pandas share the Lowland Gardens with birds and butterflies.

DREAMWORLD
GOLD COAST, QUEENSLAND, AUSTRALIA

WHY IT'S COOL Tired of roller coasters? Dreamworld has more than just rides. Get up close and personal with Aussie animals such as kangaroos, crocodiles, and koalas.

SIGNATURE RIDE Thrill seekers plummet 39 stories in five seconds on Giant Drop, the world's tallest free-fall ride.

PLUS Guests love the endangered Bengal tigers that romp around on Dreamworld's Tiger Island.

> Waterslides made out of stainless steel are faster than those that are made out of fiberglass.

> Tropical Islands is built inside a former airship hangar.

TROPICAL ISLANDS
KRAUSNICK, GERMANY

WHY IT'S COOL The biggest indoor water park in the world, Tropical Islands has soaring slides and plenty of pools, plus an indoor rain forest with real animals.

SIGNATURE RIDE The high-speed turbo slide has riders zipping down at speeds over 40 mph/70 km/h!

PLUS The Magical Lagoon features a jungle setting, complete with a cascading waterfall.

MORE MUST-SEE SITES

Ageless Time

The famous astronomical clock, built in 1410 in Prague, Czech Republic, has an astronomical dial on top of a calendar dial. Together they keep track of time, as well as the movement of the sun, moon, and stars.

Cathedral on the Square

The onion-dome-topped towers of St. Basil's are a key landmark on Moscow's Red Square in Russia. Built between 1554 and 1560 to commemorate military campaigns by Ivan the Terrible, the building is rich in Christian symbolism.

The Upright Stuff

The Tower of Pisa in Italy started tilting soon after its construction began more than 800 years ago. It was built on an ancient riverbed, which proved to be a foundation too soft to support a structure weighing 21 million pounds (9.5 million kg)! By 1990, Italy's famously tilted landmark leaned so much that officials closed it to visitors, fearing it might fall over. But after years of repair work, the marble monument is again open. And although you can't see the difference, it now leans 19 inches (48 cm) less. To straighten it, some 80 tons (73 t) of soil was dug from below the side opposite the lean. When the ground underneath settled, the tower corrected itself slightly. Officials say it should be safe for tourists to walk up for another 200 years. That gives you plenty of time to plan a visit!

1 More than **80 percent** of the country's population **lives in cities.**

2 To **celebrate** the first **full moon** of the new lunar year, South Koreans **release kites** to drive away **bad luck.**

3 Jeju Island's haenyeo, or "sea women," are fisherwomen who can hold their breath for up to **two minutes** while diving for shellfish underwater.

4 Siberian tigers represented mountain gods in South Korean folklore.

5 About 90 percent of a duck species called **Baikal teals** spend their winters in the **Geumgang estuary.**

20 Cool THINGS ABOUT

6 The **Asiatic black bear** —found in South Korea— is also called a **moon bear** because of the **crescent-shaped** mark on its chest.

7 A festival celebrating the country's **cherry blossom trees** attracts about **a million tourists** each spring.

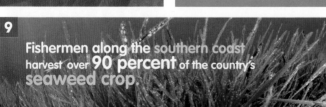

8 The **number four** is regarded as **unlucky** in traditional South Korean culture.

9 Fishermen along the southern coast harvest over **90 percent** of the country's **seaweed crop.**

10 The national dish— called **kimchi**— is mostly made of **cabbage.**

11 Located off the country's northwest coast, **Ganghwado Island** is home to about **80 stone tombs** dating back to prehistoric times.

12 You can get **pizza** topped with **sweet potato** there.

13 Some South Korean cafés have **nap stations** where customers can **snooze.**

14 A total of **7,500 torchbearers** took turns carrying the **Olympic torch** between the cities of Incheon and Pyeongchang before the start of the 2018 Winter Games.

15 Living in South Korea's mountain forests, **Siberian musk deer** have tusklike **canine teeth** sticking out below their lower jaws.

SOUTH KOREA

16 Found in South Korea, the **least weasel** doesn't dig its own den. It nests in the abandoned burrows of other animals.

17 The **oldest Buddhist canon**—a book of sacred texts—is found in this country.

18 The crane, an important symbol in **Korean culture,** is featured in architecture, stationery, and clothing there.

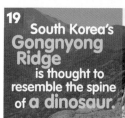

19 South Korea's **Gongnyong Ridge** is thought to resemble the spine of **a dinosaur.**

20 Traditional **Korean roofs** are curved at the corners and appear as if they're **smiling.**

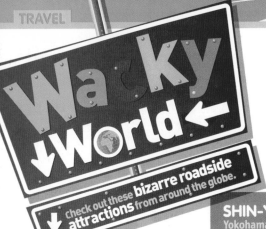

Hop in your car and get out your camera—you'll definitely want some selfies with these strange sights. Found all over the globe, bizarre roadside attractions draw visitors who want to add a little wackiness to their vacations. Take a glimpse at five of the world's weirdest stop-and-stare spots.

Check out the book!

SHIN-YOKOHAMA RAMEN MUSEUM
Yokohama, Japan
Slurp up some fun at a museum dedicated to the beloved noodle dish. Popular in Japan for more than half a century, ramen today comes in different styles specific to the country's regions. Taste them all at the museum's nine restaurants, decide which you like best, and then purchase as many packets as you like to take home. In between bites, watch how the noodles are made, read about their history, and stroll sets made to mimic a 1950s Tokyo neighborhood.

SUSPENDED WATER TAP
Ypres, Belgium
What's the trick to this floating faucet? A clear pipe inside the falling water creates the illusion. The supportive pipe carries water from a pool on the ground to the rear of the faucet. The water loops around and is spewed back out into the pool. That's why it looks like an unending flow of water. Now we're thirsty.

DRAGON BRIDGE
Da Nang, Vietnam
Drivers cruising through one Vietnamese metropolis can see a pretty epic sight: a mythical monster perched on one of the city's bridges. The six-lane crossing, which is the length of 55 school buses, was designed to resemble a dragon. (In Vietnamese culture, dragons symbolize good fortune.) The beastly bridge even "breathes" fire! A blowtorch-like device in the dragon's mouth can be timed to spew flames. This dragon-shaped bridge is really slaying it.

Over the years, Lucy has withstood fires, hurricanes, and raging parties in her belly.

LUCY THE ELEPHANT
Margate City, New Jersey, U.S.A.

No, you're not seeing things. That is a giant elephant on the horizon at the Jersey Shore. Her name is Lucy, and she's not your average pachyderm. All elephants are huge, but Lucy, made of wood and tin, stands 65 feet (19.8 m) high—taller than a six-story building. Built in 1881, Lucy has served as a jumbo-size billboard, a beach house, and a tavern. How do visitors get in? Her 22-foot (6.7-m)-tall legs hide spiral staircases that lead the way.

"Floating" faucets can also be found in Canada, England, Spain, Switzerland, and the United States.

The sculpture is as tall as some trees, but this tree won't be doing any growing.

TRAFFIC LIGHT TREE
London, England, U.K.

Money doesn't grow on trees—but traffic lights might! This 26-foot (8-m)-high treelike structure is made of 75 sets of traffic lights controlled by computers. The sculpture, created by a French artist to represent the energy of the city around it, has been a big hit with locals. Sounds like this fake tree has really taken root.

HOW TALL IS IT?

Burj Khalifa, located in Dubai in the United Arab Emirates, soars over half a mile (0.8 km) high. But how does that compare to other cool sights around the globe? Check out this lineup to find out!

The Willis Tower has **16,100** windows.

More than **36,000 stones** make up the Washington Monument.

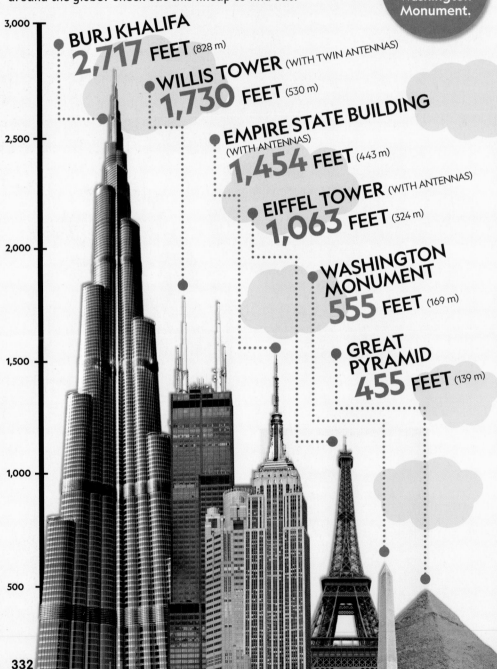

BURJ KHALIFA
2,717 FEET (828 m)

WILLIS TOWER (WITH TWIN ANTENNAS)
1,730 FEET (530 m)

EMPIRE STATE BUILDING (WITH ANTENNAS)
1,454 FEET (443 m)

EIFFEL TOWER (WITH ANTENNAS)
1,063 FEET (324 m)

WASHINGTON MONUMENT
555 FEET (169 m)

GREAT PYRAMID
455 FEET (139 m)

3,000
2,500
2,000
1,500
1,000
500

NUMBER **CASCADE**

Victoria Falls, fed by the Zambezi River and located on the border of Zambia and Zimbabwe, is one of Africa's most famous and natural wonders and one of the most impressive waterfalls found on Earth. Explore some of the amazing stats behind this thunderous wall of water, which has shaped the land and ecosystem for millions of years.

142.7 BILLION GALLONS
of water drop over the falls per minute when the river is in full flood
(540 billion L)

354 FEET HIGH
(108 M)

5,538 FEET WIDE
(1,688 M)

1.25 MILES
(2 KM) width of Zambezi River at the falls

0.3 MILE HIGH
(0.5 KM) maximum height of the spray plume

12 MILES
(20 KM) distance mist can be seen for

2,000,000 YEARS AGO
time when the falls started to form

3,000,000 YEARS OLD
age of stone artifacts made by early humans found near the falls

EXTREME
WEIRDNESS

VADER RULES THE SKY

WHAT León International Balloon Festival

WHERE León, Mexico

DETAILS This might be the Rebels' worst nightmare. Participants at this festival soared across the sky in giant hot-air balloons, such as this one shaped like Darth Vader's mask. More than a hundred balloons fly each year—anything from pandas to bees to scarecrows. But don't worry. This Vader's only full of hot air.

THE FORCE IS STRONG WITH THIS ONE.

DON'T MOW THIS GRASS.

WEAR YOUR LAWN

WHAT Grass-covered flip-flops

WHERE New South Wales Coast, Australia

DETAILS Want to feel the grass between your toes? Just plant your feet in these grass-topped flip-flops, designed to give you the sensation of being outdoors anytime. Don't worry about watering the sandals—the grass is actually a layer of artificial turf. You'll have some happy feet!

YOU'RE IN THE COLD SEAT.

ICE CUBE ON WHEELS

WHAT Truck made of ice

WHERE Hensall, Canada

DETAILS It's going to be an icy ride. This functional truck has a body made of 11,000 pounds (4,990 kg) of ice. Built over a base frame with wheels, the icy exterior covers a real engine, brakes, and steering wheel. It runs on a battery that's specially designed to start in frigid conditions that would keep most cars from revving up. The car can only go short distances—but what a great place to chill!

WILD VACATION

ENTER HERE!

SLEEP HERE!

Tree Hotel
NESTLING INTO NATURE

WHERE Dalat, Vietnam

HOW MUCH About $35 to $80 a night

WHY IT'S COOL One look at this hotel and you'll understand its nickname: "Crazy House." The bizarre lodging is designed to resemble a giant tree stump from the outside. The structure's cozy interior is filled with twisting passageways and 10 cavelike rooms, each with a different animal, insect, or plant theme. Visitors can unwind next to a fireplace shaped like a kangaroo or drift to sleep while staring at the stars through skylights in the Gourd Room. Guests can also wander through the garden, where eerie metal spiderwebs hang. More daring individuals can climb the winding walkways to the roof of the building and take in views of the surrounding city. From top to bottom, this hotel is insanely awesome.

COOL THINGS ABOUT VIETNAM

About 40 percent of the people in Vietnam have the last name Nguyen.

Grilled squid teeth are a popular snack in the country's coastal towns.

Vietnam is only 30 miles (48 km) wide at its narrowest point.

THINGS TO DO IN VIETNAM

Explore the bustling Cai Rang floating market, where boats are colorfully packed with fruits and vegetables for sale.

Sample traditional noodle soup called pho (pronounced FUH) from shops in Hanoi, the country's capital city.

Discover the palaces of former emperors inside the walls of the Hue Citadel, along the Perfume River.

QUIZ WHIZ

Is your geography knowledge off the map? Quiz yourself to find out!

Write your answers on a piece of paper. Then check them below.

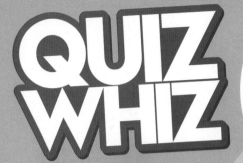

1 Each year, monarch butterflies migrate from Mexico to _____.
a. Europe
b. Canada and the United States
c. Asia
d. Australia

2 A 5,500-year-old leather _____ was once discovered in an Armenian cave.
a. handbag
b. briefcase
c. shoe
d. wallet

3 The Traffic Light Tree is a wacky roadside attraction found in which city?
a. London, England
b. Chicago, Illinois
c. Prague, Czech Republic
d. Lima, Peru

4 **True or false?** An adult gentoo penguin makes as many as 450 dives a day looking for food.

5 Which speedy animal lives in Africa?
a. cheetah
b. antelope
c. wildebeest
d. all of the above

Not STUMPED yet? Check out the *NATIONAL GEOGRAPHIC KIDS QUIZ WHIZ* collection for more crazy GEOGRAPHY questions!

ANSWERS:
1. b; 2. c; 3. a; 4. True; 5. d

HOMEWORK HELP

Finding Your Way Around

Every map has a story to tell, but first you have to know how to read one. Maps represent information by using a language of symbols. Knowing how to read these symbols provides access to a wide range of information. Look at the scale and compass rose or arrow to understand distance and direction (see box below).

To find out what each symbol on a map means, you must use the key. It's your secret decoder—identifying information by each symbol on the map.

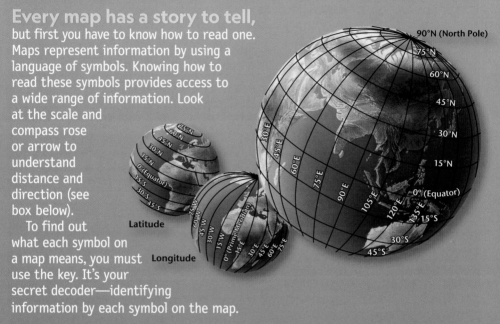

Latitude

Longitude

LATITUDE AND LONGITUDE

Latitude and longitude lines (above) help us determine locations on Earth. Every place on Earth has a special address called absolute location. Imaginary lines called lines of latitude run west to east, parallel to the Equator. These lines measure distance in degrees north or south from the Equator (0° latitude) to the North Pole (90° N) or to the South Pole (90° S). One degree of latitude is approximately 70 miles (113 km).

Lines of longitude run north to south, meeting at the poles. These lines measure distance in degrees east or west from 0° longitude (prime meridian) to 180° longitude. The prime meridian runs through Greenwich, England.

SCALE AND DIRECTION

The scale on a map can be shown as a fraction, as words, or as a line or bar. It relates distance on the map to distance in the real world. Sometimes the scale identifies the type of map projection. Maps may include an arrow or compass rose to indicate north on the map.

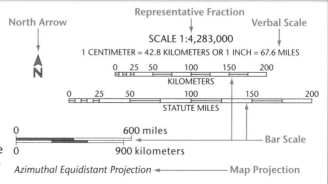

North Arrow

Representative Fraction

Verbal Scale

SCALE 1:4,283,000

1 CENTIMETER = 42.8 KILOMETERS OR 1 INCH = 67.6 MILES

N

0   25   50   100   150   200
KILOMETERS

0   25   50   100   150   200
STATUTE MILES

0   600 miles
0   900 kilometers

Bar Scale

Azimuthal Equidistant Projection ← Map Projection

337

GAME ANSWERS

What in the World?
page 164

Top row: mud, snowdrifts, lava
Middle row: moss, stones, palm leaf
Bottom row: tree trunk, iceberg, sand
dunes

Find the Hidden Animals
page 165

1. E, 2. D, 3. A, 4. B, 5. F, 6. C

Signs of the Times
page 166

Signs 5 and 8 are fake.

Stump Your Parents
page 168

1. D, 2. B, 3. B, 4. C, 5. B, 6. C, 7. A,
8. A-5, B-4, C-2, D-3, E-1, 9. A, 10. B

What in the World?
page 170

Top row: balloon, swimming pool, dreidel
Middle row: clam, butterfly, macaw
Bottom row: stadium seats, sponge,
toothbrush

Are You a Garbage Genius?
page 172

1. True, 2. True, 3. B, 4. C, 5. D

Find the Hidden Animals
page 173

1. B, 2. D, 3. E, 4. F, 5. A, 6. C

Stump Your Parents
page 175

1. C, 2. C, 3. D, 4. A, 5. B, 6. A, 7. D,
8. C, 9. C, 10. B

Movie Madness
page 176

What in the World?
page 178

Top row: galaxy, astronaut, moon
Middle row: space shuttle, sun, comet
Bottom row: Saturn, Mars rover,
satellite

Want to Learn More?

Find more information about topics in this book in these National Geographic Kids resources.

Absolute Expert series

Weird But True series

Just Joking series

5,000 Awesome Facts (About Everything!) series

The Ultimate Book of Sharks
Brian Skerry
May 2018

Animal Smackdown
Emily Krieger
August 2018

Why Not?: Over 1,111 Answers to Everything
Crispin Boyer
August 2018

Dog Science Unleashed
Jodi Wheeler-Toppen
August 2018

How Things Work: Then and Now
T. J. Resler
October 2018

1,000 Facts About Ancient Egypt
Nancy Honovich
February 2019

Funny Animals
April 2019

125 True Stories of Amazing Animal Friendships
May 2018

Extreme Records
Julie Beer and Michelle Harris
June 2018

Animal Zombies!
Chana Stiefel
August 2018

Food Fight!
Tanya Steel
September 2018

Ultimate Predatorpedia
Christina Wilsdon
October 2018

Abbreviations:
AL: Alamy Stock Photo
DRMS: Dreamstime
GI: Getty Images
IS: iStockphoto
MP: Minden Pictures
NGIC: National Geographic Image Collection
SS: Shutterstock

All Maps
By National Geographic unless otherwise noted

All Illustrations & Charts
By Stuart Armstrong unless otherwise noted

Front Cover
(bear), Donald M. Jones/MP; (macaw), Rinus Baak/DRMS; (hoverboard), Zinkevych/GI

Spine
Donald M. Jones/MP

Back Cover
(Earth), Alex Staroseltsev/SS; (robot), julos/IS/GI; (dolphin), Donhype/IS; (spinning Earth), Johan Swanepoel/SS; (VR goggles), izusek/GI; (Roman Colosseum), Marco Rubino/SS; (red-eyed tree frog), Photolukacs/SS

Front Matter (2-7)
2-3, Katherine Feng/MP; 5 (UP LE), Image Source RF/Justin Lewis/GI; 5 (UP CTR LE), Sean Crane/MP; 5 (LO CTR LE), e-volo/Cover Images/Newscom; 5 (LO LE), Stefano Boeri Archietti; 5 (LO RT), Rebecca Hale/NG Staff; 6 (UP LE), Douglas Peebles/GI; 6 (UP RT), Zee/AL; 6 (UP CTR LE), SpaceX/GI; 6 (UP CTR RT), Don Smith/GI; 6 (LO CTR LE), Anup Shah/MP; 6 (LO CTR RT), Dan Sipple; 6 (LO LE), Pat Morrow/NGIC; 6 (LO RT), Brian J. Skerry/NGIC; 7 (UP LE), Room RF/GI; 7 (UP RT), Mike Hill/GI; 7 (CTR LE), IS/GI; 7 (LO LE), MelindaChan/GI

Your World 2020 (8-17)
8-9, Image Source/GI; 10 (UP LE), Katherine Feng/MP; 10 (UP RT), Bill Ingalls/NASA; 10 (LO LE), Reinhard Dirscherl/ullstein bild/GI; 10 (LO RT), R.M. Nunes/SS; 11 (UP LE), Joel_420/SS; 11 (UP RT), Lori Epstein/NG Staff; 11 (CTR LE), PictureLux/The Hollywood Archive/AL; 11 (CTR RT), Tui De Roy/MP; 11 (LO LE), Mark Agnor/SS; 11 (LO CTR), Mark Agnor/SS; 11 (LO RT), pictoKraft/AL; 12 (UP), Peter Jolly Northpix; 12 (LO LE), Omar Marques/Anadolu Agency/GI; 12 (LO RT), Piotr Nowak/AFP/GI; 13 (UP), The Asahi Shimbun/GI; 13 (CTR CTR), Tony Duffy/GI Sport/GI; 13 (CTR RT), Steve Russell/Toronto Star/GI; 13 (LO LE), Kyodo News Stills/GI; 13 (LO RT), Mark Ralston/AFP/GI; 14 (UP & CTR), ©2016 BRAVE ROBOTICS Inc., Asratec Corp./J-deite Ride JH-001Project; 14 (LO), Susan Schmitz/SS; 15 (UP), Tom Hartman/Dearhearts Wildlife Photography; 15 (LO), Anthony Quintano; 16 (UP CTR), Johnfoto/DRMS; 16 (UP LE), Tim Pelling/First Light/GI; 16 (UP RT), Simon Balson/AL; 16 (CTR LE), Kurit afshen/SS; 16 (CTR RT), Tracy Whiteside/SS; 16 (LO CTR LE), Shane Myers Photography/SS; 16 (LO CTR RT), Joseph Sohm/SS; 16 (LO LE), amenic181/SS; 16 (LO RT), GeniusKp/SS; 17 (UP), Louis B. Ruediger/Pittsburgh

Tribune-Review/AP Photo; 17 (CTR), Roland Weihrauch/picture

Amazing Animals (18-73)
18-19, Sean Crane/MP; 20 (LE), Felis Images-Robin Darius Conz; 20 (RT), Shekar Dattatri/NGIC; 21 (UP), Tdee Photo-cm/SS; 21 (LO), Colette3/SS; 22 (UP & CTR), Shelly Roche; 22 (LO), AP Photo/Frogwatch, HO; 23 (UP), Kaïl Marie, Director/CEO; 23 (LO), Karine Aigner/NG Staff; 24 (both), Rebecca Grunwell/The Gisborne Herald; 25 (both), Conny Schmidt/Caters News Agency; 26 (UP), buteo/SS; 26 (CTR), DioGen/SS; 26 (LO), Nick Garbutt; 27 (UP LE), Kant Liang/EyeEm/GI; 27 (UP RT), reptiles4all/SS; 27 (CTR LE), Hiroya Minakuchi/MP; 27 (CTR RT), FP media/SS; 27 (LO), Aleksandar Dickov/SS; 28 (UP), Photoshot License Ltd/AL; 28 (LO), Steve Winter/NGIC; 29 (LE), Tom Brakefield/Corbis/GI; 29 (RT), James Kaiser; 30 (UP), Stephen Belcher/MP; 30 (LO), Royal Veterinary College, University of London; 31, Chris Johns/NG Staff; 32 (UP), Klein and Hubert/MP; 32 (LO LE), Stephen Dalton/MP; 32 (LO RT), Christian Ziegler/MP; 33 (UP RT), Paul Souders/GI; 33 (LO LE), Juan Carlos Muñoz/GI; 33 (all others), Ingo Arndt/MP; 34 (UP), Paul Souders/GI; 34 (CTR LE), EcoPrint/SS; 34 (LO LE), Age Fotostock/SuperStock; 34 (LO RT), Beverly Joubert/NGIC; 35 (UP), Andy Rouse/Stone/GI; 35 (LO), Albert Froneman; 36 (LO LE), Maria Diekmann/REST; 36 (LO LE inset), Jamie Trueblood/Columbia Pictures/Courtesy Everett Collection; 36 (LO RT), Suzi Eszterhas/MP; 36 (LO RT inset), 20th Century Fox/Entertainment Pictures/ZUMAPRESS; 37 (UP), Christian Boix/Africa Geographic; 37 (LO CTR LE), imageBROKER/AL; 37 (UP CTR LE & UP CTR RT), J Dennis Nigel/GI; 37 (LO CTR), Walt Disney Studios Motion Pictures/Courtesy Everett Collection; 37 (LO CTR RT), Marvel Studios/Collection Christophel/AL; 38-39 (background), Flip Nicklin/MP; 38 (LO), Brandon Cole/AL; 39 (LE), Doug Perrine/Seapics.com; 39 (RT), Tom & Pat Leeson/Ardea; 40 (UP LE), Donald M Jones/MP; 40 (UP RT), Milo Burcham/Design Pics INC/AL; 40 (LO LE), Doc White/Nature Picture Library; 40 (LO RT), Enrique R Aguirre Aves/GI; 41 (UP), John C. Lewis/SeaPics.com; 41 (CTR LE & CTR RT), Gary Bell/oceanwideimages.com; 41 (LO LE), Jeff Rotman/SeaPics.com; 41 (LO RT), Doug Perrine/SeaPics.com; 42 (UP), Norbert Wu/MP; 42 (LO), Claudio Contreres/NPL/MP; 43 (UP & LO RT), Doug Perrine/naturepl.com; 43 (CTR RT), SA Team/Foto Nature/MP; 43 (CTR LE), Claudio Contreras/Nature Picture Library; 44 (UP), Kevin Elsby/AL; 44 (CTR), Solent News and Photos; 44 (LO LE), Steve Parish; 44-45 (LO), Photo by Newspix/Rex USA; 45 (UP), Lynn M. Stone/Nature Picture Library; 45 (CTR), Reuters/ChinaDaily; 46 (UP LE), Mark Carwardine/ARDEA; 46 (UP RT & LO), Steven J. Kazlowski/AL; 47 (all), Adrian Bailey; 48 (UP RT), Cosmin Manci/SS; 48 (UP CTR LE), Ingo Arndt/naturepl.com; 48 (UP CTR RT), Dr. James L. Castner/Visuals Unlimited, Inc.; 48 (LO CTR LE), Alex Hyde/naturepl.com; 48 (LO LE), NHPA/SuperStock; 48 (LO RT), Chris Mattison/FLPA/MP; 49 (UP LE), Alex Hyde/

NaturePL.com/GI; 49 (UP RT), PREMAPHOTOS/naturepl.com; 49 (CTR LE), Christopher Smith/AL; 49 (CTR RT), Kazuo Unno/Nature Production/MP; 49 (LO), NH/SS; 50 (UP LE), Brian Kenney; 50 (UP RT), Art Wolfe/Stone/GI; 50 (LO), Ingo Arndt/MP; 51, Vicki Beaver/AL; 52 (CTR), James L. Stanfield/NGIC; 52 (LO RT), AP Images/Wide World Photos; 53 (UP), David Martinez; 53 (LO), Tom Kochel; 54-55 (both), Matthew Rakola; 56 (UP), AnetaPics/SS; 56 (LO), Suzi Eszterhas/MP; 57 (LO LE), Gerard Lacz/PhotoLibrary/GI; 57 (LO RT), ZSSD/MP; 57 (UP), Shin Yoshino/MP; 58 (UP LE), Eastcott Momatiuk/GI; 58 (LO LE), Gerry Ellis/Digital Vision; 58 (RT), Suzi Eszterhas/MP; 59 (UP), Jim Zuckerman/Kimball Stock; 59 (LO), Cincinnati Zoo; 60, Marion Vollborn/BIA/MP; 61 (UP LE), Suzi Eszterhas/MP; 61 (UP RT), Thomas Mangelsen/MP; 61 (LO LE), Grambo/GI; 61 (LO RT), Bengt Lundberg/naturepl.com; 62 (UP LE), Cabrillo Marine Aquarium/Caters News; 62 (UP RT), Karl Ammann/npl/MP; 62 (LO), Tui De Roy/MP; 63 (UP), Donald M. Jones/MP; 63 (LO), Ingo Arndt/Nature Picture Library; 64 (UP), Chris Butler/Science Photo Library/Photo Researchers, Inc.; 64 (CTR), Publiphoto/Photo Researchers, Inc.; 64 (LO), Pixeldust Studios/NGIC; 65 (A, D), Publiphoto/Photo Researchers, Inc.; 65 (B), Laurie O'Keefe/Photo Researchers, Inc.; 65 (C), Chris Butler/Photo Researchers, Inc.; 65 (E), image courtesy of Project Exploration; 66 (both), Andrea Meyer/SS; 67 (UP LE), Photo courtesy of the Royal Tyrrell Museum of Palaeontology, Drumheller, Alberta; 67 (LO), Andrew McAfee, Carnegie Museum of Natural History; 67 (LO), Peter Trusler; 68 (both), Franco Tempesta; 69 (UP), Catmando/SS; 69 (CTR), Franco Tempesta; 69 (LO), Leonello Calvetti/SS; 70 (UP & CTR), Franco Tempesta; 70 (LO), Photo by Roderick Mickens, American Museum of Natural History; 71 (LO LE), Julius Csotonyi; 71 (all others), Franco Tempesta; 72 (UP RT), Milo Burcham/Design Pics INC/AL; 72 (UP LE), Christian Ziegler/MP; 72 (CTR RT), Lionello Calvetti/SS; 72 (LO LE), Kant Liang/EyeEm/GI/GI; 73, GOLFX/SS

Science and Technology (74-99)
74-75, e-volo/Cover Images/Newscom; 76 (UP), Kakani Katija; 76 (inset), Todd Walsh/MBARI; 77 (UP), Peter Bennett/Universal Images Group Editorial/GI; 77 (CTR), Kim Reisenbichler/MBARI; 77 (LO), Kakani Katija; 78 (UP & UP CTR), VINCENT CALLEBAUT ARCHITECTURES, PARIS; 78 (LO CTR RT & LO RT), Foldimate; 78 (LO LE UP), Hammacher Schlemmer; 78 (LO LE LO), tassel78/SS; 79 (UP LE & UP CTR), PancakeBot; 79 (UP RT & CTR RT), Oombrella; 79 (LO CTR RT), Airbus; 79 (LO), Martin Heltai of Perlan Project; 80-83, Mondolithic Studios; 84, Ted Kinsman/Science Source; 85 (A), Sebastian Kaulitzki/SS; 85 (B), Steve Gschmeissner/Photo Researchers, Inc.; 85 (C), Volker Steger/Christian Bardele/Photo Researchers, Inc.; 85 (LO CTR LE), ancelpics/SS; 85 (LO CTR RT), sgame/SS; 85 (LO LE), puwanai/SS; 85 (LO RT), kwest/SS; 86 (UP), FotografFFF/SS; 86 (LO),

Craig Tuttle/Corbis/GI; 87 (UP), Lori Epstein/ NG Staff; 87 (LO LE), Lori Epstein/NG Staff; 87 (LO RT), Science Picture Co/Collection Mix: Subjects RM/GI; 87 (CTR), Lori Epstein/NG Staff; 88-89, Simon Fraser/Science Source; 90 (UP), Roger Harris/Science Source; 90 (LO), Shaber/SS; 91, Tim Vernon/SPL/ Science Source; 92 (UP), Cynthia Turner; 92 (LO), cobalt88/SS; 93 (CTR), Heritage Image Partnership Ltd/AL; 93 (LO), bgblue/IS/GI; 94 (UP LE), Dimarion/SS; 94 (UP RT), Eraxion/IS; 94 (CTR LE), Microfield Scientific Ltd./Science Source; 94 (CTR), mrfiza/SS; 94 (LO), iLexx/IS; 95 (UP), Jani Bryson/IS; 95 (CTR), MyImages - Micha/SS; 95 (LO), RapidEye/IS; 96-97 (all), Matthew Rakola; 98 (UP), FotograFFF/SS; 98 (CTR RT), Ted Kinsman/Science Source; 98 (LO LE), VINCENT CALLEBAUT ARCHITECTURES, PARIS; 99, Klaus Vedfelt/GI

Going Green (100–115)

100-101, Stefano Boeri Architetti; 102 (UP), Gemma Atwal; 102 (inset), Peter Anthony; 103 (UP), Streliuk Aleksei/DRMS; 103 (LO), Todd Paris/UAF; 104-105 (background), Wildlife in Crisis; 104 (UP), Wildlife in Crisis; 105 (UP & CTR LE), Marie De Stefanis/The Marine Mammal Center; 105 (CTR RT & LO), Wildlife in Crisis; 106 (UP), Scanrail/DRMS; 106 (CTR), Sean Pavone/DRMS; 106 (LO), Rodrigo Kristensen/SS; 107 (background), Caters News Agency; 107 (CTR RT), Jamie Squire/ GI; 107 (CTR), Joao Sabino/Solent News/REX/ SS; 107 (LO RT), Courtesy of Austin-Mergold; 107 (LO LE), Dirty Sugar Photography; 108, Cnora/GI; 109 (UP), Rich Carey/SS; 109 (LO), Jimmy Cumming/GI; 111 (UP), James Stone/ Chasing Light Photography/GI; 111 (LO), James Balog/NGIC; 112 (CTR), Rebecca Hale/ NG Staff; 112 (photo collage—redwood), FogStock LLC/Index Stock; 112 (photo collage—cat), Digital Vision/Punchstock; 112 (photo collage—ball), Royalty-Free/Corbis; 112 (photo collage—ice cream), Photodisc Green/GI; 112 (photo collage—dog), Royalty-Free/Corbis; 112 (photo collage—fire hydrant), Burke/Triolo/Brand X Pictures/ Jupiter Images; 112 (photo collage—genie lamp), Burke/Triolo/Brand X Pictures/ Jupiter Images; 112 (photo collage—girl), Rubberball Productions/GI; 112 (photo collage—WHOA sign), Thinkstock/Jupiter Images; 113, Rebecca Hale/NG Staff; 114 (UP), Scanrail/DRMS; 114 (CTR), Jim Cumming/GI; 114 (LO), Rich Carey/SS

Culture Connection (116–139)

116-117, Douglas Peebles/GI; 118 (UP), Nick Kato; 118 (inset), Kauila Barber; 119 (UP), Nick Kato; 119 (LO), Elizabeth Lindsey; 120-121 (UP), fotohunter/SS; 120 (UP LE), CreativeNature.nl/SS; 120 (UP RT), pat-tarastock/SS; 120 (LO LE), Tubol Evgeniya/ SS; 120 (LO RT), imageBROKER/AL; 121 (UP), Jeremy Villasis/Demotix/Corbis; 121 (CTR), Zee/AL; 121 (LO), wacpan/SS; 122 (UP), Ajay Verma/Reuters; 122 (LO), Rubens Chaves/ Tips Italia/Photolibrary; 123, Chonnanit/SS; 124 (UP LE), Splash News/NewsCom; 124 (UP RT), Fuse/GI; 124 (LO LE), Timothy A. Clary/ AFP/GI; 124 (LO RT), Timothy A. Clary/AFP/

GI; 125-127 (all), Rebecca Hale/NG Staff; 128 (UP LE), Ivan Vdovin/AL; 128 (UP CTR), maogg/ GI; 128 (UP RT), Paul Poplis/GI; 128 (CTR LE), Mlenny/IS; 128 (CTR RT), Jack Guez/AFP/ GI; 128 (LO LE), Courtesy of The Banknote Book; 128 (LO RT), Ninette Maumus/AL; 129 (UP LE), Numismatic Guaranty Corporation (NGC); 129 (UP RT), Comstock/GI; 129 (UP CTR LE), Igor Stramyk/SS; 129 (LO CTR LE), Splash News/Newscom; 129 (LO CTR RT), D. Hurst/ AL; 129 (LO CTR), "MoneyDress" with "Colonial Dress" behind. Paper currency and frame, Lifesize © Susan Stockwell 2010. © photo Colin Hampden-White 2010; 129 (LO RT), Kelley Miller/NG Staff; 130, Mark Thiessen/ NG Staff; 131 (both), Mark Thiessen/NG Staff; 133, fcknimages/IS/GI; 134 (LE), John Hazard; 134 (RT), Jose Ignacio Soto/SS; 135 (LE), Corey Ford/DRMS; 135 (RT), Photosani/SS; 136 (UP), Randy Olson; 136 (LO LE), Martin Gray/NGIC; 136 (LO RT), Sam Panthaky/AFP/GI; 137 (UP), Filippo Monteforte/GI; 137 (LO LE), Reza/NGIC; 137 (LO RT), Richard Nowitz/NGIC; 138 (UP), fcknimages/IS/GI; 138 (LO LE), "MoneyDress" with "Colonial Dress" behind. Paper currency and frame, Lifesize © Susan Stockwell 2010. © photo Colin Hampden-White 2010; 138 (LO RT), Mark Thiessen/NG Staff; 139 (UP LE), spa-tuletail/SS; 139 (UP RT), PictureLake/GI; 139 (CTR), cifotart/SS; 139 (LO), zydesign/SS

Space and Earth (140–161)

140-141, SpaceX/GI; 142 (UP), Kim Huppert; 142 (inset), Jordan Krcmaric; 143 (UP), Rafal Cichawa/SS; 143 (CTR & LO), Christine Y. Chen; 144-145 (CTR), Mark Garlick/Science Photo Library; 144 (LO), NASA/CXC/IOA/A FABIAN ETAL/Science Photo Library; 145 (UP), NASA, ESA and M.J. Jee (Johns Hopkins University); 145 (LO), M. Markevitch/CXC/ CFA/NASA/Science Photo Library; 146-147, David Aguilar; 148 (UP), David Aguilar; 149 (all), Mondolithic Studios; 150 (background UP), Alexxandar/GI; 150 (UP RT), Walter Myers/ Stocktrek Images/Corbis/GI; 150 (CTR RT), Tony & Daphne Hallas/Photo Researchers, Inc.; 150 (LO RT), Don Smith/GI; 151 (UP), NASA/Science Faction/SuperStock; 151 (LO), NASA; 152 (UP), Ralph Lee Hopkins/NGIC; 152 (UP LE and RT), Visuals Unlimited/GI; 152 (CTR LE), Visuals Unlimited/Corbis; 152 (CTR RT), Dirk Wiersma/Photo Researchers, Inc.; 152 (LO LE), Charles D. Winters/Photo Researchers, Inc.; 152 (LO RT), Theodore Clutter/Photo Researchers, Inc.; 153 (UP), NGIC; 154 (UP LE), Panoramic Stock Images/ NGIC; 154 (UP RT), Charles D. Winters/Photo Researchers, Inc.; 154 (CTR), Ted Clutter/ Photo Researchers, Inc.; 154 (LO LE), Jim Lopes/SS; 154 (LO RT), Jim Richardson/NGIC; 155 (UP LE), Scenics & Science/AL; 155 (UP RT), Mark A. Shneider/Photo Researchers, Inc.; 155 (UP CTR LE), Ken Lucas/Visuals Unlimited; 155 (UP CTR RT), Carsten Peter/NGIC; 155 (LO CTR), Dirk Wiersma/Photo Researchers, Inc.; 155 (LO LE), Arturo Limon/SS; 155 (LO RT), Goran Bogicevic/SS; 156, Illustration by Frank Ippolito; 157 (UP LE), All Canada Photos/ AL; 157 (UP RT), Salvatore Gebbia/National Geographic My Shot; 157 (CTR LE), NASA; 157 (CTR RT), Diane Cook & Len Jenshel/NGIC;

157 (LO LE), Image Science and Analysis Laboratory, NASA-Johnson Space Center. "The Gateway to Astronaut Photography of Earth."; 157 (LO RT), Douglas Peebles Photography/AL; 158-159 (all), Denis Budkov/ Caters News; 160 (UP), Don Smith/GI; 160 (CTR), All Canada Photos/AL; 160 (LO), Visuals Unlimited/Corbis; 161, pixhook/IS

Fun and Games (162–181)

162-163, Anup Shah/MP; 164 (UP LE), Punchstock; 164 (UP CTR), Photodisc Blue/ GI; 164 (UP RT), PictureQuest; 164 (CTR LE), Pal Hermansen/GI; 164 (CTR), Punchstock; 164 (CTR RT), Vibe Images/SS; 164 (LO LE), Anthony Ise/GI; 164 (LO CTR), Punchstock; 164 (LO RT), Denis Burdin/SS; 165 (UP LE), EEI_Tony/GI; 165 (UP RT), Joel Sartore/NGIC; 165 (CTR LE), Tui De Roy/MP; 165 (CTR RT), Jack Goldfarb/Design Pics/Corbis/GI; 165 (LO LE), Fabio Liverani/NPL/MP; 165 (LO RT), Exactostock/SuperStock; 166 (#1), Charles Gullung/GI; 166 (#2), Photo Resource Hawaii/ AL; 166 (#3), Slim Aarons/Hulton Archive/GI; 166 (#4), Joseph Sohm/Visions of America/ Corbis; 166 (#5), Thinkstock Images/Jupiter Images; 166 (#6), Owaki/Kulla/GI; 166 (#7), Jack Sullivan/AL; 166 (#8), Dale O'Dell 2008; 166 (#9), Jeff Greenberg/UIG/GI; 167, Dan Sipple; 168 (UP LE), Sergey Alimov/GI; 168 (UP RT), Sorin Rechitan/EyeEm/GI; 168 (CTR RT), NASA/Paolo Nespoli; 168 (LO RT), Globe Photos/ZUMAPRESS; 168 (LO LE), Michael and Patricia Fogden/MP; 169, Chris Ware; 170 (UP LE), artpartner-images.com/AL; 170 (UP CTR), napocska/SS; 170 (UP RT), PNC/Photodisc/GI; 170 (CTR LE), Khoroshunova Olga/SS; 170 (CTR), Dobermaraner/SS; 170 (CTR RT), Ian Duffield/ SS; 170 (LO LE), Medioimages/Jupiterimages; 170 (LO CTR), LWA/Photodisc/GI; 170 (LO RT), Esa Hiltula/AL; 171 (UP), Kitchin & Hurst/ leesonphoto; 171 (UP CTR), Elvele Images Ltd/AL; 171 (CTR LE), Pioneer111/DRMS; 171 (LO LE), Fuse/ GI; 171 (LO RT), RubberBall/SuperStock; 172 (UP CTR), Rita Kochmarjova/SS; 172 (UP RT), Autthaphol Khoonpijit/DRMS; 172 (UP CTR RT), Nerthuz/SS; 172 (CTR), Mdorottya/DRMS; 172 (CTR), Sky-pixel/DRMS; 172 (LO CTR RT), Melinda Fawver/SS; 172 (LO LE), Domiciano Pablo Romero Franco/DRMS; 172 (LO CTR), Martinmark/DRMS; 173 (UP), Robert Fowler/ SS; 173 (CTR LE), Valerie Taylor/Ardea; 173 (UP CTR RT), DARIYASINGH/IS/GI; 173 (LO LE), Iren Silence/SS; 173 (LO CTR RT), Don Johnston/ GI; 173 (LO RT), Rafael Martos Martins/SS; 174, Dan Sipple; 175 (UP LE), Rinus Baak/DRMS; 175 (UP RT), Richard Susanto/SS; 175 (CTR LE), weerapong worranam/SS; 175 (CTR RT), M. Unal Ozmen/SS; 175 (LO LE), Dobermaraner/ SS; 175 (LO RT), somchaij/SS; 176, MIGY; 177 (UP RT), Tim Laman/NGIC; 177 (A), Stephen St. John/NGIC; 177 (B), Joel Sartore/NGIC; 177 (C), Robert Harding/NGIC; 177 (UP RT inset), Uwe Bergwitz/SS; 177 (UP CTR RT), Ellen Goff/ Danita Delimont/SS; 177 (CTR LE), Westend61 Premium/SS; 177 (CTR RT), Westend61 Premium/SS; 177 (LO CTR RT), Michael Durham/MP; 178 (UP LE), David Herraez Calzada/SS; 178 (UP CTR), Andrey Armyagov/ SS; 178 (UP RT), Kei Shooting/SS; 178 (CTR LE), Mikephotos/DRMS; 178 (CTR), NASA/SDO; 178

(CTR RT), NASA/MSFC/MEO/AAron Kingery; 178 (LO LE), MarcelClemens/SS; 178 (LO CTR), NASA; 178 (LO RT), Andrey Armyagov/SS; 179, Dan Sipple; 180-181, Strika Entertainment

Awesome Exploration (182–199)

182-183, Pat Morrow/NGIC; 184 (LE), Marco Grob/NGIC; 184 (RT), Jenny Nichols; 185 (all), Brian Ford; 186-187 (UP), Brian J. Skerry/NGIC; 186 (LO), Brian J. Skerry/NGIC; 187 (CTR), Mark D. Conlin/NGIC; 187 (LO), Brian J. Skerry/NGIC; 188 (background & UP), Paul Nicklen/NGIC; 188 (LO), James C. Chatters; 189 (UP), HI-SEAS/Sian Proctor; 189 (CTR), AP Photo/Hi-Seas; 189 (LO), AP/Rex/SS; 190 (UP RT), Joel Sartore/NGIC; 190 (LO LE), Elliott Ross/NGIC; 190 (LO RT), created by John Gurche/photographed by Mark Thiessen/NGIC; 191 (UP), izusek/GI; 191 (CTR UP), Jim Cumming/GI; 191 (CTR LE), Imgorthand/GI; 191 (CTR CTR), Getman/SS; 191 (CTR RT), Tony Anderson/GI; 192 (both), Ben Arnst/Squaw Valley Alpine Meadows; 193 (UP), Renee Lynn/GI; 193 (LO), Barbara Kinney; 194 (UP LE), Pictures Colour Library/Newscom; 194 (UP RT), Marius Bøstrand; 194 (LO LE), Channi Anand/AP Photo; 194 (LO RT), Bigfoot Hostel/Barcroft Media/AL; 195 (UP LE), Michael Clark/AL; 195 (UP RT), EPA/Newscom; 195 (CTR LE), Anthony Devlin/PA Images/AL; 195 (LO RT), Lucas Jackson/Reuters; 196-197 (all), Annie Griffiths; 198 (UP), Brian J. Skerry/NGIC; 198 (CTR), AP Photo/Hi-Seas; 198 (LO), Bigfoot Hostel/Barcroft Media/AL; 199, Grady Reese/IS

Wonders of Nature (200–219)

200-201, RooM RF/GI; 202 (UP), Manu San Félix; 202 (inset), Rebecca Hale/NG Staff; 203 (all), Enric Sala/NGIC; 205 (UP), Stephanie Sawyer/GI; 205 (LO), Grant Dixon/MP; 206 (UP), Stuart Armstrong; 206 (LO), Franco Tempesta; 207 (UP LE), Leonid Tit/SS; 207 (UP RT), Lars Christensen/SS; 207 (CTR LE), Frans Lanting/NGIC; 207 (CTR RT), Daniel Loretto/SS; 207 (LO), Richard Peterson/SS; 208-209, 3dmotus/SS; 210 (UP), Stephen M. Katz/The Virginian-Pilot via AP; 210 (CTR LE), Carlos Giusti/AP; 210 (CTR RT), Melvin Levongo/AFP/GI; 210 (LO) Australia Broadcasting Corporation via AP; 211 (UP LE), Lori Mehmen/Associated Press; 211 (UP RT & RT CTR), Susan Law Cain/SS; 211 (UP CTR), Brian Nolan/IS; 211 (CTR LE), Judy Kennamer/SS; 211 (LO LE), Jim Reed; 211 (LO CTR & LO RT), jam4travel/SS; 212 (LE), AVTG/IS; 212 (RT), Brad Wynnyk/SS; 213 (UP LE), Rich Carey/SS; 213 (UP RT), Richard Walters/IS; 213 (LO LE), Karen Graham/IS; 213 (LO RT), Michio Hoshino/MP/NGIC; 214-215 (UP), Jason Edwards/NGIC; 214 (LO LE), cbpix/SS; 214 (LO RT), Mike Hill/Photographer's Choice/GI; 215 (LO LE), Wil Meinderts/Buitenbeeld/MP; 215 (LO RT), Paul Nicklen/NGIC; 216-217 (background), John A. Anderson/IS; 216 (UP), Vilainecrevette/SS; 216 (LO), Brandon Cole; 217 (UP), Paul Souders/GI; 217 (LO), Rebecca Hale/NG Staff; 218 (UP), Frans Lanting/NGIC; 218 (CTR), John A. Anderson/IS; 218 (LO), SS

History Happens (220–251)

220-221, Nicola Forenza/IS/GI; 222 (UP), Paul Nicklen/NGIC; 222 (inset), Karla Ortega; 222 (LO), Karla Ortega; 223 (UP), Paul Nicklen/NGIC; 223 (LO), Karla Ortega; 224-225 (background), Pius Lee/SS; 225 (UP LE), Providence Pictures; 225 (UP RT), HOPE PRODUCTIONS/Yann Arthus Bertrand/GI; 225 (LO RT), Hulton Archive/GI; 226 (UP), James L. Stanfield/NGIC; 226 (LO), Photoservice Electa/Universal Images/SuperStock; 227 (all), Joe Rocco; 228, Wang da Gang; 229 (UP LE, UP RT & LO RT), O. Louis Mazzatenta/NGIC; 229 (CTR RT), O. Louis Mazzatenta; 229 (LO LE), Wang da Gang; 230-231 (background), Corey Ford; 230 (LO), Disney Enterprises, Inc./Walden Media, LLC; 231 (UP RT), Ocean/Corbis; 231 (LO), Mark Thiessen/NG Staff; 232 (all), Chris Wass; 233 (UP RT), Index Stock Imagery/Jupiterimages/GI; 233 (CTR), Chip Clark/NMNH/Smithsonian Institution; 233 (LO), Superstock, Inc./SuperStock; 234, U.S. Air Force photo/Staff Sgt. Alexandra M. Boutte; 235, Corbis/GI; 238, Tom Roche/SS; 241, February/GI; 242, Anton Petrus/GI; 247, Simon Dannhauer/SS; 250 (UP), Providence Pictures; 250 (CTR), Chris Wass; 250 (LO), Photoservice Electa/Universal Images/SuperStock; 251, Christopher Furlong/GI

Geography Rocks (252–337)

252-253, MelindaChan/GI; 254 (UP), Jon Bowen; 254 (inset), Becky Hale/NG Staff; 255 (UP), International Mapping Inc/NGIC; 255 (LO), Chin Kit Sen/SS; 261 (UP RT), Lori Epstein/NG Staff; 261 (CTR LE), NASA; 262 (background), Fabiano Rebeque/GI; 262 (valley), Thomas J. Abercrombie/NGIC; 262 (river), Maria Stenzel/NGIC; 262 (mountain), Gordon Wiltsie/NGIC; 262 (glacier), James P. Blair/NGIC; 262 (canyon), Bill Hatcher/NGIC; 262 (desert), Carsten Peter/NGIC; 263, f11photo/SS; 264, Amelandfoto/SS; 265 (UP RT), Glowimages/GI; 265 (CTR LE), keyvanchan/GI; 265 (CTR RT), Jean-Jacques Hublin; 265 (LO RT), Dimitri Vervitsiotis/GI; 268, Yva Momatiuk and John Eastcott/MP; 269 (UP RT), Achim Baque/SS; 269 (CTR LE), Alex Tehrani; 269 (CTR RT), iCreative3D/SS; 269 (LO RT), Aurora Creative/GI; 272, Nguyen Anh Tuan/SS; 273 (UP RT), Jon Arnold Images/Danita Delimont.com; 273 (CTR LE), Ilin Sergey/Age Fotostock; 273 (CTR RT), Nancy Brown/Photographer's Choice/GI; 273 (LO RT), Daniel Heuclin/NPL/MP; 276, The Image Bank/GI; 277 (UP LE), Mika Stock/Danita Delimont.com; 277 (UP RT), Andrew Watson/John Warburton-Lee Photography Ltd/GI; 277 (CTR RT), FiledIMAGE/SS; 277 (LO), Robert Harding World Imagery/GI; 280, Christian Mueller/SS; 281 (UP), Roy Pedersen/SS; 281 (CTR LE), RomarioIen/SS; 281 (CTR RT), Annette Hopf/IS; 281 (LO RT), Mark Gillow/GI; 284, Stone Sub/GI; 285 (UP RT), Rodrigo Arangua/GI; 285 (CTR LE), Gail Shotlander/GI; 285 (CTR RT), Yiming Chen/GI; 285 (LO RT), Janie Blanchard/GI; 288, GI South America/GI; 289 (UP RT), Soberka Richard/hemis.fr/GI; 289 (CTR LE), David Tipling/AL; 289 (CTR RT), DC_Colombia/GI; 289 (LO RT), Walter Diaz/AFP/GI; 295, Maya Karkalicheva/GI;

296, Ondrej Prosicky/SS; 300, MehmetO/SS; 303, Tim Graham/GI; 304, EyeEm/GI; 308, Bartosz Hadyniak/GI; 311, Peter Cade/GI; 316, Westend61/GI; 318 (UP), Rosenberg Philip/Perspectives/GI; 318 (LO), Kurita KAKU/Gamma-Rapho via GI; 319 (UP), AlbertoLoyo/IS/GI; 319 (LO), Marcin Szymczak/SS; 320 (UP LE), Peter Macdiarmid/Staff/GI; 320 (UP CTR), Peter Seyfferth/Imagebroker/AL; 320 (UP RT), Alexey Senin/AL; 320 (CTR LE), Christian Wilkinson/SS; 320 (LO CTR RT), Allan Baxter/GI; 320 (LO LE), Nacho Doce/Reuters; 320 (LO LE), Charles O. Cecil/AL; 320 (LO RT), Paul Rushton/AL; 321 (UP RT), cbpix/SS; 321 (CTR RT), IS; 321 (LO LE), katyatya/IS; 321 (LO RT), SS/Bruce Rolff; 322 (UP), Krzysztof Odziomek/SS; 322 (CTR), Brian J. Skerry/NGIC; 322 (LO), Gianluca Colla/NGIC; 323 (background), avNY/Shutterstock; 323 (UP LE), kuzzie/SS; 323 (UP CTR), Vector Market/SS; 323 (UP RT), bioraven/SS; 323 (LO LE), kaisorn/SS; 323 (LO CTR), Franzi/SS; 323 (LO RT), jehsomwang/SS; 324 (UP RT), Stefen Chow/Aurora Photos; 324 (CTR RT), AP Photo/Geert Vanden Wijngaert; 324 (CTR), Tupungato/SS; 324 (LO LE), Wuttichok Panichiwarapun/SS; 324 (LO RT), Thorsten Eckert/AL; 325 (UP), David Messent/GI; 325 (LO), Kok Kai Ng/GI; 326 (UP RT), Sike Heyer/IS; 326 (CTR LE), courtesy Dream World Australia; 326 (CTR), courtesy Ocean Park Hong Kong; 326 (LO LE), Tropical Islands Holding GmbH; 327 (UP LE), Gilmanshin/SS; 327 (UP RT), Taylor S. Kennedy/NGIC; 327 (LO RT), Iouril Tcheka/SS; 328 (UP LE), Sean Pavone/SS; 328 (UP RT), Chung Sung-Jun/GI; 328 (UP CTR LO), Ondrej Prosicky/SS; 328 (CTR RT), Daniel Prudek/SS; 328 (LO CTR LE), Anan Kaewkhammul/SS; 328 (LO CTR RT), Guitar photographer/SS; 328 (LO LE), Rich Carey/SS; 328 (LO RT), Jiang Hongyan/SS; 329 (UP LE), JIPEN/SS; 329 (UP CTR), StockFood/GI; 329 (UP RT), Kyodo News via GI; 329 (UP CTR LO), Redmond O. Durrell/AL; 329 (LO CTR LE), Menno Schaefer/SS; 329 (LO CTR), Sung-bong/EPA/REX/SS; 329 (LO CTR RT), photomaster/SS; 329 (LO LE), Maxim Tupikov/SS; 329 (LO RT), Katvic/SS; 330 (UP), Tony McNicol/AL; 330 (CTR), Pioneron/SS; 330-331 (LO), Bob Henry/AL; 331 (UP), Walter Bibikow/GI; 331 (CTR LE), Alistair Scott/AL; 331 (LO RT), Stuart Miles/DRMS; 332 (LE), Ilona Ignatova/SS; 332 (CTR LE), Songquan Deng/SS; 332 (CTR), Bokic Bojan/SS; 332 (CTR RT), Roman Sigaev/SS; 332 (LO CTR RT), lesapi images/SS; 332 (LO RT), Brian Kinney/SS; 333, Galyna Andrushko/SS; 334 (UP), Shane Talbot/Solent News/REX/SS; 334 (CTR), Mario Armas/Reuters/AL; 334 (LO), ZJAN/Canadian Tire Corporation/WENN/Newscom; 335 (UP), John S Lander/LightRocket/AL; 335 (inset UP), John S Lander/LightRocket/GI; 335 (inset LO), WENN Ltd/AL; 336 (UP), Janie Blanchard/GI; 336 (CTR), Stuart Miles/DRMS; 336 (LO), keyvanchan/GI

Since 1888, the National Geographic Society has funded more than 12,000 research,
exploration, and preservation projects around the world.
The Society receives funds from National Geographic Partners, LLC,
funded in part by your purchase. A portion of the proceeds from this book
supports this vital work. To learn more, visit natgeo.com/info.

NATIONAL GEOGRAPHIC and Yellow Border Design are trademarks of the
National Geographic Society, used under license.

For more information, visit nationalgeographic.com,
call 1-800-647-5463, or write to the following address:

National Geographic Partners
1145 17th Street N.W.
Washington, D.C. 20036-4688 U.S.A.

Visit us online at nationalgeographic.com/books

For librarians and teachers: ngchildrensbooks.org

More for kids from National Geographic: natgeokids.com

National Geographic Kids magazine inspires children to explore their world with fun
yet educational articles on animals, science, nature, and more. Using fresh storytelling and
amazing photography, Nat Geo Kids shows kids ages 6 to 14 the fascinating truth about
the world—and why they should care. **kids.nationalgeographic.com/subscribe**

For information about special discounts for bulk purchases, please contact
National Geographic Books Special Sales: specialsales@natgeo.com

For rights or permissions inquiries, please contact
National Geographic Books Subsidiary Rights: bookrights@natgeo.com

Designed by Kathryn Robbins and Ruthie Thompson

**National Geographic supports K–12 educators with ELA Common Core Resources.
Visit natgeoed.org/commoncore for more information.**

Trade paperback ISBN: 978-1-4263-3284-5

Printed in the United States of America
19/WOR-PCML/1

The publisher would like to thank everyone who worked to make this book come together:
Angela Modany, associate editor; Mary Jones, project editor; Sarah Wassner Flynn,
writer; Michelle Harris, researcher; Lori Epstein, photo director; Hillary Leo, photo editor;
Mike McNey, map production; Stuart Armstrong, illustrator; Sean Philpotts, production
director; Anne LeongSon and Gus Tello, design production assistants;
Sally Abbey, managing editor; Joan Gossett, editorial production manager;
and Alix Inchausti and Molly Reid, production editors.